FANCY FREE

A TALE TOLD

An unusual anthology of narrative poems. Contains poems by Auden, Belloc, Binyon, Blunden, de la Mare, T. S. Eliot, D. H. Lawrence, C. Day Lewis, Plomer, Sassoon and other contemporary poets, in addition to many story-poems by earlier writers.

Opinions from those who are using the book:

"Heartiest congratulations on the originality, variety and sanity of this book."—*Sheffield*

"An excellent selection—breaks entirely new ground, bringing a freshness into appreciation."—*Nottingham*

"I find it a splendid selection of narrative poems for all moods, by a wide variety of authors, and containing many poems not generally known."—*Chiswick*

"Mr. Bebbington has given teachers the stimulus of much new material."—*Letchworth*

". . . a very lively and interesting collection, with a great range of mood and manner."—*London*

Sixth Impression

FANCY FREE

A SELECTION OF SHORT STORIES

MADE AND EDITED

BY

W. G. BEBBINGTON

LONDON

GEORGE ALLEN & UNWIN LTD

FIRST PUBLISHED IN 1949
SECOND IMPRESSION 1950
THIRD IMPRESSION 1954
FOURTH IMPRESSION 1960

PRINTED IN GREAT BRITAIN
in 11 Point Baskerville Type
BY BRADFORD AND DICKENS
LONDON, W.C.1

Dedicated to all
"Ye who listen with credulity to
the whispers of fancy"

ACKNOWLEDGMENTS

THE Editor and Publishers acknowledge with pleasure their indebtedness to the following for permission to include copyright stories :

Messrs. Ernest Benn Ltd. for "The Ghost Ship," Messrs. Chatto and Windus for "A Horseman in the Sky," Lord Dunsany and Messrs. Putnam & Co. for "How Jembu played for Cambridge" from *Travel Tales of Mr. Joseph Jorkens,* Mr. E. M. Forster and Messrs. Sidgwick & Jackson Ltd. for "The Celestial Omnibus," Messrs. Charles Lavell Ltd. for "Wottie," Mr. Linklater and Messrs. Jonathan Cape Ltd. for "The Dancers" from *God Likes Them Plain,* Mr. John Pudney and Messrs. John Lane Ltd. for "Uncle Arthur" from *It Breathed Down My Neck,* The Society of Authors as literary representative of the Trustees of the estate of the late W. W. Jacobs for "Over the Side," and Mrs. Marjorie Wells for "The Truth about Pyecraft."

"When Mrs. Jones opened the door she saw a small
boy standing outside.
'Please, mum, can I have my ball back?' he said.
'Where is it?' she asked.
'In your kitchen.'
'In my kitchen? But how did it get there?'
'Through the window.' "

THERE, surely, is the perfection of story-telling, in
forty-three words. Everything has stopped still, time and
space have lost relevance, the atmosphere is tense to
breaking-point, but relief comes only when it must—at
the end, when all is explained and nothing is settled.
Analyse the form, from the introduction of Mrs. Jones,
to the boy, the ball, the kitchen and—dreadful con-
clusion—the window, and you understand why there is
perfection : for form and content are mutually condi-
tional. We have been spellbound into fancy's world, and
when we return to our own world again we make but
fools of ourselves if we begin to explain, ask questions,
'fill in the blanks' or wonder how much it costs to mend
a broken window.

Yet no-one discusses the anecdote as literature, and it
has its own non-literary role to play after dinner and
behind the footlights. We are, moreover, concerned in this
book with the short story, which is literature and of
which, let it be admitted, the anecdote is only a *reductio
ad absurdum,* serving to illustrate an extreme of process.

At the other end of the scale is the novel, which also
may be a *reductio ad absurdum* of the short story and
which serves to illustrate the other extreme of process.
And somewhere between the forty-three words of our
anecdote and the scores of thousands of words of a novel

stands the short story, exactly placed, but we cannot tell exactly where. Its length may vary, but so may an anecdote's or a novel's : for length is of no consequence in and of itself : what makes one species of prose fiction a short story and neither an anecdote nor a novel is, simultaneously, what it is about and how it is about it, for these things are nowhere else to be found. It merely happens that they do not make for extreme brevity or extreme length : the stories in this book do not differ very much in size.

They do not differ at all in purpose or method. Whatever else one may read of, it is "absolutely nothing to the things that happen" in them. That is their purpose, to narrate the unique, and the anecdote and the novel are not fitted for that : *theirs* is a general purpose : the peculiar, the eccentric, is the short story's especial province. And if time is to stop and we are to join eternity ; if space is to cease and we are to join infinity ; then we need a certain minimum of time and space to accustom ourselves to the abnormal experience ; at the same time, however, we do not want too much of so good a thing. That is the method of the stories in this book. We who read certainly want to see the fairies at the bottom of the garden and so must go down the garden-path ; but we have to go back to the kitchen to make tea.

Such is the dual personality of the short story as it is seen at its best in the type of which these nine stories are examples—call it the fantastic type, the fanciful, the whimsical, what you will. There are fairies, but there are also kitchens ; there is story, but there is also a lesson to be learnt ; there is part, and there is whole ; there is nothing and everything ; there is economy and fulness, precision and suggestion ; neither too much nor too little ; there are a hundred questions which could be asked and none which should be. And there is fulfilment of the deep yearning in us all to have our legs pulled so that it does us good. Anecdotes and novels are not fitted to perform that very paradoxical function.

There are, of course, other types of short story, but none demonstrates or demands the short-story technique so triumphantly. We are not necessarily concerned with events on the Great Gromboolian Plain, however, for there is method in this madness, a reason for it all. Nothing ever happened like what happens in these pages —that is true; but, after all, you do require needles to play records.

W.G.B.

CONTENTS

JOHN PUDNEY

UNCLE ARTHUR

"OH, MOTHER, MOTHER! Look at the elephant coming down the garden," cried Lily. Her mother was thinking just then, however, and disregarded Lily's remark. Her mother was thinking about possessions.

So Lily ran and opened the front door, ready to let the elephant in. She was thrilled at the unusual visitor; though, judging by her mother's reticence, she should not have shown excitement. She had rarely seen elephants. Though she was receiving a normal education, regular nourishment, and a proper home environment, her opportunities of seeing them were almost negligible.

Something had happened at last: she had always known that it would.

She opened the door wide and smiled. She heard the gentle, rather ponderous breathing and the muffled but eager tread. She was impressed by the physical dimensions. She noticed that the eyes were twinkling like raindrops.

"I'm your Uncle Arthur," said the elephant.

"Oh, Mother, Mother! The elephant that has come says that he is Uncle Arthur!"

There was no reply. Her mother must be thinking. How rude. Lily smiled at the visitor who was standing patiently upon the threshold, completely filling it. Then she popped her head round the sitting-room door and interrupted her mother's thoughts.

"He says he's Uncle Arthur," she said.

"Who does?" said Mrs. Albion.

"Sh!" Lily made a polite gesture. "The elephant."

"What elephant, Lily?" Her mother looked cross.

"The elephant I told you about, who has just called."

"Lily! Come right in." Mother was wasting time, but she was very cross. "Now tell me: who is at the door?"

"Uncle Arthur."

Mrs. Albion winced. The child was imaginative, of course, that was the danger—a misfortune, in fact. *Uncle Arthur.* "I'll go to the door myself," she said.

They found the elephant wedged. Mrs. Albion screamed. Lily felt sorry for him, and frightened. He was stuck fast, more in than out.

"Help!" cried Mrs. Albion. "A zoo's escaped. Help! We shall be trampled underfoot!"

"Oh, Mother! He's terribly stuck. What can we do for him?"

"Come away, Lily. Quick! Run round to the Bridies and telephone. Call the police—for its keeper. I'll come with you. What a horrid great ugly brute!" For a moment she hesitated, to convince herself that he was wedged. She snatched an umbrella from the hall stand. She was outraged—she would defend her home.

She had half-turned towards the back door when she heard the kindly voice of the elephant again: "I'm your Uncle Arthur."

Mrs. Albion stopped. It was all very well for Lily, who was an imaginative child, to see elephants and hear them talk, but she was proud of the fact that she herself was practical. She had never heard elephants talk. She disbelieved them. There was no doubt, however, that an elephant was wedged in her front door.

"I'm your Uncle Arthur," he repeated.

A grey fear then enveloped her. When the Albions feared, it was grey and bleak in the house, like a November fog outside in the streets. The sitting-room sweated an emulsion of mistrust from its scrolled, crenellated and patterned content. The hall stand wilted in abject submission : the stairs looked weak and rickety at the first fearful thought. Then Mrs. Albion, in a grey voice, addressed the elephant.

"Will you repeat that, please?" she said through clenched teeth. She was desperate. One thought had taken the place of all others. It was a legend in the family that Uncle Arthur—whose uncle he was had never been clear—had been sent to prison for a long term, convicted of an unmentionable crime. That thought alone induced Mrs. Albion to address the elephant.

"He's said it twice, Mother," cried Lily; "and he must be terribly uncomfortable. . . ."

"Quiet, Lily! I wish him to repeat that remark."

The elephant eased his position. He regretted his haste in accepting Lily's invitation to come in. "I'm your Uncle Arthur," he repeated with some lack of enthusiasm. But Lily clapped her hands and danced round in front of him.

"I'm Lily!" she cried. "Little Lily!" Her voice rang out bravely against the grey pallor of the lincrusta in the hall. The bead curtains danced with her.

"But this is absurd. What will the neighbours think? Stop dancing, Lily! Go and play quietly out at the back." Mrs. Albion slammed the umbrella into the wickerwork stand. Her worst fears were realized, though she was satisfied now that she was in no danger of

3

physical attack. "And, Lily! Not a word of this, mind. If the Bridie kids are nosey, you had better ignore them. Now, out you go, and let me think in peace."

* * * *

"Good-bye, Uncle Arthur!" She ran out into the cold afternoon sunshine. How rude Mother had been. Uncle Arthur was standing there so meekly. Probably he was most uncomfortable, too. The least one could have done would have been to offer him a bun.

Lily was a kind, sweet-tempered child, in spite of Mrs. Albion's vigilance. It took more than a church-going mother and her rigid interpretations of truth to discover, much less disturb, the child's convictions. Lily had always believed that an amazing event would happen one wet afternoon. Hundreds of times she had imagined visitors such as Uncle Arthur appearing at the front door. Now it had happened, quite suddenly. A new truth had been added to life.

While Mother was trying to fit the visitor into the anxious interior of 'The Croft,' she would run out of the 'Tradesmen Only' and buy him a bun—or two, for there was twopence in her savings-box. She was not afraid of Uncle Arthur being sent away, because there had been undeniable anxiety in her mother's voice. It meant that the front door must be shut at once, before the Starks, from opposite, saw in. Besides, Uncle Arthur was wedged more in than out. It would be a job to get him out again.

So Lily skipped off through the 'Tradesmen Only,' and ran to the baker's shop, ignoring the Bridie children who called after her at the corner.

Mrs. Albion stood alone with the elephant in the frightened house. She was trying to calculate.

4

It was more difficult than calculating the hire-purchase terms of a mahogany radiogram (like the Bridies', only better): more difficult than finding the money for the motor-car insurance (the Starks had only a three-wheeler).

Mrs. Albion was trying to calculate the exact dimensions of the rumour she remembered hearing in family circles concerning Uncle Arthur and his unmentionable crime. It had not been mentioned for ten years. George had always declared, looking down his nose, that there were ugly things in many families which never need come to light if they were never mentioned in any circumstances. One must never take a risk with a thing like that, he had said. It led to loss of prestige, goodwill, and —inevitably—clientele.

And then, of course, there were the neighbours. Look at Mrs. Carver, when her sister was divorced. She was hardly able to go out of the house: and everyone sent her anonymous letters. Mrs. Albion turned over in her grey-curtained mind the words, "I'm your Uncle Arthur." There was something sinister, something irrevocably destructive, about them. From an elephant, too.

She was now satisfied that the patient beast that stood in front of her had said these words, and might say them again. She had heard, too, of elephants trumpeting, particularly when cornered. There was no time to be lost. The Bridies, the Starks, or (heaven forbid!) one of the snooty Miss Carvers, might at any moment pass, and, looking through the laurels, see the elephant. Worse still, they might hear him repeat his declaration.

"Come in," she said, "if you must. I'll put you into the conservatory till George comes home from work."

Wherever he had come from, Uncle Arthur could

never have encountered a less gracious invitation. The front door was pressed right back on its hinges as he strained to squeeze his hindquarters through. Mrs. Albion, her hands clumsy with fear and disgust, fretted with the bead curtains, and opened invitingly wide the double doors leading to the conservatory.

It was fortunate that for privacy George had white-washed the conservatory glass. At one time the neighbours had seemed to live upon the doorstep of the sitting-room which could be seen through the glass. George had determined that there were limits to neighbourliness: there was a point when you must keep yourself to your-self. That determination, Mrs. Albion reflected, had risen at the time he had become junior churchwarden. Now the whitened panes were to succour them in a situation which might imperil the very foundations of life at 'The Croft.' It showed, in a way, how guidance, and a little common sense, sometimes followed services unstintingly given: services which, at the time of their being offered to George, were considered to be of questionable value, as the Carvers were the only people in the road who went to church, and they alone were witness to the dignity of his duties.

Mrs. Albion sighed. There were no plants in the con-servatory; nothing but a few gardening tools and Lily's pram. She quickly moved these to one side. The elephant was still straining at the front door. Every moment jeo-pardized her position.

The latter end of that elephant writhing in her front door, were any of the neighbours or the tradesmen to catch sight of it, would give rise to endless rumour and speculation. Sooner or later Uncle Arthur's name would be mentioned.

No. Emergency action was necessary. Her own hat

hung upon the kitchen door. In another moment she had withdrawn one of its pins and was out through the 'Tradesmen Only.' There she met Lily carrying her little bag of buns.

"Oh, Mother, what are you going to do?" cried Lily, waving her bag. "Oh, Mother, I am excited!"

"Sh-sh! Remember what I told you about keeping to yourself. You'd better stay quietly in the kitchen till I call you."

"But you're not going to hurt Uncle Arthur with that pin?"

"Be quiet and mind your own business." Mrs. Albion's voice swept through the shrubberies like the grey wind.

"Shan't!" cried Lily defiantly. The shrubberies were lit with tinsel, like Christmas-trees. The 'Tradesmen Only' swung musically upon its hinges, twinkling with iridescent red like a huge garnet brooch. Uncle Arthur was just round the corner!

"What, Lily!" Mrs. Albion, half-stifled by the heavy air of the frightened shrubberies, was suddenly at a loss for words. She turned quickly and ran to the front door, from which the straining bulk of the elephant's haunches still protruded. All was lost if anyone should see her now, or overhear the cries of Lily. She staked her all on the efficacy of the hatpin, which she jabbed into a soft part of the great mammal which was inflicting such terror upon her home.

Immediately there was a roar, and the next moment the elephant was inside the house. With the voice of a church organ he emitted peal upon peal of sound.

"I'm your Uncle Arthur—Ouh!" he trumpeted. "I'm your Uncle Arthur—Ouh!" Mrs. Albion slammed the door after him. He went through the hall into the conservatory. But he continued to cry out. The neighbours could hardly fail to hear those cries from the conservatory. The elephant sat down on the place where she had jabbed him.

"Can't you be quiet now?" shouted Mrs. Albion.

The trumpetings continued.

What have we done, thought Mrs. Albion, that we should have been visited in this way? She thought of a dozen mean things she had done during the last few weeks. Not one of them seemed to justify the visitation of an elephant.

The trumpeting filled the house. The glass of the conservatory rattled. Lily came running in from the kitchen. Mrs. Albion made as if to slap her daughter for disobedience, for spending her pocket-money, and because she was afraid to slap the elephant. But Lily was too quick for her.

"Poor Uncle Arthur," she cried, going into the conservatory. "But look what I've brought for you. Buns!"

The trumpeting ceased.

With a benign expression, Uncle Arthur reached out his trunk and took the buns. He was satisfied: he liked buns. "Run round to the baker's and get half a dozen more, Lily. No, seven—for sixpence." Mrs. Albion could not conceal her relief. Seven buns, though extravagant, was not an impossible price to pay for security, till George came home from work. "And if you meet anybody, and they ask you what the noise was, say it was the wireless."

"Don't go and hurt him again while I'm gone, Mother. It's going to be such fun having him." The colours and shapes of a tropical jungle danced in profusion around her as she passed up the few yards of drive to the front gate. The late afternoon light which laved the tidy avenue in pungent ordinariness, swirled about her in magical effulgence.

Something had happened. The avenue, the drive, the front door, the wicker hat stand, and, most of all, the whitewashed conservatory, would never be the same again. An elephant had come.

"Lily, dear!" Mrs. Bridie leant over her gate. "Are you all right at home? We thought we heard such a funny sound just now. I was just going to send to see. . . ."

"Mother says it's our wireless." Nobody could tell an untruth and be aware of the glory of the afternoon.

"Oh a *new* wireless?" Mrs. Bridie felt that she had not been kept abreast with local affairs. Lily skipped on towards the baker's. Even her father passed unnoticed. Uncle Arthur will have had nine buns, she thought: how satisfied he will feel.

But all was not well at 'The Croft.'

George Albion, on his return from business, had not expected to find his wife conversing with an elephant.

"You had no business to come here," she was saying. "I don't care whether you starve or what happens. I'm not going to be made the talk, and, of course, the laughing-stock of the whole avenue. . . ." George stood still. It was not an elephant: it couldn't be.

"What *are* you talking about?" he asked, ignoring the elephant altogether.

"Can't you see, George?" snapped Mrs. Albion.

"Yes," he said, relieved that she saw it too. "An elephant."

"I should think it *is* an elephant."

"But what made you get it?" George Albion was losing his self-control. All things considered, his business reputation, his authority, his office in the church. . . .

"It came. It walked in." Hysterically she turned again to address the elephant. "I don't care whether you say you're Uncle Arthur, or not. . . ."

"I am your Uncle Arthur," said the elephant.

Mrs. Albion faced her husband as she would have faced death. There was no pride or arrogance or even cunning left in her demeanour. She looked sallow, rutted with anxiety: and all the Albions' fears emerged from their hiding-places behind the bead curtains.

"Does anyone know?" said Albion at last.

"Only Lily."

"Where is she?"

"Buying buns."

Mr. Albion glared. Buns on Sundays, yes—but on weekdays it was just the kind of extravagance he was determined to put down. His small anger vented his huge quaking fear. "Why buns?" he roared.

"For the elephant."

Mrs. Albion's words laid him like ashes. Nobody spoke till Lily returned. Nobody answered when she asked if she should give Uncle Arthur the buns. They watched her feed sixpennyworth of buns to the elephant. Then George announced that he would speak to the elephant alone. The legend about Uncle Arthur's crime had been unmentionable.

When they had gone, he lit the gas and questioned the elephant for an hour. He asked every question that a careful business man could ask an elephant. There was no reply at all. Then, looking closely at his visitor, he noticed that the small eyes were closed. The elephant was asleep.

That night, the Albions came to the most critical decision of their lives; they decided to keep Uncle Arthur concealed in the conservatory. It was the only safe course. With constant attention and vigilance they would be able to protect themselves from a danger which both agreed would destroy those virtues more precious than life itself, the respect of their neighbours, financial stability, and the support of the church. In the course of time the elephant might be induced to explain himself.

"Shall I buy some more buns for Uncle Arthur?" said Lily at breakfast.

"Yes, dear. Run and get seven more."

With the sixpence warm in her hand, Lily ran out into the bright new morning.

"What, more buns?" said the baker's wife. "You are a hungry girl, Lily."

"We shall need plenty of buns just now," replied Lily, with joy in her voice which the baker's wife failed to understand.

Plenty of buns were needed at 'The Croft.'

During the next fortnight they tried every form of food, from dog-biscuits to rice-pudding. Uncle Arthur disliked them all. With anything but buns he grew restless, muttering to himself, and threatening to trumpet as he had done when Mrs. Albion jabbed him. He needed plenty of buns. It varied from three to four dozen. It was no good running and buying them by the bag. They were sent round by special delivery.

"And the more buns they has," said the baker's wife to Mrs. Bridie, "the thinner they gets. Like a pair of shadows, though Lily don't seem to suffer. . . ."

Mrs. Bridie nodded. "I shouldn't wonder," she said, "if there's not something going on. Just what it is, I can't get at. . . ."

Everybody suspected something, but nobody suspected that the Albions were keeping an elephant.

Uncle Arthur said very little for three weeks, but he seemed to think his own thoughts, not snatchily as Lily had seen her mother think about possessions, but rhythmically like rain on wet afternoons. He was a pleasure to watch.

George Albion took to sitting by the conservatory door in the evenings, at first in order to carry on interrogation, but later because he, too, found pleasure in watching Uncle Arthur think. Sometimes he caught himself thinking himself: and one evening he read a book to Lily and the elephant.

Mrs. Albion did not join them until a week or so later, when the intensity of local gossip drove her out of the sitting-room. They gave up lighting the gas there because people were always calling on some pretext or other and mentioning casually the subject of buns.

Three to four dozen buns a day for three people.

Every other evening one of the Miss Carvers would call to see if her cat had strayed. Young Stark would pop in to borrow insulating tape. The Bridies—any pretext was enough for them.

Mrs. Albion became much kindlier when she met them all in the street, however: and everyone agreed that Lily was radiant. Lily had lost her spots: and that couldn't be buns.

Mrs. Albion found that sitting with Uncle Arthur calmed her. Sometimes she held Lily's hand and sometimes when they were all sitting round together she sang rather sentimental songs. The bead curtains clicked merrily and Uncle Arthur's eyes twinkled.

Except for the expense of buying buns, fears and anxieties vanished from the Albions' home. They had sold the car and sold the wireless set, and were wondering what to give Uncle Arthur for Christmas, when they realized that they had very little money left.

"Though we shall always be quite happy on what I earn," beamed George Albion.

"I think it's time Uncle Arthur worked for his living, too," said Lily. "I'll tell him there's no more buns, and see what he does."

"He's a lazy old thing, bless him," sighed Mrs. Albion. "It's a pity he costs us so much in buns; but then, I must say I don't grudge it."

That night Lily told the elephant that there were no more buns when she went to kiss him good-night. They all laughed when she said it. They wondered if it would make him think of something new to say. But he thought ponderously that evening and went to sleep early.

In the morning he had gone.

"How he went through that door beats me!" muttered Albion.

"We shall have to tell the baker not to send the buns," sighed Mrs. Albion.

Lily cried a little at first. But the world had not changed: it was still full of surprise. Something had happened. They bought her a small grey toy elephant for Christmas. But her father and mother laughed more often now, and they all agreed that it was not a good substitute for Uncle Arthur, so they burnt it.

In the avenue and round the corner, the inhabitants discussed the Albions' order for buns, whenever more than one of them was gathered together. Its sudden cessation did nothing to diminish speculation. It gave the story a finality which added to its relish.

They discuss it still: and if the Albions overhear them, they just laugh.

AMBROSE BIERCE

A HORSEMAN IN THE SKY

ONE sunny afternoon in the autumn of the year 1861, a soldier lay in a clump of laurel by the side of a road in Western Virginia. He lay at full length, upon his stomach, his feet resting upon the toes, his head upon the left forearm. His extended right hand loosely grasped his rifle. But for the somewhat methodical disposition of his limbs and a slight rhythmic movement of the cartridge box at the back of his belt, he might have been thought to be dead. He was asleep at his post of duty. But if detected he would be dead shortly afterwards, that being the just and legal penalty of his crime.

The clump of laurel in which the criminal lay was in the angle of a road which, after ascending, southward, a steep acclivity to that point, turned sharply to the west, running along the summit for perhaps one hundred yards. There it turned southwards again and went zigzagging downward through the forest. At the salient of that second angle was a large flat rock, jutting out from the ridge to the northward, overlooking the deep valley from which the road ascended. The rock capped a high cliff; a stone dropped from its outer edge would have fallen sheer downward one thousand feet to the tops of the pines. The angle where the soldier lay was on another spur of the same cliff. Had he been awake he would have commanded a view, not only of the short arm of the road and jutting rock but of the entire profile of the cliff below it. It might well have made him giddy to look.

The country was wooded everywhere except at the bottom of the valley to the northward, where there was a small natural meadow, through which flowed a stream scarcely visible from the valley's rim. This open ground looked hardly larger than an ordinary door-yard, but was really several acres in extent. Its green was more vivid than that of the enclosing forest. Away beyond it rose a line of giant cliffs similar to those upon which we are supposed to stand in our survey of the savage scene, and through which the road had somehow made its climb to the summit. The configuration of the valley, indeed, was such that from our point of observation it seemed entirely shut in, and one could not but have wondered how the road which found a way out of it had found a way into it, and whence came and whither went the waters of the stream that parted the meadow two thousand feet below.

No country is so wild and difficult but men will make it a theatre of war; concealed in the forest at the bottom of that military rat-trap, in which half a hundred men in possession of the exits might have starved an army to submission, lay five regiments of Federal infantry. They had marched all the previous day and night and were resting. At nightfall they would take to the road again, climb to the place where their unfaithful sentinel now slept, and, descending the other slope of the ridge, fall upon a camp of the enemy at about midnight. Their hope was to surprise it, for the road led to the rear of it. In case of failure their position would be perilous in the extreme; and fail they surely would should accident or vigilance apprise the enemy of the movement.

15

The sleeping sentinel in the clump of laurel was a young Virginian named Carter Druse. He was the son of wealthy parents, an only child, and had known such ease and cultivation and high living as wealth and taste were able to command in the mountain country of Western Virginia. His home was but a few miles from where he now lay. One morning he had risen from the breakfast table and said, quietly but gravely, "Father, a Union regiment has arrived at Grafton. I am going to join it."

The father lifted his leonine head, looked at the son a moment in silence, and replied, "Go, Carter, and, whatever may occur, do what you conceive to be your duty. Virginia, to which you are a traitor, must get on without you. Should we both live to the end of the war, we will speak further of the matter. Your mother, as the physician has informed you, is in a most critical condition; at the best she cannot be with us longer than a few weeks, but that time is precious. It would be better not to disturb her."

So Carter Druse, bowing reverently to his father, who returned the salute with a stately courtesy which masked a breaking heart, left the home of his childhood to go soldiering. By conscience and courage, by deeds of devotion and daring, he soon commended himself to his fellows and his officers; and it was to these qualities and to some knowledge of the country that he owed his selection for his present perilous duty at the extreme outpost. Nevertheless, fatigue had been stronger than resolution, and he had fallen asleep. What good or bad angel came in a dream to rouse him from his state of crime who shall say? Without a movement, without a sound, in the profound silence and the languor of the later afternoon, some invisible messenger of fate touched with unsealing finger the eyes of his consciousness—whispered into the ear of his spirit the mysterious awakening word which no human lips have ever spoken, no human memory ever has recalled. He quietly raised his forehead from his arm and looked between the masking stems of the laurels, instinctively closing his right hand about the stock of his rifle.

His first feeling was a keen artistic delight. On a colossal pedestal, the cliff, motionless at the extreme edge of the capping rock and sharply outlined against the sky, was an equestrian statue of impressive dignity. The figure of the man sat the figure of the horse, straight and soldierly, but with the repose of a Grecian god carved in the marble which limits the suggestion of activity. The grey costume harmonized with its aerial background; the metal of accoutrement and caparison was softened and subdued by the shadow; the animal's skin had no points of high light. A carbine, strikingly foreshortened, lay across the pommel of the saddle, kept in place by the right hand grasping it at the 'grip'; the left hand, holding the bridle rein, was invisible. In silhouette against the sky, the profile of the horse was cut with the sharpness of a cameo; it looked across the heights of air to the confronting cliffs beyond. The face of the rider, turned slightly to the left, showed only an outline of temple and beard; he was looking downward to the bottom of the valley. Magnified by its lift against the sky and by the soldier's testifying sense of the formidableness of a near enemy, the group appeared of heroic, almost colossal, size.

For an instant Druse had a strange, half-defined feeling that he had slept to the end of the war and was looking upon a noble work of art reared upon that commanding eminence to commemorate the deeds of an heroic past of which he had been an inglorious part. The feeling was dispelled by a slight movement of the group; the horse, without moving its feet, had drawn its body slightly backward from the verge; the man remained immobile as before. Broad awake and keenly alive to the significance of the situation, Druse now brought the butt of his rifle against his cheek by cautiously pushing the barrel forward through the bushes, cocked the piece, and, glancing through the sights, covered a vital spot of the horseman's breast. A touch upon the trigger and all would have been well with Carter Druse. At that instant the horseman turned his head and looked in the direction of his concealed foeman—seemed to look into his very face, into his eyes, into his brave, compassionate heart.

Is it, then, so terrible to kill an enemy in war—an enemy who has surprised a secret vital to the safety of one's self and comrades—an enemy more formidable for his knowledge than all his army for its numbers? Carter Druse grew deathly pale ; he shook in every limb, turned faint, and saw the statuesque group before him as black figures, rising, falling, moving unsteadily in arcs of circles in a fiery sky. His hand fell away from his weapon, his head slowly dropped until his face rested on the leaves in which he lay. This courageous gentleman and hardy soldier was near swooning from intensity of emotion.

It was not for long; in another moment his face was raised from earth, his hands resumed their places on the rifle, his forefinger sought the trigger; mind, heart, and eyes were clear, conscience and reason sound. He could not hope to capture that enemy; to alarm him would but send him dashing to his camp with his fatal news. The duty of the soldier was plain : the man must be shot dead from ambush—without warning, without a moment's spiritual preparation, with never so much as an unspoken prayer, he must be sent to his account. But no—there is a hope; he may have discovered nothing—perhaps he is but admiring the sublimity of the landscape. If permitted he may turn and ride carelessly away in the direction whence he came. Surely it will be possible to judge at the instant of his withdrawing whether he knows. It may well be that his fixity of attention—Druse turned his head and looked below, through the deeps of air downward, as from the surface to the bottom of a translucent sea. He saw creeping across the green meadow a sinuous line of figures of men and horses—some foolish commander was permitting the soldiers of his escort to water their beasts in the open, in plain view from a hundred summits!

Druse withdrew his eyes from the valley and fixed them again upon the group of man and horse in the sky, and again it was through the sights of his rifle. But this time his aim was at the horse. In his memory, as if they were a divine mandate, rang the words of his father at their parting, "Whatever may occur, do what you conceive to be your duty." He was calm now. His teeth were firmly but not rigidly closed; his nerves were as tranquil as a sleeping babe's—not a tremor affected any muscle of his body; his breathing, until suspended in the act of taking aim, was regular and slow. Duty had conquered; the spirit had said to the body, "Peace, be still." He fired.

At that moment an officer of the Federal force, who, in a spirit of adventure or in quest of knowledge, had left the hidden *bivouac* in the valley, and, with aimless feet, had made his way to the lower edge of a small open space near the foot of the cliff, was considering what he had to gain by pushing his exploration further. At a distance of a quarter-mile before him, but apparently at a stone's throw, rose from its fringe of pines the gigantic face of rock, towering to so great a height above him

that it made him giddy to look up to where its edge cut
a sharp, rugged line against the sky. At some distance
away to his right it presented a clean, vertical profile
against a background of blue sky to a point half of the
way down, and of distant hills hardly less blue thence to
the tops of the trees at its base. Lifting his eyes to the
dizzy altitude of its summit, the officer saw an astonishing
sight—a man on horseback riding down into the valley
through the air!

Straight upright sat the rider, in military fashion, with
a firm seat in the saddle, a strong clutch upon the rein
to hold his charger from too impetuous a plunge. From
his bare head his long hair streamed upward, waving
like a plume. His right hand was concealed in the cloud
of the horse's lifted mane. The animal's body was as level
as if every hoof stroke encountered the resistant earth.
Its motions were those of a wild gallop, but even as the
officer looked they ceased, with all the legs thrown
sharply forward as in the act of alighting from a leap.
But this was a flight!

Filled with amazement and terror by this apparition
of a horseman in the sky—half believing himself the
chosen scribe of some new Apocalypse, the officer was
overcome by the intensity of his emotions; his legs failed
him and he fell. Almost at the same instant he heard a
crashing sound in the trees—a sound that died without
an echo, and all was still.

The officer rose to his feet, trembling. The familiar
sensation of an abraded shin recalled his dazed faculties.
Pulling himself together, he ran rapidly obliquely away
from the cliff to a point a half-mile from its foot; thereabout he expected to find his man; and thereabout he
naturally failed. In the fleeting instant of his vision his
imagination had been so wrought upon by the apparent

grace and ease and intention of the marvellous performance that it did not occur to him that the line of march of aerial cavalry is directed downward, and that he could find the objects of his search at the very foot of the cliff. A half-hour later he returned to camp.

This officer was a wise man; he knew better than to tell an incredible truth. He said nothing of what he had seen. But when the commander asked him if in his scout he had learned anything of advantage to the expedition, he answered:

"Yes, sir; there is no road leading down into this valley from the southward."

The commander, knowing better, smiled.

After firing his shot Private Carter Druse reloaded his rifle and resumed his watch. Ten minutes had hardly passed when a Federal sergeant crept cautiously to him on hands and knees. Druse neither turned his head nor looked at him, but lay without motion or sign of recognition.

"Did you fire?" the sergeant whispered.

"Yes."

"At what?"

"A horse. It was standing on yonder rock—pretty far out. You see it is no longer there. It went over the cliff."

The man's face was white but he showed no other sign of emotion. Having answered, he turned away his face and said no more. The sergeant did not understand.

"See here, Druse," he said, after a moment's silence, "it's no use making a mystery. I order you to report. Was there anybody on the horse?"

"Yes."

"Who?"

"My father."

The sergeant rose to his feet and walked away. "Good God!" he said.

H. G. WELLS

THE TRUTH ABOUT PYECRAFT

H E sits not a dozen yards away. If I glance over my shoulder I can see him. And if I catch his eye—and usually I catch his eye—it meets me with an expression.

It is mainly an imploring look—and yet with suspicion in it.

Confound his suspicion! If I wanted to tell on him I should have told long ago. I don't tell and I won't tell, and he ought to feel at his ease! As if anything so gross and fat as he could feel at ease. Who would believe me if I did tell?

Poor old Pyecraft! Great, uneasy jelly of substance. The fattest clubman in London.

He sits at one of the little club tables in the huge bay by the fire, stuffing. What is he stuffing? I glance judiciously and catch him biting at a round of hot buttered tea-cake, with his eyes on me. Confound him! —with his eyes on me!

That settles it, Pyecraft! Since you *will* be abject, since you *will* behave as though I was not a man of honour, here, right under your embedded eyes, I write the thing down—the plain truth about Pyecraft. The man I helped, the man I shielded, and who has requited me by making my club unendurable, absolutely unendurable, with his liquid appeal, with the perpetual "don't tell" of his looks.

And, besides, why does he keep on eternally eating?

Well, here goes for the truth, the whole truth, and nothing but the truth!

Pyecraft—I made the acquaintance of Pyecraft in this very smoking-room. I was a young, nervous new member, and he saw it. I was sitting all alone, wishing I knew more of the members, and suddenly he came, a great rolling front of chins and abdomina, towards me, and grunted and sat down in a chair close by me and wheezed for a space, and scraped for a space with a match and lit a cigar, and then addressed me. I forget what he said —something about the matches not lighting properly, and afterwards as he talked he kept stopping the waiters one by one as they went by, and telling them about the matches in that thin, fluty voice he has. But, anyhow, it was in some such way we began our talking.

He talked about various things and came round to games. And thence to my figure and complexion. "You ought to be a good cricketer," he said. I suppose I am slender, slender to what some people would call lean, and I suppose I am rather dark, still—I am not ashamed of having a Hindu great-grandmother, but, for all that, I don't want casual strangers to see through me at a glance to *her*. So that I was set against Pyecraft from the beginning.

But he only talked about me in order to get to himself.

"I expect," he said, "you take no more exercise than I do, and probably you eat no less." (Like all excessively obese people he fancied he ate nothing.) "Yet"—and he smiled an oblique smile—"we differ."

And then he began to talk about his fatness and his fatness; all he did for his fatness and all he was going to do for his fatness; what people had advised him to do for his fatness and what he had heard of people doing for fatness similar to his. *"A priori,"* he said, "one would think a question of nutrition could be answered by dietary and a question of assimilation by drugs." It was stifling. It was dumpling talk. It made me feel swelled to hear him.

One stands that sort of thing once in a way at a club, but a time came when I fancied I was standing too much. He took to me altogether too conspicuously. I could never go into the smoking-room but he would come wallowing towards me, and sometimes he came and gormandized round and about me while I had my lunch. He seemed at times almost to be clinging to me. He was a bore, but not so fearful a bore as to be limited to me; and from the first there was something in his manner—almost as though he knew, almost as though he penetrated to the fact that I might—that there was a remote, exceptional chance in me that no one else presented.

"I'd give anything to get it down," he would say— "anything," and peer at me over his vast cheeks and pant.

Poor old Pyecraft! He had just gonged, no doubt to order another buttered tea-cake!

He came to the actual thing one day. "Our Pharmacopoeia," he said, "our Western Pharmacopoeia is anything but the last word of medical science. In the East, I've been told—"

He stopped and stared at me. It was like being at an aquarium.

I was quite suddenly angry with him. "Look here," I said, "who told you about my great-grandmother's recipes?"

"Well," he fenced.

"Every time we've met for a week," I said—"and

we've met pretty often—you've given me a broad hint or so about that little secret of mine."

"Well," he said, "now the cat's out of the bag, I'll admit, yes, it is so. I had it—"

"From Pattison?"

"Indirectly,"he said, which I believe was lying, "yes."

"Pattison," I said, "took that stuff at his own risk."

He pursed his mouth and bowed.

"My great-grandmother's recipes," I said, "are queer things to handle. My father was near making me promise—"

"He didn't?"

"No. But he warned me. He himself used one—once."

"Ah! . . . But do you think—? Suppose—suppose there did happen to be one—"

"The things are curious documents," I said. "Even the smell of 'em. . . . No!"

But after going so far Pyecraft was resolved I should go farther. I was always a little afraid if I tried his patience too much he would fall on me suddenly and smother me. I own I was weak. But I was also annoyed with Pyecraft. I had got to that state of feeling for him that disposed me to say, "Well, *take* the risk." The little affair of Pattison to which I have alluded was a different matter altogether. What it was doesn't concern us now, but I knew, anyhow, that the particular recipe I used then was safe. The rest I didn't know so much about, and, on the whole, I was inclined to doubt their safety pretty completely.

Yet even if Pyecraft got poisoned—

I must confess the poisoning of Pyecraft struck me as an immense undertaking.

That evening I took that queer, odd-scented sandal-wood box out of my safe and turned the rustling skins over. The gentleman who wrote the recipes for my great-grandmother evidently had a weakness for skins of a miscellaneous origin, and his handwriting was cramped to the last degree. Some of the things are quite unreadable to me—though my family, with its Indian Civil Service associations, has kept up a knowledge of Hindustani from generation to generation—and none are absolutely plain sailing. But I found the one that I knew was there soon enough, and sat on the floor by my safe for some time looking at it.

"Look here," said I to Pyecraft next day, and snatched the slip away from his eager grasp.

"So far as I can make it out, this is a recipe for Loss of Weight. ("Ah!" said Pyecraft.) I'm not absolutely sure, but I think it's that. And if you take my advice you'll leave it alone. Because, you know—I blacken my blood in your interest, Pyecraft—my ancestors on that side were, so far as I can gather, a jolly queer lot. See?"

"Let me try it," said Pyecraft.

I leant back in my chair. My imagination made one mighty effort and fell flat within me. "What in Heaven's name, Pyecraft," I asked, "do you think you'll look like when you get thin?"

He was impervious to reason. I made him promise never to say a word to me about his disgusting fatness again whatever happened—never, and then I handed him that little piece of skin.

"It's nasty stuff," I said.

"No matter," he said, and took it.

He goggled at it. "But—but—" he said.

He had just discovered that it wasn't English.

"To the best of my ability," I said, "I will do you a translation."

I did my best. After that we didn't speak for a fortnight. Whenever he approached me I frowned and motioned him away, and he respected our compact, but at the end of the fortnight he was as fat as ever. And then he got a word in.

"I must speak," he said. "It isn't fair. There's something wrong. It's done me no good. You're not doing your great-grandmother justice."

"Where's the recipe?"

He produced it gingerly from his pocket-book.

I ran my eye over the items. "Was the egg addled?" I asked.

"No. Ought it to have been?"

"That," I said, "goes without saying in all my poor dear great-grandmother's recipes. When condition or quality is not specified you must get the worst. She was drastic or nothing. . . . And there's one or two possible alternatives to some of these other things. You got *fresh* rattlesnake venom?"

"I got a rattlesnake from Jamrach's. It cost—it cost—"

"That's your affair, anyhow. This last item—"

"I know a man who—"

"Yes. H'm. Well, I'll write the alternatives down. So far as I know the language, the spelling of this recipe is particularly atrocious. By the bye, dog here probably means pariah dog."

For a month after that I saw Pyecraft constantly at the club and as fat and anxious as ever. He kept our treaty, but at times he broke the spirit of it by shaking his head despondently. Then one day in the cloakroom he said, "Your great-grandmother—"

"Not a word against her," I said; and he held his peace.

I could have fancied he had desisted, and I saw him

one day talking to three new members about his fatness as though he was in search of other recipes. And then, quite unexpectedly, his telegram came.

"Mr. Formalyn!" bawled a page-boy under my nose, and I took the telegram and opened it at once.

"For Heaven's sake come—Pyecraft."

"H'm," said I, and to tell the truth I was so pleased at the rehabilitation of my great-grandmother's reputation this evidently promised that I made a most excellent lunch.

I got Pyecraft's address from the hall porter. Pyecraft inhabited the upper half of a house in Bloomsbury, and I went there so soon as I had done my coffee and Trappistine. I did not wait to finish my cigar.

"Mr. Pyecraft?" said I, at the front door.

They believed he was ill; he hadn't been out for two days.

"He expects me," said I, and they sent me up.

I rang the bell at the lattice-door upon the landing.

"He shouldn't have tried it, anyhow," I said to myself. "A man who eats like a pig ought to look like a pig."

An obviously worthy woman, with an anxious face and a carelessly placed cap, came and surveyed me through the lattice.

I gave my name and she opened his door for me in a dubious fashion.

"Well?" said I, as we stood together inside Pyecraft's piece of the landing.

"'E said you was to come in if you came," she said, and regarded me, making no motion to show me anywhere. And then, confidentially, "'E's locked in, sir."

"Locked in?"

"Locked himself in yesterday morning and 'asn't let anyone in since, sir. And ever and again *swearing*. Oh, my!"

I stared at the door she indicated by her glances. "In there?" I said.

"Yes, sir."

"What's up?"

She shook her head sadly. "'E keeps on calling for vittles, sir. *'Eavy* vittles 'e wants. I get 'im what I can. Pork 'e's 'ad, sooit puddin', sossiges, noo bread. Everythink like that. Left outside, if you please, and me go away. 'E's eatin', sir, somethink *awful*."

There came a piping bawl from inside the door: "That Formalyn?"

"That you, Pyecraft?" I shouted, and went and banged the door.

"Tell her to go away."

I did.

Then I could hear a curious pattering upon the door, almost like someone feeling for the handle in the dark, and Pyecraft's familiar grunts.

"It's all right," I said, "she's gone."

But for a long time the door didn't open.

I heard the key turn. Then Pyecraft's voice said, "Come in."

I turned the handle and opened the door. Naturally I expected to see Pyecraft.

Well, you know, he wasn't there!

I never had such a shock in my life. There was his sitting-room in a state of untidy disorder, plates and dishes among the books and writing things, and several chairs overturned, but Pyecraft—

"It's all right, o' man; shut the door," he said, and then I discovered him.

There he was right up close to the cornice in the corner by the door, as though someone had glued him to the ceiling. His face was anxious and angry. He panted and gesticulated. "Shut the door," he said. "If that woman gets hold of it—"

I shut the door, and went and stood away from him and stared.

"If anything gives way and you tumble down," I said, "you'll break your neck, Pyecraft."

"I wish I could," he wheezed.

"A man of your age and weight getting up to kiddish gymnastics—"

"Don't," he said, and looked agonized. "Your damned great-grandmother—"

"Be careful," I warned him.

"I'll tell you," he said, and gesticulated.

"How the deuce," said I, "are you holding on up there?"

And then abruptly I realized that he was not holding on at all, that he was floating up there—just as a gas-filled bladder might have floated in the same position. He began a struggle to thrust himself away from the ceiling and to clamber down the wall to me. "It's that prescription," he panted, as he did so. "Your great-gran—"

"*No!*" I cried.

He took hold of a framed engraving rather carelessly as he spoke and it gave way, and he flew back to the ceiling again, while the picture smashed on to the sofa. Bump he went against the ceiling, and I knew then why he was all over white on the more salient curves and angles of his person. He tried again more carefully, coming down by way of the mantel.

It was really a most extraordinary spectacle, that great, fat, apopletic-looking man upside down and trying to get from the ceiling to the floor. "That prescription," he said. "Too successful."

"How?"

"Loss of weight—almost complete."

And then, of course, I understood.

"By Jove, Pyecraft," said I, "what you wanted was a cure for fatness! But you always called it weight. You would call it weight."

Somehow I was extremely delighted. I quite liked Pyecraft for the time. "Let me help you!" I said, and took his hand and pulled him down. He kicked about, trying to get foothold somewhere. It was very like holding a flag on a windy day.

"That table," he said, pointing, "is solid mahogany and very heavy. If you can put me under that—"

I did, and there he wallowed about like a captive balloon, while I stood on his hearthrug and talked to him.

I lit a cigar. "Tell me," I said, "what happened?"

"I took it," he said.

"How did it taste?"

"Oh, *beastly!*"

I should fancy they all did. Whether one regards the ingredients or the probable compound or the possible results, almost all my great-grandmother's remedies appear to me at least to be extraordinarily uninviting. For my own part—

"I took a little sip first."

"Yes?"

"And as I felt lighter and better after an hour, I decided to take the draught."

"My dear Pyecraft!"

"I held my nose," he explained. "And then I kept on getting lighter and lighter—and helpless, you know."

He gave way suddenly to a burst of passion. "What the goodness am I to *do?*" he said.

"There's one thing pretty evident," I said, "that you mustn't do. If you go out of doors you'll go up and up." I waved an arm upward. "They'd have to send Santos-Dumont after you to bring you down again."

"I suppose it will wear off?"

I shook my head. "I don't think you can count on that," I said.

And then there was another burst of passion, and he kicked out at adjacent chairs and banged the floor. He behaved just as I should have expected a great, fat, self-indulgent man to behave under trying circumstances—that is to say, very badly. He spoke of me and of my great-grandmother with an utter want of discretion.

"I never asked you to take the stuff," I said.

And generously disregarding the insults he was putting upon me, I sat down in his arm-chair and began to talk to him in a sober, friendly fashion.

I pointed out to him that this was a trouble he had brought upon himself, and that it had almostly an air of poetical justice. He had eaten too much. This he disputed, and for a time we argued the point.

He became noisy and violent, so I desisted from this aspect of his lesson. "And then," I said, "you committed the sin of euphuism. You called it, not Fat, which is just and inglorious, but Weight. You—"

He interrupted to say that he recognized all that. What was he to *do?*

I suggested he should adapt himself to his new conditions. So we came to the really sensible part of the business. I suggested that it would not be difficult for him to learn to walk about on the ceiling with his hands—

"I can't sleep," he said.

But that was no great difficulty. It was quite possible, I

pointed out, to make a shake-up under a wire mattress, fasten the under things on with tapes, and have a blanket, sheet, and coverlet to button at the side. He would have to confide in his housekeeper, I said; and after some squabbling he agreed to that. (Afterwards it was quite delightful to see the beautifully matter-of-fact way with which the good lady took all these amazing inversions.) He could have a library ladder in his room, and all his meals could be laid on the top of his bookcase. We also hit on an ingenious device by which he could get to the floor whenever he wanted, which was simply to put the *British Encyclopædia* (tenth edition) on the top of his open shelves. He just pulled out a couple of volumes and held on, and down he came. And we agreed there must be iron staples along the skirting, so that he could cling to those whenever he wanted to get about the room on the lower level.

As we got on with the thing I found myself almost keenly interested. It was I who called in the housekeeper and broke matters to her, and it was I chiefly who fixed up the inverted bed. In fact, I spent two whole days at his flat. I am a handy, interfering sort of man with a screwdriver, and I made all sorts of ingenious adaptations for him—ran a wire to bring his bells within reach, turned all his electric lights up instead of down, and so on. The whole affair was extremely curious and interesting to me, and it was delightful to think of Pyecraft like some great, fat blow-fly, crawling about on his ceiling and clambering round the lintel of his doors from one room to another, and never, never, never coming to the club any more. . . .

Then, you know, my fatal ingenuity got the better of me. I was sitting by his fire drinking his whisky, and he was up in his favourite corner by the cornice, tacking a

Turkey carpet to the ceiling, when the idea struck me. "By Jove, Pyecraft!" I said, "all this is totally unnecessary."

And before I could calculate the complete consequences of my notion I blurted it out. "Lead underclothing," said I, and the mischief was done.

Pyecraft received the thing almost in tears. "To be right ways up again—" he said.

I gave him the whole secret before I saw where it would take me. "Buy sheet lead," I said, "stamp it into discs. Sew 'em all over your underclothes until you have enough. Have lead-soled boots, carry a bag of solid lead, and the thing is done! Instead of being a prisoner here you may go abroad again, Pyecraft; you may travel—"

A still happier idea came to me. "You need never fear a shipwreck. All you need do is just slip off some or all of your clothes, take the necessary amount of luggage in your hand, and float up in the air—"

In his emotion he dropped the tack-hammer within an ace of my head. "By Jove!" he said, "I shall be able to come back to the club again."

The thing pulled me up short. "By Jove!" I said, faintly, "Yes. Of course—you will."

He did. He does. There he sits behind me now, stuffing—as I live!—a third go of buttered tea-cake. And no one in the whole world knows—except his housekeeper and me—that he weighs practically nothing; that he is a mere boring mass of assimilatory matter, mere clouds in clothing, *niente, nefas,* the most inconsiderable of men. There he sits watching until I have done this writing. Then, if he can, he will waylay me. He will come billowing up to me. . . .

He will tell me over again all about it, how it feels, how it doesn't feel, how he sometimes hopes it is passing off a little. And always somewhere in that fat, abundant discourse he will say, "The secret's keeping, eh? If anyone knew of it—I should be so ashamed. . . . Makes a fellow look such a fool, you know. Crawling about on a ceiling and all that. . . ."

And now to elude Pyecraft, occupying, as he does, an admirable strategic position between me and the door.

ERIC LINKLATER

THE DANCERS

MR. G. P. POMFRET was a wealthy man and the centre of as large a circle of friends and relations as the junior partner in a prosperous brewery might reasonably expect to be. But, until he disappeared, he was not famous. Then he became a household word, and the five members of his family—consanguineous, allied and presumptively allied—who disappeared with him, all earned pages in those indefatigable supplements to our national biography, the Sunday newspapers. For with Mr. Pomfret there also vanished Mrs. Pomfret his wife; Lt.-Commander Hugo Disney and Mrs. Disney (*née* Pomfret); Miss Joan Pomfret; and Mr. George Otto Samways, her fiancé.

The circumstances of their joint occultation were remarkable, and as the geographical environment was sufficiently and yet not immeasurably remote from the more advertised holiday haunts of man, the affair took to itself a halo of romance that was entirely different from the hectic nimbus which ever and again makes some obscure police-court luminous.

It has been said that Mr. Pomfret was wealthy. He had inherited a large number of shares in an excellent brewery and with them a sanguine and speculative temperament. His fortune persuaded the members of his family, initial and contributory, readily to accept a certain imperiousness of temper which Mr. Pomfret occasionally exhibited; and so when one evening early in June he said, from the top of his dinner-table, "I intend, subject to your approval, to take you all with me on a somewhat unusual holiday," his household (including Lt.-Commander Hugo Disney) and the solitary guest (Mr. George Otto Samways) accepted the invitation in the manner of a royal command.

"Where are we going, daddy?" asked Joan, adeptly disengaging the integument of her peach.

"To Orkney, my dear," replied Mr. Pomfret, and surveyed with benign amusement the expressions of surprise which impinged upon or flitted across the faces of his domestic audience.

Lt.-Commander Disney alone showed no amazement. "That's excellent," he said heartily, "I've meant for long enough to go back there."

Orkney is worthy of some attention. The islands have a romantic appeal as the home of lost races. The Vikings settled there, and before the Vikings there was a mysterious people, Picts or such, little men who vanished and left few traces of their occupation. At some time Culdee monks from Ireland went there; and went again as silently. Stewart earls ruled the islands like young pagan emperors. When the Great War began the British Fleet chose Scapa Flow, in the heart of the Orkneys, as its headquarters and battle haven. Later the German Fleet also rested there; but at the still bottom, not on the wind-flawed surface of the waters.

It was, however, the excellence of the trout-fishing which led Lt.-Commander Disney to applaud Mr. Pomfret's decision. He had spent the less active intervals in three years of naval warfare in Scapa Flow, and had become acquainted with the opportunities of sport which the island lochs offered to a fisherman robust enough to disregard occasional inclemencies of weather. Frequently he had spoken to Mr. Pomfret of brown trout and sea trout, praising their strain of fishy pugnacity and the delicate savour of their flesh; praising too the lure of sunny waters under a canopy of brilliant sky all painted with cloud galleons, porpoises and swimming dolphins of cloud, and at evening gorgeous with the barred crimson and gold, the errant greens, the daffodil hues, the rosy outflung feathers, of the sun sliding backwards behind the enormous wall of the Atlantic. And these conversations, moving like yeast in Mr. Pomfret's brain, had finally given rise to this momentous decision.

It is unnecessary to consider the manner of the journey north, which was complicated. Mr. Pomfret had rented for two months a large house called Swandale, in one of the seaward parishes in the northern part of the mainland of Orkney; it was considered advisable to take, as well as his family, a motor-car, a chauffeur and three maids. The first week or so of their residence passed pleasantly enough. They were enraptured with the scenery, the vast stretches of ever-changing sea, the majestic cliffs loud with the ceaseless activity of gulls; they watched the diving gannets, the ludicrous earnest puffins, the graceful terns, and hysterical oyster-catchers. They were delighted with the shy and independent islanders. They enjoyed the novelty of peat-fires blazing in an open hearth. Lt.-Commander Disney and Mrs. Disney fished with notable success in the neighbouring lochs. Mr. Pomfret walked and inquired diligently into local traditions and history. And Mrs. Pomfret read the works of Lord Lytton, to which she was ineradicably addicted. Joan Pomfret and Otto Samways occupied themselves in ways apparently satisfactory, and certainly remote from the rest of the family.

The holiday would probably have continued on these pleasant and harmless lines had it not been for the imaginative temperament (excited by love and romantic surroundings) of Miss Joan Pomfret. It suddenly occurred to her that they were rapidly approaching Midsummer Day.

Now the summer solstice has, or had, its appropriate festivals. In the northern parts of Britain the sun used indisputably to reign supreme, and, at such times as his presence blessed the earth almost throughout the circle of day and night, it was proper to honour him with dancing and other devout festivities. In Orkney he succeeds at Midsummer in banishing the thief of night for all but a dim hour or so from the dominion of his majesty. There is light on the islands, benign and irresistible, except for one or perhaps two shadowed hours in the cycle of twenty-four.

Something of this was in Joan's mind when she said over the marmalade one morning, "Daddy, the day after to-morrow is Midsummer. Let's celebrate it properly."

"How, my dear?" asked Mr. Pomfret, putting down the toast which was within an inch of his mouth.

"By a midnight picnic. We'll spend the night on an island—on Eynhallow—and see the dawn come up before the afterglow is out of the sky. And we'll dance when the sun shows himself again."

"I haven't danced for years," said Mrs. Pomfret pathetically, "and don't you think the grass would be damp?"

"Tut!" said Mr. Pomfret. "Grass damp? Pouf!" Spousal resistance invariably excited him to action, and he had, it may be remembered, a sanguine nature.

"I should like a chance to watch the birds on Eyn-hallow," said Lt.-Commander Disney. "They're interesting in the early morning. And we could take plenty of rugs, and a flask, you know, in case it is cold."

"Of course we could." Mr. Pomfret was in a singularly eupeptic mood that morning. He felt positively boyish. "Do you remember, Mother"—he called Mrs. Pomfret Mother when he felt particularly young and could think good-naturedly of her growing a little mature—"Do you remember that bicycling tour I did once in Cornwall? Excellent fun it was, Hugo. It must be twenty-five years ago, and I often wish that I had found an opportunity to repeat it. This idea of yours is splendid, Joan, my dear. Dancing to the Midsummer Sun—Ha! I shall show you all how to dance. Hugo, my boy, will you see about a boat?"

Eynhallow is a small uninhabited island between the mainland of Orkney and the island of Rousay. It is surrounded by unruly tides, but to the fishermen who know them it is not difficult to land, provided the weather is calm. Those definitely in favour of the expedition were Mr. Pomfret, Lt.-Commander Disney, Joan, and naturally, since Joan would be there, Otto Samways. Mrs. Disney shrugged her shoulders and said, "It will mean the first late night I've had for a fortnight and the first woollen undies I've worn for years. I don't mind, though." Poor Mrs. Pomfret sighed and returned to *The Last Days of Pompeii*.

Hugo Disney persuaded a local fisherman, John Corrigall, that it would be more profitable than lobster-fishing to sail the Pomfret party to Eynhallow and call for them on the following morning, and so the preliminaries of the excursion were successfully completed. John Corrigall was privately convinced that they were all mad—except Mrs. Pomfret, whom he found to be an unwilling victim—but refrained from saying so, except in the privacy of his own family; for a madman's money is as good as that of a man dogmatically and indecently sane, and, indeed, more easily earned.

On Midsummer Eve then, after dinner, the Pomfrets set sail. They carried baskets of food, for a night in the open is a potent ally of hunger, but no instrument of fire, such as a primus stove, for that, Joan said, would be an insult to the omnipotence of the sun, who should rule alone. They took rugs and cushions, and Mrs. Pomfret wore a fur coat and Russian boots. They set a portable gramophone—for they were to dance—in the stern of the boat, and Otto Samways carried two albums of records. There was a heavy cargo aboard when John Corrigall hauled his sheet and brought the boat's head round for Eynhallow. He landed them, without more incident than a faint protest from Mrs. Pomfret, on a shingle beach, and left them.

And that is the last that has been seen of them.

When Corrigall returned to Eynhallow in the morning, he found the island deserted. He shouted, and there was no answer, he walked round the island, which is small, and found no trace of the midnight visitors. He sat on a rock and struggled heavily with thought, and then, because he was anxious to get back before the tide turned, he sailed home again.

It is, of course, an ingrained belief in the mind of the northern Scot that the English are a flighty, unreliable race. They travel far from home when there is no need to travel, they are wantonly extravagant (John Corrigall had been paid in advance), and their actions spring from impulse instead of emanating slowly from cautious deliberation. They are volatile (as the English say the

French are volatile), and their volatility makes them difficult to understand. So John Corrigall said nothing, except to his wife, of the disappearance of the Pomfrets. He had no intention of making a fool of himself by raising what was possibly a false alarm, and the whole day, which might have been profitably spent on investigation, was wasted.

In the evening the chauffeur, an energetic man when aroused, went to make inquiries, and was astounded to hear that his master had apparently vanished. With the decision of a man who had lived in cities and learnt, before he took to driving one, the art of evading motor-cars, he told a little girl who happened to be at hand to summon the village constable, and ordered Corrigall to make his boat ready for sea. The latter protested, for the wind and tide were at odds and a pretty sea was breaking round Eynhallow. But the chauffeur was like adamant, and drove the constable and John Corrigall to the shore, helped to push out the boat, and after a stormy crossing landed, wet through, on the island. A thorough search was made, and not a sign of the Pomfrets could be found; nothing, that is, except a little tag of bright metal which was found lying on the grass, the significance of which was unknown to Corrigall and the policeman, who had no experience of modern toilets, and to the chauffeur, who was virtuous and unmarried. Later it was identified simultaneously by the maids as the end, the catch or hatch as it were, of a stocking-suspender such as many ladies wear. If Miss Joan had been dancing vigorously, it might have sprung asunder from the rest of the article and fallen to the ground, they said.

The three maids became hysterical soon after they learnt of the mystery; John Corrigall went home to his bed, convinced that it did not concern him; the constable was useless, having encountered no such case in his previous professional experience; and it was left to the chauffeur to devise a course of action.

He persuaded the constable to cycle to Kirkwall, the capital and cathedral city of Orkney, and report to such superior officers as he might discover there. He insisted on the local telegraph office opening after hours, and sent an expensive message to the newspaper which guided the thought and chronicled the deeds of the town in which Mr. Pomfret had prominently lived. And he made a careful inventory of everything that the unfortunate party had taken with them. Then he sat down to compose a long letter to the newspaper already mentioned.

The assistant-editor of the paper made instant and magnificent use of the chauffeur's telegram. Times were dull, and his chief was away on holiday. The chief sub-editor was a man of consummate craft and no conscience. Between them they splashed a throbbing, breath-taking story over the two main news columns. They flung across the page a streaming head-line that challenged the hearts of their readers like a lonely bugle sounding on a frosty night. Eynhallow became a Treasure Island encircled by northern mists, and the sober citizens who read this strange story of the disappearance of people whom they knew so well (by sight), whose motor-cars they had envied, and whose abilities they had derided, felt creeping into their souls an Arctic fog of doubt, a cold hush of suspense, a breath of icy wind from the waste seas of mystery. Which was precisely the effect intended by the enterprising assistant-editor and the highly competent sub-editor.

This was the beginning of the story which subsequently took all England by the ears, and echoed, thinly or tumultuously, in ribald, hushed, or strident accents, in railway carriages and on the tops of buses, at street-corners and over dinner-tables, at chamber-concerts and through brass-band recitals, in all places where two or three newspaper-readers were gathered together, and finally in one or two topically-inclined pulpits and behind the footlights of the variety stage.

The assistant-editor sent hurrying northwards a young and alert reporter, and it was not his fault that an emissary of a great London evening paper arrived in Orkney before him. For the latter travelled by aeroplane, the evening paper being wealthy and its editor having been noticeably impressed by the provincial report. The first general information, therefore, that Britain had of the Great Pomfret Mystery was a brightly written account of the long flight of Our Special Investigator.

Within twenty-four hours every self-respecting news-sheet in the country had published a map of Orkney, on which the approximate position of Eynhallow was surrounded by a black circle. The more erudite contributed brief historical sketches of the islands, and a few discovered that a church or monastery had once been built on the particular islet of mystery. Brief descriptions of Mr. Pomfret with at least the names, Christian names, and ages of his party appeared in all the papers. Two offered ready-made solutions to the problem, three laughed at it, and one rashly cited as a parallel case the vanishing crew of the *Marie Celeste*.

On the following day a Paymaster-Commander wrote to say that he had once, during the War, motored from Scapa to Swandale (Mr. Pomfret's house), and distinctly remembered seeing Eynhallow. "A charming, sea-girt, romantic-looking island," he wrote, "with the appearance of having withstood a thousand storms and blossomed with a thousand green springtimes." Subsequently an Admiral, who had also been in Scapa during the War, corroborated this, writing to say that he had seen the island himself. Thereafter its actual existence was not doubted.

In a short time photographs began to appear, photographs of Mr. Pomfret and his family, one of Lt.-Commander Disney in uniform, and a charming picture of Miss Joan Pomfret playing in a local tennis tournament. The two reporters sent long descriptive stories about nothing in particular, and their respective sub-editors garnished them with suggestive and arresting headlines. Several papers remembered that the *Hampshire,* with Lord Kitchener aboard, had been sunk on the other side of Orkney, and "A Student of Crime" wrote to suggest that a floating mine, one of the chain responsible for that dire catastrophe, had survived to be washed up on Eynhallow, and had blown the Pomfrets into minute and undiscoverable fragments. No sound of an explosion, however, had startled Orkney, and no trace of such a convulsion was apparent on the island. A photograph of John Corrigall and his boat appeared, an artistic camera study with an admirable sky effect. Several stories of mysterious yachts cruising in the vicinity were mooted, and the yachts were all satisfactorily identified as trawlers.

On the second Sunday after the disappearance, when the mystery had been deepened by time and even the most ingenious could offer no likely solution, an eminent clergyman, a staunch supporter of temperance, publicly warned the country against the danger of owning breweries. Mr. Pomfret, he said, was widely known as a brewer, one who had made his fortune out of beer, that enemy of man and canker in the home. And Mr. Pomfret had disappeared. Divine vengeance, he said, cometh like a thief in the night. To-day we are here, in the midst of our wickedness, and to-morrow we are plucked up and cast into the oven. Let all, he concluded, who own breweries consider the appalling fate of George Plover Pomfret, and mend their ways by honest repentance while there is yet time.

And then the London paper had a scoop. Its reporter discovered that during all this bustle of conjecture, doubt and query, investigation and disappointment, a German professor had quietly been living, as a summer boarder, in a farmhouse not two miles distant from Swandale. His own explanation of his presence so near the scene of supposed tragedy was that he was collecting and examining survivals of Norse influence in the Orkney dialect; but his story, especially when it was printed alongside his own photograph, met with derisive incredulity, and in the natural excitement that followed this disclosure there was not a little sturdy denunciation of the Hidden Hand. The professor was detained in custody, and was released only on the telegraphic intervention of the German Foreign Secretary, who personally vouched for his honesty and innocence. This again deepened the suspicions of many newspaper readers.

The local police, meanwhile, reinforced by an inspector from Edinburgh and a detective from Scotland Yard, had quietly and systematically established that there were no clues to the whereabouts of Mr. Pomfret and his friends, and no solution to the mystery of their disappearance. It was impossible for anyone to get on to or off the island without a boat, and no boat could easily have landed, owing to the state of the tide, between the hour at which the Pomfrets were disembarked and the morning visit of John Corrigall. No strange vessel had been seen in the vicinity. The Pomfrets could not have made a raft, as some hundreds of people had suggested, because they had nothing out of which to make one, except two luncheon baskets, a gramophone, some records, and a box of gramophone needles which were, it must be admitted, too small to nail together pieces of driftwood, supposing suitable planks to have been present on the beach. Nor, unless they had been attacked by an epidemic mania, a surging and contagious Sindbad complex, was there any particular reason why they should have wanted to make a raft. No clear evidence even of their presence on the island, except an integral portion of a lady's stocking-suspender, was found, and some people suggested that John Corrigall was a liar and that the Pomfrets had never gone there. But the circumstantial evidence of the servants was in Corrigall's favour, and he had not, it was found, the mental ability successfully to dispose of six adult bodies.

Investigation of a practical kind came to an end. There was no one to question and nothing to find. Even the spiritualistic mediums who offered their services were of no real assistance, though some of them claimed to have established communication with Miss Joan Pomfret, who told them that everything was for the best in the best of all possible Beyonds. Mrs. Pomfret, it was reported, had said, "Sometimes it is light here and sometimes it is dark. I have not seen Bulmer, but I am happy." There was a little discussion on the significance of *Bulmer,* till a personal friend suggested that it was a mis-tapping for the name of Mrs. Pomfret's favourite author, but the general mystery was in danger of being forgotten, dismissed as insoluble.

It was about this time that Mr. Harold Pinto left Kirkwall in the Orkneys for Leith, sailing on the s.s.

St. Giles. Mr. Pinto was a commercial traveller, more silent than many of his class, a student of human nature, and in his way an amateur of life.

When the *St. Giles* was some four hours out of Kirkwall he stepped into the small deckhouse which served as a smoking-room, and, pressing a bell, presently ordered a bottle of beer. There were, in the smoking-room, two other commercial travellers with whom he was slightly acquainted, the reporter of the provincial newspaper which had first heard of the Pomfret case, an elderly farmer who said he was going to South Africa, and a young, bright-eyed man, carelessly dressed, distinguished by a short, stubbly beard. He looked, thought Mr. Pinto, as though he might be a gentleman. His nails were clean; but his soft collar was disgustingly dirty and his clothes had evidently been slept in. He asked for Bass, at the same time as Mr. Pinto, in an educated and pleasant voice, but when the beer came he merely tasted it, and an expression of disgust passed over his face. He took no part in the general conversation, though Mr. Pinto noticed that he followed the talk actively with his eyes—very expressive eyes they were, full, at times, of an almost impish merriment.

The conversation naturally centred round the Pomfret Mystery, and the reporter very graphically told the story from the beginning, embellished with certain details which had not been published. "There are some things," he said, "which I wouldn't willingly tell outside this company. It's my private belief that old Pomfret took drugs. Don't ask me for proof, because I'm not going to tell you. And there's another thing. Joan Pomfret once asked the gardener at Swandale—he's a local man— whether he knew of any really lonely places near by. The sort of places where there were likely to be no casual passers-by. I didn't send that piece of news to my paper because I'm still waiting for the psychological moment at which to make it public. But you'll admit that it's significant."

The other commercial travellers both contributed theories, at which the reporter scoffed, but Mr. Pinto was almost as silent as the young man with the beard.

"Mass suicide won't do," said the reporter, "however much you talk about crowd psychology; and mass murder, followed by the suicide of the murderer, won't do either. None of them was likely to run amok. And where are the bodies? One at least would have been washed up before now. No, it's my opinion that there's an international gang at the bottom of it, and one of the party—at least one—was either a confederate or a fugitive from the justice of the gang."

The man who was going to South Africa said that he had a cousin who had once disappeared in Mashonaland. He was about to tell the story more fully when the two commercial travellers and the reporter discovered that they were sleepy—and it was nearly midnight—and went hurriedly below. And after a minute or two the man with the cousin in Mashonaland followed them.

The young man with the stubbly beard sat still, staring at nothing with eyes that were alert and full of comprehension. He seemed to be listening to the throb of the steamer's screw and the answering wash of the sea. His lips moved slightly when a wave, louder than the others, ran with a slithering caress along the ship's side, and he smiled engagingly, looking at Mr. Pinto as though he expected an answering smile.

"The Möder Di,"[1] he said, "laughing at fishermen's

---

[1] Möder Di: The Ninth Wave.

wives. All summer she laughs lightly, but the laughter of her winter rut is like icebergs breaking."

Mr. Pinto, remarking that it seemed to be a fine night, stepped out on the deck.

"Oh, a glorious night," said the young man with the beard, following him. "Look at the clouds, like grey foxes running from the moon!"

"Indeed, there is one extraordinarily like a fox," replied Mr. Pinto politely.

"She is hunting to-night," said the young man. "Foxes and grey wolves. And see, there's a stag in the west. A great night for hunting, and all the sky to run through."

Mr. Pinto and his friend had the deck to themselves, and Mr. Pinto began to feel curiously lonely in such strange company.

"Listen," said the young man, pointing over the rail. "Do you hear a shoal of herring talking out there? There's a hum of fear in the air. Perhaps a thresher-shark is coming through the Firth."

Mr. Pinto, convinced that he had a lunatic to deal with, was considering an excuse for going below when the young man said, "I saw you sitting silent while those fools were talking about Pomfret's disappearance. Why did you say nothing?"

"Because I didn't think any of their theories were good enough," answered Mr. Pinto, feeling a little easier, "and because I had no theory of my own to offer."

"What do you think? You must think something?"

Mr. Pinto blinked once or twice, and then diffidently suggested, "'There are more things in heaven and earth,' you know; it sounds foolish, after having been quoted so often and so unnecessarily, but—"

"It does not sound foolish. Those others were fools.

You, it seems, are not yet a fool; though you will be, if you live to grow old and yet not old enough. If you like, I will tell you what happened to George Pomfret and his friends. Sit there."

Mr. Pinto, rather subdued, sat; and the young man walked once or twice up and down, his hair flying like a black banner in the wind, turned his face up to the moon to laugh loudly and melodiously, and suddenly said, "They landed on Eynhallow in the quietness of a perfect evening. The tide was talking to the shore, telling it the story of the Seven Seals who went to Sule Skerry, but they could not hear it then. A redshank whistled 'O Joy! look at them!' as they stepped ashore. But they did not know that either. They made a lot of noise as they walked up the shingle beach, and the rabbits in the grass, because they made a noise, were not frightened, but only ran a little way and turned to look at them.

"Mrs. Pomfret was not happy, but they let her sit on the rugs and she fell asleep. The others walked round the island—it is not big—and threw stones into the sea. The sea chuckled and threw more stones on the beach; but they did not know that. And the sea woke birds who were roosting there, and the birds flew round and laughed at them. By and by the shadow of night came—it was not really night—and they sat down to eat. They ate for a long time, and woke Mrs. Pomfret, who said she could never eat out of doors, and so they let her sleep again. The others talked. They were happy, in a way, but what they talked was nonsense. Even Joan, who was in love, talked nonsense which she does not like to think about now."

"Then—" Mr. Pinto excitedly tried to interrupt, but the young man went imperturbably on.

"Disney said one or two things about the birds which were true, but they did not listen to him. And by and by—the hours pass quickly on Midsummer night—it was time to dance. They had taken a gramophone with them, and Joan had found a wide circle of turf, as round as a penny and heavenly smooth, with a square rock beside it. They put the gramophone on the rock and played a fox-trot or some dance like that. Disney and Norah Disney danced together, and Joan danced with Samways. Two or three times they danced, and old Pomfret made jokes and put new records on.

"And then Joan said, 'These aren't proper dances for Eynhallow and Midsummer Eve. I hate them.' And she stopped the gramophone. She picked up the second album of records and looked for what she wanted; it was light enough to read the names if she held them close to her eyes. She soon found those she was looking for."

The young man looked doubtfully at Mr. Pinto and asked, "Do you know the music of Grieg?"

"A little of it," said Mr. Pinto. "He composed some Norwegian dances. One of them goes like this." And he whistled a bar or two, tunefully enough.

The young man snapped his fingers joyously and stepped lightly with adept feet on the swaying deck.

"That is it," he cried, and sang some strange-sounding words to the tune. "But Grieg did not make it. He heard it between a pine-forest and the sea and cleverly wrote it down. But it was made hundreds of years ago, when all the earth went dancing, except the trees, and their roots took hold of great rocks and twined round the rocks so that they might not join the dance as they wished. For it was forbidden them, since they had to grow straight and tall that ships might be made out of them."

The young man checked himself. "I was telling you about the Pomfrets," he said.

"Joan found these dances that she loved, and played first one and then the other. She made them all dance to the music, though they did not know what steps were in it, nor in what patterns they should move. But the tunes took them by the heels and they pranced and bowed and jumped, laughing all the time. Old Pomfret capered in the middle, kicking his legs, and twirling round like a top. And he laughed; how he laughed! And when he had done shaking with laughter he would start to dance again.

"'This is too good for Mother to miss,' he said, 'we must wake her and make her dance too.' So they woke Mrs. Pomfret, and there being then six of them they made some kind of a figure and started to dance in earnest. Mrs. Pomfret, once she began, moved as lightly as any of them except Joan, who was like thistledown on the grass and moonlight on the edge of a cloud.

"And then, as the music went on, they found that they were dancing in the proper patterns, for they had partners who had come from nowhere, who led them first to the right and then to the left, up the middle and down the sides, bowing, and knocking their heels in the air. As the tune quickened they turned sometimes head over heels, even Mrs. Pomfret, who held her sides and laughed to see old Pomfret twirling on one toe. And the gramophone never stopped, for a little brown man was sitting by it and now and again turning the handle, and singing loudly as he sat.

"So they danced while the sky became lighter and turned from grey to a shining colour like mackerel; and then little clouds like roses were thrown over the silver, and at last the sun himself, daffodil gold, all bright and new, shot up and sent the other colours packing.

"And everybody shouted and cheered like mad, and

for a minute danced more wildly than ever, turning catherine-wheels, fast and faster in a circle, or shouting 'Hey!' and 'Ho!' and 'Ahoi! Ahoi! A-hoi!'

"Then they sank to the ground exhausted, and the Pomfrets looked at their partners who had come from nowhere; and were suddenly amazed.

"'Well, I'm damned!' said old Pomfret, and all the little brown men rolled on the grass and laughed as though they would burst.

"'Oh, they're the Wee Folk, the Peerie [2] Men!' cried Joan delightedly, clapping her hands. 'Peerie Men, Peerie Men, I've found you at last!'

"And again the little men laughed and hugged themselves on the grass. By and by, still laughing, they drew together and talked among themselves very earnestly, and then the biggest of them, who was as tall as a man's leg to the mid-thigh, went forward, saying his name was Ferriostok, and made a little speech explaining how delighted they were to entertain such charming guests on Eynhallow; and would they please to come in for breakfast?

"Some pushed aside the stone on which the gramophone had been standing and, as though it were the most natural thing in the world, the Pomfrets went down rock stairs to a long, sandy hall, lit greenly by the sea, and full, at that time, of the morning song of the North Tide of Eynhallow. They sat down, talking with their hosts, and then two very old little men brought stone cups full of a yellow liquor that smelt like honey and the first wind after frost. They tasted it, curiously, and old Pomfret—he was a brewer, you know—went red all over and said loudly, 'I'll give every penny I have in the world for the recipe!' For he guessed what it was.

[2] Peerie: Little.

54

"And the little men laughed louder than ever, and filled his cup again. One said, 'The Great King offered us Almain for it eleven hundred years ago. We gave him one cup for love, and no more. But you, who have brought that music with you, are free to our cellar. Stay and drink with us, and to-night we shall dance again.'

"No one of them had any thought of going, for it was heather ale they drank. Heather ale! And the last man who tasted it was Thomas of Ercildoune. It was for heather ale that the Romans came to Britain, having heard of it in Gaul, and they pushed northwards to Mount Graupius in search of the secret. But they never found it. And now old Pomfret was swilling it, his cheeks like rubies, because Joan had brought back to the Peerie Men the music they had lost six hundred years before, when their oldest minstrel died of a mad otter's bite.

"Disney was talking to an old grey seal at the sea-door, hearing new tales of the German war, and Joan was listening to the Reykjavik story of the Solan Geese which three little men told her all together, so excited they were by her beauty and by the music she had brought them. At night they danced again, and Joan learnt the Weaving of the Red Ware, the dance that the red shore-seaweed makes for full-moon tides. The Peerie Men played on fiddles cut out of old tree-roots, with strings of rabbit-gut, and they had drums made of shells and rabbit-skins scraped as thin as tissue with stone knives. They hunt quietly, and that is why the rabbits are frightened of silence, but were not afraid of the Pomfrets, who made a noise when they walked. The Peerie Men's music was thin and tinkly, though the tunes were as strong and sweet as the heather ale itself, and always they turned again to the gramophone which Joan had brought, and danced as madly as peewits in April, leaping like winter spring, and clapping their heels high in the air. They danced the Merry Men of Mey and the slow sad Dance of Lofoden, so that everybody wept a little. And then they drank more ale and laughed again, and as the sun came up they danced the Herring Dance, weaving through and through so fast that the eye could not follow them.

"Now this was the third sunrise since the Pomfrets had gone to the island, for the first day and the second night and the second day had passed like one morning in the sandy hall of the Little Men; so many things were there to hear, and such good jokes an old crab made, and so shockingly attractive was a mermaid story that the afternoon tide told. Even the sand had a story, but it was so old that the Peerie Men themselves could not understand it, for it began in darkness and finished under a green haze of ice. And since the Pomfrets were so busy there they heard no sound of the chauffeur's visit and the Peerie Men said nothing of it. They had taken below all the rugs and cushions and hampers and gramophone records, and brushed the grass straight, so that no trace was left of the Midsummer dancing—except the tag of Joan's stocking-suspender, which was overlooked, so it seems.

"The old grey seal told them, in the days that followed, of all that was going on by land, and even Mrs. Pomfret laughed to hear of the bustle and stir they had created. There was no need, the Peerie Men found, to make them hide when more searchers came, for none of the Pomfrets had any wish to be found. Disney said he was learning something about the sea for the first time in his life (and he had followed the sea all his life), and Norah sang Iceland cradle-songs all day. Old Pomfret swilled his ale, glowing like a ruby in the green cave, and

Joan—Joan was the queen of the Peerie Men, and the fosterling of the old grumbling sand, and the friend of every fish that passed by the sea-door. And at night they danced, to the music of tree-root fiddles and pink shell-drums, and above all to that music which you think was made by Grieg. They danced, I tell you! . . ."

The young man tossed up his arms and touched his fingers above his head; he placed the flat of his foot on the calf of the other leg; twirled rapidly on his toes. "Danced, I say! Is there anything in the world but dancing?" And he clapped his heels together, high in the air, first to one side and then to the other, singing something fast and rhythmic and melodious.

Mr. Pinto coughed nervously—he was feeling cold—and said: "That is an extraordinarily interesting story. But, if you will pardon my curiosity, do you mind telling me what reason you have for thinking that this actually happened to Mr. Pomfret and his friends?"

"Reason!" said the young man, staring at him. His hair blew out on the wind like a black banner, and he laughed loud and melodiously.

"This reason," he said, "that I am Otto Samways!" And he turned, very neatly, a standing somersault on the deck and came up laughing.

"They sent me away to buy something," he said, "and when I have bought it I am going back to Eynhallow to dance the Merry Men, and the Herring Dance, and the Sea Moon's Dance with Joan."

And once again he sang, very melodiously, and turned a rapid series of catherine-wheels along the deck.

"To buy what?" shouted Mr. Pinto, as he disappeared.

"Gramophone needles!" bellowed the young man, laughing uproariously.

RICHARD MIDDLETON

THE GHOST SHIP

FAIRFIELD is a little village lying near the Portsmouth
Road about half-way between London and the sea.
Strangers who find it by accident now and then, call it
a pretty, old-fashioned place; we, who live in it and call
it home, don't find anything very pretty about it, but we
should be sorry to live anywhere else. Our minds have
taken the shape of the inn and the church and the green,
I suppose. At all events we never feel comfortable out of
Fairfield.

Of course the Cockneys, with their vasty houses and
their noise-ridden streets, can call us rustics if they
choose, but for all that Fairfield is a better place to live
in than London. Doctor says that when he goes to
London his mind is bruised with the weight of the houses,
and he was a Cockney born. He had to live there himself when he was a little chap, but he knows better now.
You gentlemen may laugh—perhaps some of you come
from London way—but it seems to me that a witness like
that is worth a gallon of arguments.

Dull? Well, you might find it dull, but I assure you
that I've listened to all the London yarns you have spun
to-night, and they're absolutely nothing to the things that
happen at Fairfield. It's because of our way of thinking
and minding our own business. If one of your Londoners

were set down on the green of a Saturday night when the ghosts of the lads who died in the war keep tryst with the lasses who lie in the churchyard, he couldn't help being curious and interfering, and then the ghosts would go somewhere where it was quieter. But we just let them come and go and don't make any fuss, and in consequence Fairfield is the ghostiest place in all England. Why, I've seen a headless man sitting on the edge of the well in broad daylight, and the children playing about his feet as if he were their father. Take my word for it, spirits know when they are well off as much as human beings.

Still, I must admit that the thing I'm going to tell you about was queer even for our part of the world, where three packs of ghost-hounds hunt regularly during the season, and blacksmith's great-grandfather is busy all night shoeing the dead gentlemen's horses. Now that's a thing that wouldn't happen in London, because of their interfering ways, but blacksmith he lies up aloft and sleeps as quiet as a lamb. Once when he had a bad head he shouted down to them not to make so much noise, and in the morning he found an old guinea left on the anvil as an apology. He wears it on his watch-chain now. But I must get on with my story; if I start telling you about the queer happenings at Fairfield I'll never stop.

It all came of the great storm in the spring of '97, the year that we had two great storms. This was the first one, and I remember it very well, because I found in the morning that it had lifted the thatch of my pigsty into the widow's garden as clean as a boy's kite. When I looked over the hedge, widow—Tom Lamport's widow that was—was prodding for her nasturtiums with a daisy-grubber. After I had watched her for a little I went down to the Fox and Grapes to tell landlord what she had said to me. Landlord he laughed, being a married man and at ease with the sex. "Come to that," he said, "the tempest has blowed something into my field. A kind of a ship I think it would be."

I was surprised at that until he explained that it was only a ghost-ship and would do no hurt to the turnips. We argued that it had been blown up from the sea at Portsmouth, and then we talked of something else. There were two slates down at the parsonage and a big tree in Lumley's meadow. It was a rare storm.

I reckon the wind had blown our ghosts all over England. They were coming back for days afterwards with foundered horses and as footsore as possible, and they were so glad to get back to Fairfield that some of them walked up the street crying like little children. Squire said that his great-grandfather's great-grandfather hadn't looked so dead-beat since the battle of Naseby, and he's an educated man.

What with one thing and another, I should think it was a week before we got straight again, and then one afternoon I met the landlord on the green and he had a worried face. "I wish you'd come and have a look at that ship in my field," he said to me; "it seems to me it's leaning real hard on the turnips. I can't bear thinking what the missus will say when she sees it."

I walked down the lane with him, and sure enough there was a ship in the middle of his field, but such a ship as no man had seen on the water for three hundred years, let alone in the middle of a turnip-field. It was all painted black and covered with carvings, and there was a great bay window in the stern for all the world like the Squire's drawing-room. There was a crowd of little black cannon on deck and looking out of her portholes, and she was anchored at each end to the hard ground. I have

seen the wonders of the world on picture-postcards, but
I have never seen anything to equal that.

"She seems very solid for a ghost-ship," I said, seeing
the landlord was bothered.

"I should say it's a betwixt and between," he
answered, puzzling it over, "but it's going to spoil a
matter of fifty turnips, and missus she'll want it moved."
We went up to her and touched the side, and it was as
hard as a real ship. "Now there's folks in England would
call that very curious," he said.

Now I don't know much about ships, but I should
think that that ghost-ship weighed a solid two hundred
tons, and it seemed to me that she had come to stay, so
that I felt sorry for landlord, who was a married man.
"All the horses in Fairfield won't move her out of my
turnips," he said, frowning at her.

Just then we heard a noise on her deck, and we looked
up and saw that a man had come out of her front cabin
and was looking down at us very peaceably. He was
dressed in a black uniform set out with rusty gold lace,
and he had a great cutlass by his side in a brass sheath.
"I'm Captain Bartolomew Roberts," he said, in a gentleman's voice, "put in for recruits. I seem to have brought
her rather far up the harbour."

"Harbour!" cried landlord; "why, you're fifty miles
from the sea."

Captain Roberts didn't turn a hair. "So much as that,
is it?" he said coolly. "Well, it's of no consequence."

Landlord was a bit upset at this. "I don't want to be
unneighbourly," he said, "but I wish you hadn't brought
your ship into my field. You see, my wife sets great store
on these turnips."

The captain took a pinch of snuff out of a fine gold
box that he pulled out of his pocket, and dusted his

fingers with a silk handkerchief in a very genteel fashion. "I'm only here for a few months," he said; "but if a testimony of my esteem would pacify your good lady I should be content," and with the words he loosed a great gold brooch from the neck of his coat and tossed it down to landlord.

Landlord blushed as red as a strawberry. "I'm not denying she's fond of jewellery," he said, "but it's too much for half a sackful of turnips." And indeed it was a handsome brooch.

The captain laughed. "Tut, man," he said, "it's a forced sale, and you deserve a good price. Say no more about it"; and nodding good-day to us, he turned on his heel and went into the cabin. Landlord walked back up the lane like a man with a weight off his mind. "That tempest has blowed me a bit of luck," he said; "the missus will be main pleased with that brooch. It's better than the blacksmith's guinea any day."

Ninety-seven was Jubilee year, the year of the second Jubilee, you remember, and we had great doings at Fairfield, so that we hadn't much time to bother about the ghost-ship, though anyhow it isn't our way to meddle in things that don't concern us. Landlord, he saw his tenant once or twice when he was hoeing his turnips and passed the time of day, and landlord's wife wore her new brooch to church every Sunday. But we didn't mix much with the ghosts at any time, all except an idiot lad there was in the village, and he didn't know the difference between a man and a ghost, poor innocent! On Jubilee Day, however, somebody told Captain Roberts why the church bells were ringing, and he hoisted a flag and fired off his guns like a loyal Englishman. 'Tis true the guns were shotted, and one of the round shot knocked a hole in Farmer Johnstone's barn, but nobody thought much of that in such a season of rejoicing.

It wasn't till our celebrations were over that we noticed that anything was wrong in Fairfield. 'Twas shoemaker who told me first about it one morning at the Fox and Grapes. "You know my great great-uncle?" he said to me.

"You mean Joshua, the quiet lad," I answered, knowing him well.

"Quiet!" said shoemaker indignantly. "Quiet you call him, coming home at three o'clock every morning as drunk as a magistrate and waking up the whole house with his noise."

"Why, it can't be Joshua!" I said, for I knew him for one of the most respectable young ghosts in the village.

"Joshua it is," said shoemaker; "and one of these nights he'll find himself out in the street if he isn't careful."

This kind of talk shocked me, I can tell you, for I don't like to hear a man abusing his own family, and I could hardly believe that a steady youngster like Joshua had taken to drink. But just then in came butcher Aylwin in such a temper that he could hardly drink his beer. "The young puppy! the young puppy!" he kept on saying; and it was some time before shoemaker and I found out that he was talking about his ancestor that fell at Senlac.

"Drink?" said shoemaker hopefully, for we all like company in our misfortunes, and butcher nodded grimly.

"The young noodle," he said, emptying his tankard.

Well, after that I kept my ears open, and it was the same story all over the village. There was hardly a young man among all the ghosts of Fairfield who didn't roll home in the small hours of the morning the worse for liquor. I used to wake up in the night and hear them stumble past my house, singing outrageous songs. The

worst of it was that we couldn't keep the scandal to ourselves, and the folk at Greenhill began to talk of 'sodden
Fairfield' and taught their children to sing a song
about us:

> Sodden Fairfield, sodden Fairfield, has no use for
> bread-and-butter,
> Rum for breakfast, rum for dinner, rum for tea, and
> rum for supper!

We are easy-going in our village, but we didn't like that.

Of course we soon found out where the young fellows
went to get the drink, and landlord was terribly cut up
that his tenant should have turned out so badly, but his
wife wouldn't hear of parting with the brooch, so that
he couldn't give the Captain notice to quit. But as time
went on, things grew from bad to worse, and at all hours
of the day you would see those young reprobates sleeping
it off on the village green. Nearly every afternoon a
ghost-wagon used to jolt down to the ship with a lading
of rum, and though the older ghosts seemed inclined to
give the Captain's hospitality the go-by, the youngsters
were neither to hold nor to bind.

So one afternoon when I was taking my nap I heard
a knock at the door, and there was parson looking very
serious, like a man with a job before him that he didn't
altogether relish. "I'm going down to talk to the Captain
about all this drunkenness in the village, and I want you
to come with me," he said straight out.

I can't say that I fancied the visit much myself, and I
tried to hint to parson that as, after all, they were only
a lot of ghosts, it didn't very much matter.

"Dead or alive, I'm responsible for their good conduct," he said, "and I'm going to do my duty and put a
stop to this continued disorder. And you are coming with

me, John Simmons." So I went, parson being a per-
suasive kind of man.

We went down to the ship, and as we approached her
I could see the Captain tasting the air on deck. When he
saw parson he took off his hat very politely, and I can
tell you that I was relieved to find that he had a proper
respect for the cloth. Parson acknowledged his salute and
spoke out stoutly enough. "Sir, I should be glad to have
a word with you."

"Come on board, sir, come on board," said the Captain, and I could tell by his voice that he knew why we
were there. Parson and I climbed up an uneasy kind of
ladder, and the Captain took us into the great cabin at
the back of the ship, where the bay-window was. It was
the most wonderful place you ever saw in your life, all
full of gold and silver plate, swords with jewelled scab-
bards, carved oak chairs, and great chests that looked as
though they were bursting with guineas. Even parson was
surprised, and he did not shake his head very hard when
the Captain took down some silver cups and poured us
out a drink of rum. I tasted mine, and I don't mind
saying that it changed my view of things entirely. There
was nothing betwixt and between about that rum, and I
felt that it was ridiculous to blame the lads for drinking
too much of stuff like that. It seemed to fill my veins with
honey and fire.

Parson put the case squarely to the Captain, but I
didn't listen much to what he said; I was busy sipping
my drink and looking through the window at the fishes
swimming to and fro over landlord's turnips. Just then
it seemed the most natural thing in the world that they
should be there, though afterwards, of course, I could
see that that proved it was a ghost-ship.

But even then I thought it was queer when I saw a

drowned sailor float by in the thin air with his hair and beard all full of bubbles. It was the first time I had seen anything quite like that at Fairfield.

All the time I was regarding the wonders of the deep, parson was telling Captain Roberts how there was no peace or rest in the village owing to the curse of drunkenness, and what a bad example the youngsters were setting to the older ghosts. The Captain listened very attentively, and only put in a word now and then about boys being boys and young men sowing their wild oats. But when parson had finished his speech he filled up our silver cups and said to parson, with a flourish, "I should be sorry to cause trouble anywhere where I have been made welcome, and you will be glad to hear that I put to sea to-morrow night. And now you must drink me a prosperous voyage." So we all stood up and drank the toast with honour, and that noble rum was like hot oil in my veins.

After that Captain showed us some of the curiosities he had brought back from foreign parts, and we were greatly amazed, though afterwards I couldn't clearly remember what they were. And then I found myself walking across the turnips with parson, and I was telling him of the glories of the deep that I had seen through the window of the ship. He turned on me severely. " If I were you, John Simmons," he said, "I should go straight home to bed." He has a way of putting things that wouldn't occur to an ordinary man, has parson, and I did as he told me.

Well, next day it came on to blow, and it blew harder and harder, till about eight o'clock at night I heard a noise and looked out into the garden. I dare say you won't believe me, it seems a bit tall even to me, but the wind had lifted the thatch of my pigsty into the widow's garden a second time. I thought I wouldn't wait to hear what widow had to say about it, so I went across the green to the Fox and Grapes, and the wind was so strong that I danced along on tiptoe like a girl at the fair. When I got to the inn landlord had to help me shut the door; it seemed as though a dozen goats were pushing against it to come in out of the storm.

"It's a powerful tempest," he said, drawing the beer. "I hear there's a chimney down at Dickory End."

"It's a funny thing how these sailors know about the weather," I answered. "When Captain said he was going to-night, I was thinking it would take a capful of wind to carry the ship back to sea, but now here's more than a capful."

"Ah, yes," said landlord, "it's to-night he goes true enough, and, mind you, though he treated me handsome over the rent, I'm not sure it's a loss to the village. I don't hold with gentrice who fetch their drink from London instead of helping local traders to get their living."

"But you haven't got any rum like his," I said to draw him out.

His neck grew red above his collar, and I was afraid I'd gone too far; but after a while he got his breath with a grunt.

"John Simmons," he said, "if you've come down here this windy night to talk a lot of fool's talk, you've wasted a journey."

Well, of course, then I had to smooth him down with praising his rum and Heaven forgive me for swearing it was better than Captain's. For the like of that rum no living lips have tasted save mine and parson's. But somehow or other I brought landlord round, and presently we must have a glass of his best to prove its quality.

"Beat that if you can!" he cried, and we both raised our glasses to our mouths, only to stop half-way and look at each other in amaze. For the wind that had been howling outside like an outrageous dog had all of a sudden turned as melodious as the carol-boys of a Christmas Eve.

"Surely that's not my Martha," whispered landlord; Martha being his great-aunt that lived in the loft overhead.

We went to the door, and the wind burst it open so that the handle was driven clean into the plaster of the wall. But we didn't think about that at the time; for over our heads, sailing very comfortably through the windy stars, was the ship that had passed the summer in landlord's field. Her portholes and her bay-window were blazing with lights, and there was a noise of singing and fiddling on her decks. "He's gone," shouted landlord above the storm, "and he's taken half the village with him!" I could only nod in answer, not having lungs like bellows of leather.

In the morning we were able to measure the strength of the storm, and over and above my pigsty there was damage enough wrought in the village to keep us busy. True it is that the children had to break down no branches for the firing that autumn, since the wind had strewn the woods with more than they could carry away. Many of our ghosts were scattered abroad, but this time very few came back, all the young men having sailed with Captain; and not only ghosts, for a poor half-witted lad was missing, and we reckoned that he had stowed himself away or perhaps shipped as cabin-boy, not knowing any better.

What with the lamentations of the ghost-girls and the grumblings of families who had lost an ancestor, the village was upset for a while, and the funny thing was that it was the folk who had complained most of the carryings-on of the youngsters, who made most noise now that they were gone. I hadn't any sympathy with shoemaker or butcher, who ran about saying how much they missed their lads, but it made me grieve to hear the poor bereaved girls calling their lovers by name on the village green at nightfall. It didn't seem fair to me that they should have lost their men a second time, after giving up life in order to join them, as like as not. Still, not even a spirit can be sorry for ever, and after a few months we made up our mind that the folk who had sailed in the ship were never coming back, and we didn't talk about it any more.

And then one day, I dare say it would be a couple of years after, when the whole business was quite forgotten, who should come trapesing along the road from Portsmouth but the daft lad who had gone away with the ship, without waiting till he was dead to become a ghost. You never saw such a boy as that in all your life. He had a great rusty cutlass hanging to a string at his waist, and he was tattooed all over in fine colours, so that even his face looked like a girl's sampler. He had a handkerchief in his hand full of foreign shells and old-fashioned pieces of small money, very curious, and he walked up to the well outside his mother's house and drew himself a drink as if he had been nowhere in particular.

The worst of it was that he had come back as soft-headed as he went, and try as we might we couldn't get anything reasonable out of him. He talked a lot of gibberish about keel-hauling and walking the plank and crimson murders—things which a decent sailor should know nothing about, so that it seemed to me that for all his manners Captain had been more of a pirate than a gentleman mariner. But to draw sense out of that boy was as hard as picking cherries off a crab-tree. One silly tale he had that he kept on drifting back to, and to hear him you would have thought that it was the only thing that happened to him in his life. "We was at anchor," he would say, "off an island called the Basket of Flowers, and the sailors had caught a lot of parrots and we were teaching them to swear. Up and down the decks, up and down the decks, and the language they used was dreadful. Then we looked up and saw the masts of the Spanish ship outside the harbour. Outside the harbour they were, so we threw the parrots into the sea and sailed out to fight. And all the parrots were drownded in the sea and the language they used was dreadful." That's the sort of boy he was, nothing but silly talk of parrots when we asked him about the fighting. And we never had a chance of teaching him better, for two days after he ran away again, and hasn't been since since.

That's my story, and I assure you that things like that are happening at Fairfield all the time. The ship never come back, but somehow as people grow older they seem to think that one of these windy nights, she'll come sailing in over the hedges with all the lost ghosts on board. Well, when she comes, she'll be welcome. There's one ghost-lass that has never grown tired of waiting for her lad to return. Every night you'll see her out on the green, straining her poor eyes with looking for the mast-lights among the stars. A faithful lass you'd call her, and I'm thinking you'd be right.

Landlord's field wasn't a penny the worse for the visit, but they do say that since then the turnips that have been grown in it have tasted of rum.

LORD DUNSANY

HOW JEMBU PLAYED FOR CAMBRIDGE

THE next time that Murcote brought me again to his Club we arrived a little late. Lunch was over, and nine or ten of them were gathered before that fireplace they have; and that talk of theirs had commenced, the charm of which was that there was no way of predicting upon what topics it would touch. It all depended upon who was there, and who was leading the talk, and what his mood was; and of course on all manner of irrelevant things besides, such as whisky, and the day's news or rumour.

But to-day they had evidently all been talking of cricket, and the reason of that was clearer than men usually seem to think such reasons are. I seemed to see it almost the moment that I sat down; and nobody told it me, but the air seemed heavy with it. The reason that they talked about cricket was that there was a group there that day that were out of sympathy with Mr. Jorkens; bored perhaps by his long reminiscences, irritated by his lies, or disgusted by the untidy mess that intemperance made of his tie. Whatever it was it was clear enough that they were talking vigorously of cricket because they felt sure that that topic, if well adhered to, must keep the old fellow away from the trackless lands and jungles, and that, if he must talk of Africa, it could only be of some tidy trim well-ordered civilized part of it that he could get from the subject of cricket. They felt so sure of this.

They had evidently been talking of cricket for some time, and were resolute to keep on it, when shortly after I sat down among them one turned to Jorkens himself and said, "Are you going to watch the match at Lord's?"

"No, no," said Jorkens, sadly, "I never watch cricket now."

"But you used to a good deal, didn't you?" said another, determined not to let Jorkens get away from cricket.

"Oh yes," said Jorkens, "once; right up to that time when Cambridge beat Surrey by one run." He sighed heavily and continued: "You remember that?"

"Yes," said someone. "But tell us about it."

They thought they were on safe ground there. And so they started Jorkens upon a story, thinking they had him far from the cactus jungles. But that old wanderer was not kept so easily in English fields, his imagination to-day or his memory or whatever you call it, any more than his body had been in the old days, of which he so often told.

"It's a long story," said Jorkens. "You remember Jembu?"

"Of course," said the cricketers.

"You remember his winning hit," said Jorkens.

"Yes, a two, wasn't it?" said someone.

"Yes," said Jorkens, "it was. And you remember how he got it?"

That was too much for the cricketers. None quite remembered. And then Murcote spoke. "Didn't he put it through the slips with his knee?" he said.

"Exactly," said Jorkens. "Exactly. That's what he did. Put it through the slips with his knee. And only a leg-bye. He never hit it. Only a leg-bye." And his voice dropped into mumbles.

"What did you say?" said one of the ruthless cricketers, determined to keep him to cricket.

"Only a leg-bye," said Jorkens. "He never hit it."

"Well, he won the match all right," said one, "with that couple of runs. It didn't matter how he got them."

"Didn't it!" said Jorkens. "Didn't it!"

And in the silence that followed the solemnity of his emphasis he looked from face to face. Nobody had any answer. Jorkens had got them.

"I'll tell you whether it mattered or not, that couple of leg-byes," said Jorkens then. And in the silence he told this story:

"I knew Jembu at Cambridge. He was younger than me of course, but I used to go back to Cambridge often to see those towers and the flat fen country, and so I came to know Jembu. He was no cricketer. No, no, Jembu was no cricketer. He dressed as white men dress and spoke perfect English, but they could not teach him cricket. He used to play golf and things like that. And sometimes in the evening he would go right away by himself and sit down on the grass and sing. He was like that all his first year. And then one day they seem to have got him to play a bit, and then he got interested, probably because he saw the admiration they had for his marvellous fielding. But as for batting, as for making a run, well, his average was less than one in something like ten innings.

"And then he came by the ambition to play for Cambridge. You never know with these natives what on earth they will set their hearts on. And I suppose that if he had not fulfilled his ambition he would have died, or committed murder or something. But, as you know, he played for Cambridge at the end of his second year."

"Yes," said someone.

"Yes, but do you know how?" said Jorkens.

"Why, by being the best bat of his time, I suppose," said Murcote.

"He never made more than fifty," said Jorkens, with a certain sly look in his eye as it seemed to me.

"No," said Murcote, "but within one or two of it whenever he went to the wickets for something like two years."

"One doesn't want more than that," said another.

"No," said Jorkens. "But he did the day that they played Surrey. Well, I'll tell you how he came to play for Cambridge."

"Yes, do," they said.

"When Jembu decided that he must play for Cambridge he practised at the nets for a fortnight, then broke his bat over his knee and disappeared."

"Where did he go to?" said someone a little incredulously.

"He went home," said Jorkens.

"Home?" they said.

"I was on the same boat with him," said Jorkens drawing himself up at the sound of doubt in their voices.

"You were going to tell us how Jembu played for Cambridge," said one called Terbut, a lawyer, who seemed as much out of sympathy with Jorkens and his ways as any of them.

"Wait a moment," said Jorkens. "I told you he could not bat. Now, when one of these African natives wants to do something that he can't, you know what he always does? He goes to a witch doctor. And when Jembu made up his mind to play for Cambridge he put the whole force of his personality into that one object, every atom of will he had inherited from all his ferocious ancestors. He gave up reading divinity, and everything, and just practised at the nets as I told you, all day long for a fortnight."

"Not an easy thing to break a bat over his knee," said Terbut.

"His strength was enormous," said Jorkens. "I was more interested in cricket in those days than in anything else. I visited Jembu in his rooms just at that time. Into the room where we sat he had put the last touches of tidiness: I never saw anything so neat, all his divinity books put away trim in their shelves, he must have had over a hundred of them, and everything in the room with that air about it that a dog would recognize as foreboding a going away.

" 'I am going home,' he said.

" 'What, giving up cricket?' I asked.

" 'No,' he answered and his gaze looked beyond me as though concerned with some far-off contentment. 'No, but I must make runs.'

" 'You want practice,' I said.

" 'I want prayer,' he answered.

" 'But you can pray here,' I said.

"He shook his head.

" 'No, no,' he answered with that far-away look again.

"Well, I only cared for cricket. Nothing else interested me then. And I wanted to see how he would do it. I suppose I shouldn't trouble about it nowadays. But the memory of his perfect fielding, and his keenness for the one thing I cared about, and his tremendous ambition, as it seemed to me then, to play cricket for Cambridge, made the whole thing a quest that I must see the end of.

" 'Where will you pray?' I said.

" 'There's a man that is very good at all that sort of thing,' he answered.

" 'Where does he live?' I said.

" 'Home.'

"Well it turned out he had taken a cabin on one of the Union Castle line. And I decided to go with him. I booked my passage on the same boat; and, when we got into the Mediterranean, deck cricket began, and Jembu was always bowled in the first few balls even at that. I am no cricketer, I worshipped the great players all the more for that; I don't pretend to have been a cricketer; but I stayed at the wickets longer than Jembu every time, all through the Mediterranean till we got to the Red Sea, and it became too hot to play cricket, or even to think of it for more than a minute or two on end. The equator felt cool and refreshing after that. And then one day we came to Killindini. Jembu had two ponies to meet us there and twenty or thirty men."

"Wired to them I suppose?" said Terbut.

"No," said Jorkens. "He had wired to some sort of missionary who was in touch with Jembu's people. Jembu, you know, was a pretty important chieftain, and when anyone got word to his people that Jembu wanted them, they had to come. They had tents for us, and mattresses, and they put them on their heads and carried them away through Africa, while we rode. It was before the days of railway, and it was a long trek, and uphill all the way. We rose eight thousand feet in two hundred miles. We went on day after day into the interior of Africa: you know the country?"

"We have heard you tell of it," said someone.

"Yes, yes," said Jorkens, cutting out, as I thought, a good deal of local colour that he had intended to give us. "And one day Kenya came in sight like a head between two great shoulders; and then Jembu turned northwards. Yes, he turned northwards as far as I could make out; and travelled much more quickly; and we came to nine thousand feet, and forests of cedar. And every evening Jembu and I used to play stump cricket, and I always bowled him out in an over or two; and then the sun would set and we lit our fires."

"Was it cold?" said Terbut.

"To keep off lions," said Jorkens.

"You bowled out Jembu?" said another incredulously, urged to speech by an honest doubt, or else to turn Jorkens away from one of his interminable lion-stories.

"A hundred times," said Jorkens, "if I have done it once."

"Jembu," some of us muttered almost involuntarily, for the fame of his batting lived on, as indeed it does still.

"Wait till I tell you," said Jorkens. "In a day or two we began to leave the high ground: bamboos took the place of cedars; trees I knew nothing of took the place of bamboos; and we came in sight of hideous forests of cactus; when we burned their trunks in our camp-fires, mobs of great insects rushed out of the shrivelling bark. And one day we came in sight of hills that Jembu knew, with a forest lying dark in the valleys and folds of them, and Jembu's own honey-pots tied to the upper branches.

"These honey-pots were the principal source, I fancy, of Jembu's wealth, narrow wooden pots about three feet long, in which the wild bees lived, and guarded by men that you never see, waiting with bows and arrows. It was the harvest of these in a hundred square miles of forest that sent Jembu to Cambridge to study divinity, and learn our ways and our language. Of course he had cattle too, and plenty of ivory came his way, and raw gold now and then; and, in a quiet way, I should fancy, a good many slaves.

"Jembu's face lighted up when he saw his honey-pots, and the forest that was his home, dark under those hills that were all flashing in sunlight. But no thought of his home or his honey-pots made him forget for a single instant his ambition to play for Cambridge, and that night at the edge of the forest he was handling a bat still, and I was still bowling him out.

"Next day we came to the huts of Jembu's people. Queer people. I should have liked to have shown you a photograph of them. I had a small camera with me. But whenever I put it up they all ran away.

"We came to their odd reed huts.

"Undergrowth had been cleared and the earth stamped hard by bare feet, but they did not ever seem to have thinned the trees, and their huts were in and out among the great trunks. My tent was set up a little way from the huts, while Jembu went to his people. Men came and offered me milk and fruit and chickens, and went away. And in the evening Jembu came to me.

"'I am going to pray now,' he said.

"I thought he meant there and then, and rose to leave the tent to him.

"'No,' he said, 'one can't pray by oneself.'

"Then I gathered that by 'pray' he meant some kind of worship, and that the man he had told me of in his rooms at Cambridge would be somewhere near now. I was so keen on cricket in those days that anything affecting it always seemed to me of paramount importance, and I said, 'May I come, too?'

"Jembu merely beckoned with his hand and walked on.

"We went through the dark of the forest for some few minutes, and saw in the shade a great building standing alone. A sort of cathedral of thatch. Inside, a great space seemed bare. The walls near to the ground were of reed and ivory: above, it was all a darkness of rafters and thatch. The long, thin reeds were vertical, and every foot or so a great tusk of an elephant stood upright in the wall. Nuggets of gold here and there were fastened against the tusks by thin strands of copper. Presently I could make out that a thin line of brushwood was laid in a wide circle on the floor. Inside it Jembu sat down on the hard mud. And I went far away from it and sat in a corner, though not too near to the reeds, because, if anything would make a good home for a cobra, they would. And Jembu said never a word; and I waited.

"Then a man stepped through the reeds in the wall that Jembu was facing, dressed in a girdle of feathers hanging down from his loins, wing feathers they seemed to be, out of a crane. He went to some sort of iron pot that stood on the floor, that I had not noticed before, and lifted the lid and took fire from it, and lit the thin line of brushwood that ran round Jembu. Then he began to dance, and he danced round him in circles, or leapt is a better word, for it was too fierce for a dance. He took no notice of me. After he had been dancing some time I saw that his circles were narrowing; and presently he came to the line of brushwood at a point that the fire had not reached, and leapt through it and danced on round Jembu. Jembu sat perfectly still, with his eyes fixed. The weirdest shadows were galloping round the walls from the waving flames of the brushwood; and any man such as us must have been sick and giddy from the frightful pace of those now narrow circles that he was making round Jembu, but he leapt nimbly on. He was within a few feet of my friend now. What would he do, I was wondering, when he reached him? Still Jembu never stirred, either hand or eyelid. Stray leaves drifting up from the dancing savage's feet were already settling on Jembu. And all of a sudden the black dancer fainted.

"He lay on the ground before Jembu, his feet a yard from him, and one arm flung out away from him, so that that hand lay in the brushwood. The flames were near to the hand, but Jembu never stirred. They reached it and scorched it: Jembu never lifted a finger, and the heathen dancer neither moved nor flinched. I knew then that this swoon that he had gone into was a real swoon, whatever was happening. The flames died down round the hand, died down round the whole circle: till only a glow remained, and the shadow of Jembu was as still on the wall as a black bronze image of Buddha.

"I began to get up then, with the idea of doing something for the unconscious man, but Jembu caught the movement, slight as it was, although he was not looking at me: and, still without giving me a glance of his eye, waved me sharply away with a jerk of his left hand. So I left the man lying there, as silent as Jembu. And there I sat, while Jembu seemed not to be breathing, and the embers went out and the place seemed dimmer than ever for the light of the fire that was gone. And then the dancing man came to, and got up and bent over Jembu, and spoke to him, and turned: and all at once he was gone through the slit in the reeds by which he had entered the temple. Then Jembu turned his head, and I looked at him.

" 'He has promised,' he said.

" 'Who?' I asked.

" 'Mungo,' said Jembu.

" 'Was that Mungo?' I asked.

" 'He? No! Only his servant.'

" 'Who is Mungo?' I asked.

" 'We don't know,' said Jembu, with so much finality that I said no more of that.

"But I asked what he had promised.

" 'Fifty runs,' replied Jembu.

" 'In one innings?' I asked.

" 'Whenever I bat,' said Jembu.

" 'Whenever you bat!' I said. 'Why! That will get you into any eleven. Once or twice would attract notice, but a steady average of fifty, and always to be relied on, it mayn't be spectacular, but you'd be the prop of any eleven.'

"He seemed so sure of it that I was quite excited; I could not imagine a more valuable man to have in a team than one who could always do that, day after day, against any kind of bowling, on a good wicket or bad.

" 'But I must never make more,' said Jembu.

" 'You'll hardly want to,' I said.

" 'Not a run more,' said Jembu, gazing straight at the wall.

" 'What will happen if you do?' I asked.

" 'You never know with Mungo,' Jembu replied.

" 'Don't you?' I said.

" 'No man knows that,' said Jembu.

" 'You'll be able to play for Cambridge now,' I said.

"Jembu got up from the floor and we came away.

"He spoke to his people that evening in the firelight. Told them he was going back to Cambridge again, told them what he was going to do there, I suppose; though what they made of it, or what they thought Cambridge was, Mungo only knows. But I saw from his face, and from theirs, that he made that higher civilization, to which he was going back, very beautiful to them, a sort of landmark far far on ahead of them, to which I suppose they thought that they would one day come themselves. Fancy them playing cricket!

"Well, next day we turned round and started back again, hundreds of miles to the sea. The lions . . ."

"We've heard about them," said Terbut.

"Oh, well," said Jorkens.

But if they wouldn't hear his lion-stories they wanted to hear how Jembu played for Cambridge: it was the glamour of Jembu's name after all these years that was holding them. And soon he was back with his story of the long trek to the seas from somewhere north of a line between Kenya and the great lake.

He told us of birds that to me seemed quite incredible, birds with horny faces, and voices like organ-notes; and he told us of the cactus-forests again, speaking of cactus as though it could grow to the size of trees; and he told us of the falls of the Guaso Nyero, going down past a forest trailing grey beards of moss; there may be such falls as he told of above some such forests, but we thought more likely he had picked up tales of some queer foreign paradise, and was giving us them as geography, or else that he had smoked opium or some such drug, and had dreamed of them. One never knew with Jorkens.

He told us how they came to the coast again; and apparently there are trees in Mombasa with enormous scarlet flowers, that I have often seen made out of linen in windows in drapers' shops, but according to him they are real.

Well, I will let him tell his own story.

"We had to wait in that oven" (he meant Mombasa) "for several days before we could get a ship, and when we got home the cricket season was over. It was an odd thing, but Jembu went to the nets at once, and began hitting about, as he had been doing in the Red Sea; and there was no doubt about it that he was an unmistakable batsman. And he always stopped before there was any possibility that he could by any means be supposed to have made fifty.

"I talked to him about Mungo now and then but could get nothing out of him: he became too serious for that, whenever one mentioned Mungo, and of the dancing man in the temple I got barely a word; indeed, I never even knew his name. He read divinity still, but not with the old zest, so far as I could gather whenever I went to see him, and I think that his thoughts were far away with Mungo.

"And as soon as May came round he was back at cricket; and sure enough, as you know, he played for Cambridge. That was the year he played first; and you have only to look at old score books to see that he never made less than forty-six all that year. He always got very shy when he neared fifty: he was too afraid of a four if he passed forty-six, and that was why he always approached it so gingerly, often stopping at forty-seven, though what he liked to do was to get to forty-six and then to hit a four and hear them applauding his fifty. For he was very fond of the good opinion of Englishmen, though the whole of our civilization was really as nothing to him, compared with the fear of Mungo.

"Well, his average was magnificent; considering how often he was not out, it must have been nearly eighty. And then next year was the year he played against Surrey. All through May and June he went on with his forty-seven, forty-eight, forty-nine and fifty; and Cambridge played Surrey early in July. I needn't tell you of

that match; after Oxford *v.* Cambridge in 1870, and
Eton *v.* Harrow in 1910, I suppose it's the best-remem-
bered match in history. You remember how Cambridge
had two runs to win and Jembu was in with Halket, the
last wicket. Halket was their wicket-keeper and hardly
able to deal with this situation; at least Jembu thought
not, for he had obviously been getting the bowling all to
himself for some time. But now he had made fifty. With
the whole ground roaring applause at Jembu's fifty, and
two runs still to win I laid a pretty large bet at two to
one against Cambridge. Most of them knew his pecu-
liarity of not passing fifty, but I was the only man on the
ground that knew of his fear of Mungo. I alone had seen
his face when the dancing man went round him, I alone
knew the terms. The bet was a good deal more than I
could afford. A good deal more. Well, Jembu had the
bowling, two to win, and the first ball he stopped very
carefully; and then one came a little outside the off
stump; and Jembu put his leg across the wicket and
played the ball neatly through the slips with his knee.
They ran two, and the game was over. Jembu's score, of
course, stayed at fifty, no leg-byes could affect that, as
anyone knows who has ever heard of cricket. How could
anyone think otherwise? But that damned African spirit
knew nothing of cricket. How should he know, if you
come to think of it? Born probably ages ago in some
tropical marsh, from which he had risen to hang over
African villages, haunting old women and travellers lost
in the forest, or blessing or cursing the crops with moods
that changed with each wind, what should be know of
the feelings or rules of a sportsman? Spirits like that keep
their word as far as I've known: it was nothing but
honest ignorance; and he had credited poor Jembu with
fifty-two though not a ball that had touched his bat

that day had had any share in more than fifty runs.

"And I've learned this of life, that you must abide by the mistakes of your superiors. Your own you may sometimes atone for, but with the mistakes of your superiors, so far as they affect you, there is nothing to do but to suffer for them.

"There was no appeal for Jembu against Mungo's mistake. Who would have listened to him? Certainly no one here : certainly no one in Africa. Jembu went back to see what Mungo had done, as soon as he found out the view that Mungo had taken. He found out that soon enough, by dropping back to his old score of one and nothing in three consecutive innings. The Cambridge captain assured him that that might happen to anybody, and that he mustn't think of giving up cricket. But Jembu knew. And he went back to his forest beyond Mount Kenya, to see what Mungo had done.

"And only a few years later I came on Jembu again, in a small hotel in Marseilles, where they give you excellent fish. They have them in a little tank of water, swimming about alive, and you choose your fish and they cook it. I went there only three or four years after that match against Surrey, being in Marseilles for a day ; and a black waiter led me to the glass tank, and I looked up from the fishes, and it was Jembu. And we had a long talk, and he told me all that had happened because of those two leg-byes that had never been near his bat.

"It seems that a tribe that had never liked Jembu's people had broken into his forest and raided his honey-pots. They had taken his ivory, and burnt his cathedral of thatch, and driven off all his slaves. I knew from speeches that he had made at Cambridge that Jembu in principle was entirely opposed to slavery ; but it is altogether another matter to have one's slaves driven away, and not know where they have gone to or whether they will be well cared for. It was that that broke his heart as much as the loss of his honey-pots; and they got his wives too. His people were scattered, and all his cattle gone; there was nothing after that raid left for Jembu in Africa.

"He wandered down to the coast; he tried many jobs; but Mungo was always against him. He drifted to Port Said as a stowaway, to Marseilles as a sailor, and there deserted, and was many things more, before he rose to the position of waiter; and I question if Mungo had even done with him then. A certain fatalistic feeling he had, which he called resignation, seemed to bear him up and to comfort him. The word resignation, I think, came out of his books of divinity; but the feeling came from far back, out of old dark forests of Africa. And, wherever it came from, it cheered him awhile at his work in that inn of Marseilles, and caused him to leave gravy just where it fell, on the starched shirt-front that he wore all day. He was not unhappy, but he looked for nothing better; after all, he had won that match for Cambridge against Surrey, I don't see what more he could want, and many a man has less. But when I said good-bye to him I felt sure that Mungo would never alter his mind, either to understand, or to pardon, those two leg-byes."

"Did you ask him," said Terbut, "how Mungo knew that he got those two leg-byes?"

"No," said Jorkens, "I didn't ask him that."

A. J. ALAN

WOTTIE

THE preparatory school I went to was near Haywards Heath—about sixteen miles from Brighton—(in Sussex, you know). The Headmaster was a man called Mercer, and he knew his job.

He taught us cricket and rugger, and how to behave and (I believe) one or two other things.

There was nothing at all petty about him. He didn't make us walk two and two on Sunday afternoons, but he discouraged us from openly laughing at schools who did. If anyone attempted to put on side he promptly thrashed him. Altogether old Mercer was a sportsman and so, incidentally, was Mrs. Mercer.

As regards tuckshops we were pretty well off. There were two—Wottlespoon's and Jackson's. Wottlespoon's was the nearer to the school and the better. It was also the more expensive of the two. I mean, Russian toffee was eight a penny instead of ten, as it was at Jackson's, and you didn't get quite such a big ice for threepence, but it was cleaner.

Also there was Ma Wottlespoon. That's what she was known as, but I ought to point out that it was quite a courtesy and proleptic use of the title 'Ma.' The lady was, to the best of my belief, a complete and utter spinster. She was fair and plump but not by any means old. She was very dignified too. For instance, as soon as you got your eleven or your fifteen you could call her 'Wottie,' but not before. She was awfully decent about tick and had rather prominent front teeth.

That's the sort of person she was. We all liked her, of course, ever so, but Ackroyd major went a bit too far in my opinion, and got quite sloppy about her, and it was rather distressing because he was a particular friend of mine.

Not only that, we were both of us getting fairly senior and Old Mercer expected us to set an example to the rest of the school, so you see how difficult it was when he, Ackroyd, that is, went and developed this passion for Wottie. I was terrified that other people might notice it.

He used to give her presents. There was a perfectly appalling inkstand, I remember, and I had to present it because he was too shy. I was shy, too, of course, but not as shy as he was.

I shall never forget it. We had to wait till the shop was empty, then I went in and thrust the inkstand at her. Ackroyd hung about outside. She was perfectly charming, as always, though I'm quite sure she must have wondered what it all meant. At least I don't know. They say women understand these things. She tried to give me a sausage roll and it was dreadfully awkward. I went outside and kicked Ackroyd, and that was my first experience as liaison officer.

At all events this was the pitch things had got to just before the middle of a certain summer term.

Then there came a day of tragedy. It wasn't all tragic by any manner of means. In fact, as days go it began jolly well.

There was a whacking great thunderstorm at about six o'clock in the morning and the whole basement of the house was flooded to a depth of nearly two feet. It was owing to some grating getting stopped up. Old Mercer allowed us to bale it out in our pyjamas instead of doing early school, and there was just enough water to swim in the coal cellar. On the top of all this it was the morning we had hot rolls for breakfast and a half holiday, so what more could you want?

However, after dinner someone strolled down to Wottie's for an ice and came racing back with the news that she'd disappeared. She'd—from all accounts—got up and dressed during the night and not come back.

We naturally tore down to the shop, about twenty of us, to verify this and found her mother in a great state of mind. In another walk of life she'd have been sitting with her apron over her head—if you know what I mean. She was sure that something terrible must have happened to her daughter.

We weren't old enough to do anything but agree, so we bought a few things out of sympathy and sloped off. During the next few days sundry rumours filtered into the school via boot boys and people of woods being searched and ponds dragged, but without success.

Wottie never came back and it came to be generally accepted that she had made away with herself owing to a fruitless love-affair.

Ackroyd was nearly prostrate with grief. With any encouragement at all he'd have persuaded himself that it was entirely on his account that she'd gone out and committed this suicide. What did I think? I said I thought not, unless she'd been driven to it by the ink-stand. Whereupon we had words, in the course of which we forgot Wottie—for the time being.

I'm afraid you will have to excuse this story for being rather disjointed, but it's rather a disjointed story.

Nothing more happened for about three weeks and then something did.

You should know that Mrs. Mercer, our Headmaster's wife, was an extremely nice woman, and, like so many extremely nice women, she had an awful lot of brothers —about eight—and one or other of these brothers used to come down to the school for most week-ends.

It's a matter of considerable surprise to me that they ever came a second time in view of what they had to put up with. Reels of cotton unwound themselves in tin boxes on the tops of their wardrobes. Alarm clocks went off under their beds at 3 a.m., and those who slept with their mouths open were naturally fed with pellets of soap. In fact they were made thoroughly welcome.

Well, the one who was coming this particular Saturday was Julian. We didn't call him that, but that's who he was. He was immensely tall and bowled leg breaks.

Now it so happened that the rest of the school were being taken into Brighton to see the last day of Sussex *v.* Middlesex. Ackroyd and I weren't going because the following Saturday Old Mercer was going to take us to a place called Sheffield Park to see the South Africans. They were going to play someone or other—I've forgotten whom. So this left Ackroyd and me entirely on our own, and we thought it would be rather a wheeze to go down to the station and meet old Julian and carry his bag up. He would, or should, think how kind of us it was, and while he was still in this frame of mind we should stop for a breather just outside the tuck shop and-er-voilà !

We knew everyone's habits, and as Julian had always come by the 2.15 we duly met it, but to our extreme chagrin it arrived without him, and so did the next train, so we gave him up.

We decided that it was a beastly swizzle, all our plans being upset like this, and we promptly cast about in our minds for some mischief to get into.

Ackroyd 'voted' that we went and tried to hire the tandem from Hilton's (Hilton's was the local bicycle shop where we got our hair cut) and then rode to Blane's Hill Quarry. I said "Good egg." I said it with especial carefreedom because I hadn't any money at all, whereas I knew he'd got five bob. He was the pampered son of an only father and mother and they'd sent it him that very morning. So, as I say, I concurred with this proposal.

There was a strong element of doubt about our getting this tandem because the man hadn't ever let us have it. He said we weren't old enough. However, we were lucky. He wasn't there—it was only Mrs. Bicycle and she raised no objections. Ackroyd planked down his half-crown just as though it were a penny and away we went.

We didn't attempt to mount the machine outside the shop because we didn't know how, and the saddles were too high any way, so we just wheeled it up to Wottie's. We leant it up against the window and went inside to see how far Ackroyd's remaining half-crown could be made to go.

We got a reasonably large pork pie, which was our fashionable ' stodge ' just then, but we couldn't get any éclairs to go with it owing to Wottie herself being dead and so on, so we had to be content with half a chocolate cake for second course and four bottles of stone ginger beer.

We tied these stores about the wretched tandem until it looked like a Christmas tree, and wheeled it clear of the village.

We then proceeded to learn to ride it. Ackroyd bagged

the front seat, so I held the machine upright while he got on, and when he was on I pushed it a few yards and got on too—in perfectly good faith, but Ackroyd promptly steered us into the right-hand ditch.

There wasn't any water in it, but it was, none the less, a ditch.

Well, we picked ourselves up and brushed each other down and got on again. After all, you can't expect to be able to ride a tandem first go off, but when we continued to crash time after time into the right-hand hedge without the slightest sign of improvement I began to feel it in my bones that we weren't, somehow, getting the best out of our machine.

I raised the matter with Ackroyd the next time we fell off. I said, "I say, Ackroyd, you might let me sit in front. You can't steer for nuts."

He demurred on the grounds that it was his half-crown which had paid for the hire of the blooming thing and he could steer it if he liked.

I said he obviously couldn't and that he'd better let me have a go while the front wheel was anything like round. I also agreed to pay him one and threepence which I earmarked out of my journey money at the end of term. That did it and we swapped over.

Just as we were going to remount I noticed that the string of the pork pie parcel had somehow got looped over the front lamp-bracket and it was preventing the handle-bar from being turned to the left at all. I just unlooped it. It was no good telling Ackroyd because he'd only have wanted to try sitting in front again.

As it was we began to make progress. I don't wish to spot myself in the very least but we did get along quite well, especially on the straight, and there was only a slight falling off at one or two of the sharper corners.

Well, we got to Blane's Hill Quarry all right—it was only about four miles—and sat down on the edge to enjoy ourselves.

I should, perhaps, mention that this quarry was hopelessly out of bounds because it was extremely dangerous, which made it all the more attractive, and it was a lovely day, but the food was not all it might have been. Anything but. I don't know what the shelf life of a pork pie is, but when we came to break this one open we found a grey feathery deposit on the top of the pork. If it had been an accumulator nowadays I should have said it was sulphating.

It tasted so mouldy that we could hardly finish it, and the shortcomings of the chocolate cake made us still further deplore the death or whatnot of Wottie.

However, at the noontide of youth (we were both twelve) moods soon pass, and we looked round for some convenient method of disposing of the empty ginger beer bottles. We didn't want to leave them lying about.

Now there was a small stone hut with a slate roof down at the bottom of the quarry about fifty feet below us, and really—it might have been put there on purpose.

We registered two direct hits on it, but the roof proved obstinate and the bottles merely bounced off. Not to be borne for a moment. Ackroyd found a piece of flint about as big as a football and said, "I dare you to throw that down."

Mind you, I'm not defending my action for a moment —it was dastardly—but you know what it is when you are dared to do anything. I simple had to pitch this young boulder over and it went 'plunk' straight through the roof and left a great gaping hole in the slates.

There was no chance of hurting anyone because it was only a sort of store shed. We found out afterwards that they kept the dynamite and detonators there for blasting in the quarry, but we oughtn't to have dropped rocks on it all the same.

The next thing Ackroyd did was to fall over the edge. It was a judgment on him because he was reaching for something still larger to throw and he made a slight miscalculage and lost his balance. I thought he'd gone right to the bottom and I was a bit worried, but actually there was a ledge sticking out a few feet down, and on this ledge he—lodged. It was covered with brambles and he got so involved that I had to climb down and undo him.

While we were messing about down there we both began to notice a most peculiar—what shall I say—lack of freshness in the air. Most marked it was and it seemed to be coming from the mouth of a small tunnel driven into the face of the stone just behind us.

I said, "Something's died," and Ackroyd said, "Yes—let's go in and see what it is." I wasn't frightfully keen personally, but he would go, so I had to follow. We had to duck our heads to get in and there wasn't room to walk two abreast. It was pretty dark, too, after the glare outside, and the atmosphere—well—it was indescribable.

We'd only gone three or four yards when Ackroyd stooped over something lying on the ground—then he suddenly gave a most fearful yell and said, "By Gosh, it's Wottie—let me out," and he turned round and tried to charge past me, but the place was so beastly narrow that we almost got jammed, and while we were fighting to get free I caught a glimpse, over his shoulder, of a ghastly object with an almost black face grinning at us. It wouldn't have been recognisable at all if it hadn't been for the rather prominent front teeth. One look was enough for me—I bolted for the entrance for all I was worth with Ackroyd after me—still yelling.

It may sound cowardly now, but you understand we'd neither of us seen anyone dead before, and what with one thing and another it came as a bit of a shock. I've no recollection at all of getting back to the tandem, but I do know we rode it across a cornfield without falling off, which only shows what absolute panic will do.

We'd recovered somewhat by the time we got back to school, and we went and had a long jaw behind the pavilion about what was to be done.

If we'd been a little older we should have gone straight to old Mercer and owned up, but we were so afraid of what might happen to us for going to the quarry at all, let alone bashing in that roof, that we decided to trust to luck and keep quiet, and strange to say we were never found out.

After thirty odd years I was almost beginning to regard the incident as closed until, about a couple of months ago, I got a letter from a cousin of mine.

He lives down in Sussex, and he said, in this letter, that they'd just laid out a new golf course near his place. Would we go down for the opening and watch him miss his first tee shot. He'd been elected president of the club, or something, and had to drive off before a cheering multitude.

Well, my wife and I went down on the great day and saw him carry the first hazard of the course in brilliant fashion.

This hazard turned out to be a corner of my dear old friend, Blane's Hill Quarry. It had been disused for some years, so they told me, but there it still was, as large as life. That's the great thing about a quarry—when it's done with it's got to stop. You can't pull it down or turn it into flats. I even recognized the ruins of the old dynamite store. The historic tunnel where Ackroyd and

I had found—what we had found, was right away on the far side, and there wasn't a chance of going to look for it just then. But after dinner that night (my cousin had a lot of people there) I told them the whole story— all about Wottie and the tandem and finding the body and so on—just as I've told it to you, only they didn't believe it. They said I'd made it all up—as though one would. They were so jolly certain about it not being true that they laid me ten to one in gin and bitters that I couldn't take them to the place and show them the tunnel. I said "Done with you," and it was finally arranged for us all to meet at the Golf Club next morning, and then I was to lead them to the tragic spot. They called it the gruesome grotto.

By the by, one man dining there was the coroner for the district, and he pointed out that if we found so much as a single bone he'd have to hold an inquest. They do, you know. Why, they once found a mummy in the cloak room at King's Cross Station, and they solemnly sat on the good lady to find out what she'd died of about seven thousand years before.

At any rate, we all met next morning and walked round the edge of the quarry till we got to the point just above the ruins of the store shed. The ledge was still there and I slithered down on to it. The others were so certain that it was all a leg pull that they wouldn't come down with me. They all stood at the top and jeered. The whole place was a mass of brambles and weeds but I found the tunnel all right. That fetched 'em. They all came tumbling down and fairly fought to get the entrance clear.

As soon as it was possible my cousin and I squeezed in and we found an absolutely perfect skeleton—of a sheep.

Well, of course, they reckoned I'd won all right, and

that it was very handsome of me to have thrown in a skeleton as well, when it wasn't in the contract, even if it wasn't quite the right kind of skeleton. But up at the Club House, afterwards, over my winnings, one of them said, "It's all very well, you know, but quite apart from your being a couple of heartless young devils, I can't think why you didn't go back next day out of sheer curiosity, and then you'd have found that it was only a sheep."

And I said, "Yes, we did."

W. W. JACOBS

OVER THE SIDE

O F all classes of men, those who follow the sea are probably the most prone to superstition. Afloat upon the black waste of waters, at the mercy of wind and sea, with vast depths and strange creatures below them, a belief in the supernatural is easier than ashore, under the cheerful gas-lamps. Strange stories of the sea are plentiful, and an incident which happened within my own experience has made me somewhat chary of dubbing a man fool or coward because he has encountered something he cannot explain. There are stories of the supernatural with prosaic sequels; there are others to which the sequel has never been published.

I was fifteen years old at the time, and as my father, who had a strong objection to the sea, would not apprentice me to it, I shipped before the mast on a sturdy little brig called the *Endeavour,* bound for Riga. She was a small craft, but the skipper was as fine a seaman as one could wish for, and, in fair weather, an easy man to sail under. Most boys have a rough time of it when they first go to sea, but, with a strong sense of what was good for me, I had attached myself to a brawny, good-natured infant, named Bill Smith, and it was soon understood that whoever hit me struck Bill by proxy. Not that the crew were particularly brutal, but a sound cuffing

occasionally is held by most seamen to be beneficial to
a lad's health and morals. The only really spiteful fellow
among them was a man named Jem Dadd. He was a
morose, sallow-looking man, of about forty, with a strong
taste for the supernatural, and a stronger taste still for
frightening his fellows with it. I have seen Bill almost
afraid to go on deck of a night for his trick at the wheel
after a few of his reminiscences. Rats were a favourite
topic with him, and he would never allow one to be
killed if he could help it, for he claimed for them that
they were the souls of drowned sailors, hence their love
of ships and their habit of leaving them when they
became unseaworthy. He was a firm believer in the trans-
migration of souls, some idea of which he had, no doubt,
picked up in Eastern ports, and gave his shivering
auditors to understand that his arrangements for his own
immediate future were already perfected.

We were six or seven days out when a strange thing
happened. Dadd had the second watch one night, and
Bill was to relieve him. They were not very strict aboard
the brig in fair weather, and when a man's time was up
he just made the wheel fast, and, running for'ard,
shouted down the fo'c's'le. On this night I happened to
awake suddenly, in time to see Bill slip out of his bunk
and stand by me, rubbing his red eyelids with his
knuckles.

"Dadd's giving me a long time," he whispered, seeing
that I was awake; "it's a whole hour after his time."

He pattered up on deck, and I was just turning over,
thankful that I was too young to have a watch to keep,
when he came softly down again, and, taking me by the
shoulders, shook me roughly.

"Jack," he whispered. "Jack."

I raised myself on my elbows, and, in the light of

the smoking lamp, saw that he was shaking all over.

"Come on deck," he said, thickly.

I put on my clothes and followed him quietly to the sweet, cool air above. It was a beautiful clear night, but, from his manner, I looked nervously around for some cause of alarm. I saw nothing. The deck was deserted except for the solitary figure at the wheel.

"Look at him," whispered Bill, bending a contorted face to mine.

I walked aft a few steps, and Bill followed slowly. Then I saw that Jem Dadd was leaning forward clumsily on the wheel with his hands clenched on the spokes.

"He's asleep," said I, stopping short.

Bill breathed hard. "He's in a queer sleep," said he ; "kind o' trance more like. Go closer."

I took fast hold of Bill's sleeve, and we both went. The light of the stars was sufficient to show that Dadd's face was very white, and that his dim, black eyes were wide open, and staring in a very strange and dreadful manner straight before him.

"Dadd," said I, softly, "Dadd !"

There was no reply, and, with a view of arousing him, I tapped one sinewy hand as it gripped the wheel, and even tried to loosen it.

He remained immovable, and, suddenly with a great cry, my courage deserted me, and Bill and I fairly bolted down into the cabin and woke the skipper.

Then we saw how it was with Jem, and two strong seamen forcibly loosened the grip of those rigid fingers, and, laying him on the deck, covered him with a piece of canvas. The rest of the night two men stayed at the wheel, and, gazing fearfully at the outline of the canvas, longed for dawn.

It came at last, and, breakfast over, the body was sewn

up in canvas, and the skipper held a short service compiled from a Bible which belonged to the mate, and what he remembered of the Burial Service proper. Then the corpse went overboard with a splash, and the men, after standing awkwardly together for a few minutes, slowly dispersed to their duties.

For the rest of that day we were all very quiet and restrained; pity for the dead man being mingled with a dread of taking the wheel when night came.

"The wheel's haunted," said the cook, solemnly; "mark my words, there's more of you will be took the same way Dadd was."

The cook, like myself, had no watch to keep.

The men bore up pretty well until night came on again, and then they unanimously resolved to have a double watch. The cook, sorely against his will, was impressed into the service, and I, glad to oblige my patron, agreed to stay up with Bill.

Some of the pleasure had vanished by the time night came, and I seemed only just to have closed my eyes when Bill came, and, with a rough shake or two, informed me that the time had come. Any hope that I might have had of escaping the ordeal was at once dispelled by his expectant demeanour, and the helpful way in which he assisted me with my clothes, and, yawning terribly, I followed him on deck.

The night was not so clear as the preceding one, and the air was chilly, with a little moisture in it. I buttoned up my jacket and thrust my hands in my pockets.

"Everything quiet?" asked Bill as he stepped up and took the wheel.

"Ay, ay," said Roberts, "quiet as the grave," and, followed by his willing mate, he went below.

I sat on the deck by Bill's side as, with a light touch

on the wheel, he kept the brig to her course. It was weary work sitting there, doing nothing, and thinking of the warm berth below, and I believe that I should have fallen asleep, but that my watchful companion stirred me with his foot whenever he saw me nodding.

I suppose I must have sat there, shivering and yawning, for about an hour, when, tired of inactivity, I got up and went and leaned over the side of the vessel. The sound of the water gurgling and lapping by was so soothing that I began to doze.

I was recalled to my senses by a smothered cry from Bill, and, running to him, I found him staring to port in a very intense and uncomfortable fashion. At my approach he took one hand from the wheel, and gripped my arm so tightly that I was like to have screamed with the pain of it.

"Jack," said he, in a shaky voice, "while you was away something popped its head up and looked over the ship's side."

"You've been dreaming," said I, in a voice that was a very fair imitation of Bill's own.

"Dreaming," repeated Bill, "dreaming! Ah, *look there!*"

He pointed with outstretched finger, and my heart seemed to stop beating as I saw a man's head appear above the side. For a brief space it peered at us in silence, and then a dark figure sprang like a cat on to the deck, and stood crouching a short distance away.

A mist came before my eyes, and my tongue failed me, but Bill let off a roar such as I have never heard before or since. It was answered from below, both aft and for'ard, and the men came running up on deck just as they left their beds.

"What's up?" shouted the skipper, glancing aloft.

For answer Bill pointed to the intruder, and the men, who had just caught sight of him, came up and formed a compact knot by the wheel.

"Come over the side, it did," panted Bill, "come over like a ghost out of the sea."

The skipper took one of the small lamps from the binnacle, and, holding it aloft, walked boldly up to the cause of alarm. In the little patch of light we saw a ghastly black-bearded man, dripping with water, regarding us with unwinking eyes, which glowed red in the light of the lamp.

"Where did you come from?" asked the skipper.

The figure shook his head.

"Where did you come from?" he repeated, walking up and laying his hand on the other's shoulder.

Then the intruder spoke, but in a strange fashion and in strange words. We leaned forward to listen, but, even when he repeated them, we could make nothing of them.

"He's a furriner," said Roberts.

"Blest if I've ever 'eard the lingo afore," said Bill. "Does anybody reckernize it?"

Nobody did, and the skipper, after another attempt, gave it up, and, falling back upon the universal language of signs, pointed first to the man and then to the sea. The other understood him, and, in a heavy, slovenly fashion, portrayed a man drifting in an open boat, and clutching and clambering up the side of a passing ship. As his meaning dawned upon us, we rushed to the stern, and, leaning over, peered into the gloom, but the night was dark, and we saw nothing.

"Well," said the skipper, turning to Bill with a mighty yawn, "take him below, and give him some grub, and the next time a gentleman calls on you, don't make such a confounded row about it."

He went below, followed by the mate, and after some

slight hesitation, Roberts stepped up to the intruder and
signed to him to follow. He came stolidly enough, leaving
a trail of water on the deck, and, after changing into the
dry things we gave him, fell to, but without much
appearance of hunger, upon some salt beef and biscuit,
regarding us between his bites with black, lack-lustre
eyes.

"He seems as though he's a-walking in his sleep," said
the cook.

"He ain't very hungry," said one of the men; "he
seems to mumble his food."

"Hungry!" repeated Bill, who had just left the wheel.
"Course he ain't famished. He had his tea last night."

The men stared at him in bewilderment.

"Don't you see?" said Bill, still in a hoarse whisper;
"ain't you ever seen them eyes afore? Don't you know
what he used to say about dying? It's Jem Dadd come
back to us. Jem Dadd got another man's body, as he
always said he would."

"Rot!" said Roberts, trying to speak bravely, but he
got up, and, with the others, huddled together at the end
of the fo'c's'le and stared in a bewildered fashion at the
sodden face and short squat figure of our visitor. For his
part, having finished his meal, he pushed his plate from
him, and, leaning back on the locker, looked at the
empty bunks.

Roberts caught his eye, and, with a nod and a wave of
his hand, indicated the bunks. The fellow rose from the
locker, and, amid a breathless silence, climbed into one
of them—Jem Dadd's!

He slept in a dead sailor's bed that night, the only man
in the fo'c's'le who did sleep properly, and turned out
heavily and lumpishly in the morning for breakfast.

The skipper had him on deck after the meal, but could
make nothing of him. To all his questions he replied in

the strange tongue of the night before, and, though our
fellows had been to many ports, and knew a word or two
of several languages, none of them recognized it. The
skipper gave it up at last, and, left to himself, he stared
about him for some time, regardless of our interest in his
movements, and then, leaning heavily against the side of
the ship, stayed there so long that we thought he must
have fallen asleep.

"He's half-dead *now!*" whispered Roberts.

"Hush!" said Bill, "mebbe he's been in the water a
week or two, and can't quite make it out. See how he's
looking at it now."

He stayed on deck all day in the sun, but, as night
came on, returned to the warmth of the fo'c's'le. The
food we gave him remained untouched, and he took
little or no notice of us, though I fancied that he saw the
fear we had of him. He slept again in the dead man's
bunk, and when morning came still lay there.

Until dinner-time, nobody interfered with him, and
then Roberts, pushed forward by the others, approached
him with some food. He motioned it away with a dirty,
bloated hand, and, making signs for water, drank it
eagerly.

For two days he stayed there quietly, the black eyes
always open, the stubby fingers always on the move. On
the third morning Bill, who had conquered his fear
sufficiently to give him water occasionally, called softly
to us.

"Come and look at him," said he. "What's the matter
with him?"

"He's dying!" said the cook, with a shudder.

"He can't be going to die *yet!*" said Bill, blankly.

As he spoke the man's eyes seemed to get softer and
more lifelike, and he looked at us piteously and help-
lessly. From face to face he gazed in mute inquiry, and

then, striking his chest feebly with his fist, uttered two words.

We looked at each other blankly, and he repeated them eagerly, and again touched his chest.

"It's his name," said the cook, and we all repeated them.

He smiled in an exhausted fashion, and then, rallying his energies, held up a forefinger; as we stared at this new riddle he lowered it, and held up all four fingers, doubled.

"Come away," quavered the cook; "he's putting a spell on us."

We drew back at that, and back farther still, as he repeated the motions. Then Bill's face cleared suddenly, and he stepped towards him.

"He means his wife and younkers," he shouted eagerly. "This ain't no Jem Dadd!"

It was good then to see how our fellows drew round the dying sailor and strove to cheer him. Bill, to show he understood the finger business, nodded cheerily, and held his hand at four different heights from the floor. The last was very low, so low that the man set his lips together, and strove to turn his heavy head from us.

"Poor devil!" said Bill, "he wants us to tell his wife and children what's become of him. He must ha' been dying when he come aboard. What was his name, again?"

But the name was not easy to English lips and we had already forgotten it.

"Ask him again," said the cook, "and write it down. Who's got a pen?"

He went to look for one as Bill turned to the sailor to get him to repeat it. Then he turned round again, and eyed us blankly, for, by this time, the owner had himself forgotten it.

E. M. FORSTER

THE CELESTIAL OMNIBUS

I

THE boy who resided at Agathox Lodge, 28 Buckingham Park Road, Surbiton, had often been puzzled by the old sign-post that stood almost opposite. He asked his mother about it, and she replied that it was a joke, and not a very nice one, which had been made many years back by some naughty young men, and that the police ought to remove it. For there were two strange things about this sign-post: firstly, it pointed up a blank alley, and, secondly, it had painted on it, in faded characters, the words, "To Heaven."

"What kind of young men were they?" he asked.

"I think your father told me that one of them wrote verses, and was expelled from the University and came to grief in other ways. Still, it was a long time ago. You must ask your father about it. He will say the same as I do, that it was put up as a joke."

"So it doesn't mean anything at all?"

She sent him upstairs to put on his best things, for the Bonses were coming to tea, and he was to hand the cake-stand.

It struck him, as he wrenched on his tightening trousers, that he might do worse than ask Mr. Bons about the sign-post. His father, though very kind, always laughed at him—shrieked with laughter whenever he or any other child asked a question or spoke. But Mr. Bons was serious as well as kind. He had a beautiful house and lent one books, he was a churchwarden, and a candidate for the County Council; he had donated to the Free Library enormously, he presided over the Literary Society, and had Members of Parliament to stop with him—in short, he was probably the wisest person alive.

Yet even Mr. Bons could only say that the sign-post was a joke—the joke of a person named Shelley.

"Of course!" cried the mother; "I told you so, dear. That was the name."

"Had you never heard of Shelley?" asked Mr. Bons.

"No," said the boy, and hung his head.

"But is there no Shelley in the house?"

"Why, yes!" exclaimed the lady in much agitation. "Dear Mr. Bons, we aren't such Philistines as that. Two at the least. One a wedding present, and the other, smaller print, in one of the spare rooms."

"I believe we have seven Shelleys," said Mr. Bons, with a slow smile. Then he brushed the cake crumbs off his stomach, and, together with his daughter, rose to go.

The boy, obeying a wink from his mother, saw them all the way to the garden gate, and when they had gone he did not at once return to the house, but gazed for a little up and down Buckingham Park Road.

His parents lived at the right end of it. After No. 39 the quality of the houses dropped very suddenly, and 64 had not even a separate servants' entrance. But at the present moment the whole road looked rather pretty, for the sun had just set in splendour, and the inequalities of rent were drowned in a saffron afterglow. Small birds twittered, and the breadwinners' train shrieked musically down through the cutting—that wonderful cutting which has drawn to itself the whole beauty out of Surbiton, and clad itself like any Alpine valley, with the glory of the fir and the silver birch and the primrose. It was this cutting that had first stirred desires within the boy—desires for something just a little different, he knew not what, desires that would return whenever things were sunlit, as they were this evening, running up and down inside him, up and down, up and down, till he would feel quite unusual all over, and as likely as not would want to cry. This evening he was even sillier, for he slipped across the road towards the sign-post and began to run up the blank alley.

The alley runs between high walls—the walls of the gardens of 'Ivanhoe' and 'Belle Vista' respectively. It smells a little all the way, and is scarcely twenty yards long, including the turn at the end. So not unnaturally the boy soon came to a standstill. "I'd like to kick that Shelley," he exclaimed, and glanced idly at a piece of paper which was pasted on the wall. Rather an odd piece of paper, and he read it carefully before he turned back. This is what he read :

"S. AND C.R.C.C.

Alteration in Service

Owing to lack of patronage the Company are regretfully compelled to suspend the hourly service, and to retain only the

Sunrise and Sunset Omnibuses,

which will run as usual. It is to be hoped that the public will patronize an arrangement which is intended for their convenience. As an extra inducement, the Company will, for the first time, now issue

Return Tickets !

(available one day only), which may be obtained of the driver. Passengers are again reminded that *no tickets are issued at the other end,* and that no complaints in this connexion will receive consideration from the Company.

Nor will the Company be responsible for any negligence or stupidity on the part of the Passengers, nor for Hailstorms, Lightning, Loss of Tickets, nor for any Act of God.

For the Direction."

Now he had never seen this notice before, nor could he imagine where the omnibus went to. S. of course was for Surbiton, and R.C.C. meant Road Car Company. But what was the meaning of the other C.? Coombe and Malden, perhaps, or possibly 'City.' Yet it could not hope to compete with the South-Western. The whole thing, the boy reflected, was run on hopelessly unbusiness-like lines. Why no tickets from the other end? And what an hour to start! Then he realized that unless the notice was a hoax, an omnibus must have been starting just as he was wishing the Bonses good-bye. He peered at the ground through the gathering dusk, and there he saw what might or might not be the marks of wheels. Yet nothing had come out of the alley. And he had never seen an omnibus at any time in the Buckingham Park Road. No: it must be a hoax, like the signposts, like the fairy tales, like the dreams upon which he would wake suddenly in the night. And with a sigh he stepped from the alley—right into the arms of his father.

Oh, how his father laughed! "Poor, poor Popsey!" he cried. "Diddums! Diddums! Diddums think he'd walky-palky up to Ev-vink!" And his mother, also convulsed with laughter, appeared on the steps of Agathox Lodge. "Don't, Bob!" she gasped. "Don't be so naughty! Oh, you'll kill me! Oh, leave the boy alone!"

But all that evening the joke was kept up. The father implored to be taken too. Was it a very tiring walk? Need one wipe one's shoes on the door-mat? And the boy went to bed feeling faint and sore, and thankful for only one thing—that he had not said a word about the omnibus. It was a hoax, yet through his dreams it grew more and more real, and the streets of Surbiton, through which he saw it driving, seemed instead to become hoaxes and shadows. And very early in the morning he woke with a cry, for he had had a glimpse of its destination.

He struck a match, and its light fell not only on his watch but also on his calendar, so that he knew it to be half an hour to sunrise. It was pitch dark, for the fog had come down from London in the night, and all Surbiton was wrapped in its embraces. Yet he sprang out and dressed himself, for he was determined to settle once for all which was real: the omnibus or the streets. "I shall be a fool one way or the other," he thought, "until I know." Soon he was shivering in the road under the gas lamp that guarded the entrance to the alley.

To enter the alley itself required some courage. Not only was it horribly dark, but he now realized that it was an impossible terminus for an omnibus. If it had not been for a policeman, whom he heard approaching through the fog, he would never have made the attempt. The next moment he had made the attempt and failed. Nothing. Nothing but a blank alley and a very silly boy gaping at its dirty floor. It *was* a hoax. "I'll tell papa and mamma," he decided. "I deserve it. I deserve that they should know. I am too silly to be alive." And he went back to the gate of Agathox Lodge.

There he remembered that his watch was fast. The sun was not risen; it would not rise for two minutes. "Give the bus every chance," he thought cynically, and returned into the alley.

But the omnibus was there.

II

It had two horses, whose sides were still smoking from their journey, and its two great lamps shone through the fog against the alley's walls, changing their cobwebs and moss into tissues of fairyland. The driver was huddled up in a cape. He faced the blank wall, and how he had managed to drive in so neatly and so silently was one of the many things that the boy never discovered. Nor could he imagine how ever he would drive out.

"Please," his voice quavered through the foul brown air, "Please, is that an omnibus?"

"Omnibus est," said the driver, without turning round. There was a moment's silence. The policeman passed, coughing, by the entrance of the alley. The boy crouched in the shadow, for he did not want to be found out. He was pretty sure, too, that it was a Pirate; nothing else, he reasoned, would go from such odd places and at such odd hours.

"About when do you start?" He tried to sound nonchalant.

"At sunrise."

"How far do you go?"

"The whole way."

"And can I have a return ticket which will bring me all the way back?"

"You can."

"Do you know, I half think I'll come." The driver made no answer. The sun must have risen for he unhitched the brake. And scarcely had the boy jumped in before the omnibus was off.

How? Did it turn? There was no room. Did it go forward? There was a blank wall. Yet it was moving—moving at a stately pace through the fog, which had turned from brown to yellow. The thought of warm bed and warmer breakfast made the boy feel faint. He wished he had not come. His parents would not have approved. He would have gone back to them if the weather had not made it impossible. The solitude was terrible; he was the only passenger. And the omnibus, though well built, was cold and somewhat musty. He drew his coat round him, and in so doing chanced to feel his pocket. It was empty. He had forgotten his purse.

"Stop!" he shouted. "Stop!" And then, being of a polite disposition, he glanced up at the painted notice-board so that he might call the driver by name. "Mr. Browne! stop; Oh, do please stop!"

Mr. Browne did not stop, but he opened a little window and looked in at the boy. His face was a surprise, so kind it was and modest.

"Mr. Browne, I've left my purse behind. I've not got a penny. I can't pay for the ticket. Will you take my watch, please? I am in the most awful hole."

"Tickets on this line," said the driver, "whether single or return, can be purchased by coinage from no terrene mint. And a chronometer, though it had solaced the vigils of Charlemagne, or measured the slumbers of Laura, can acquire by no mutation the double-cake that charms the fangless Cerberus of Heaven!" So saying, he handed in the necessary ticket, and, while the boy said "Thank you," continued: "Titular pretensions, I know it well, are vanity. Yet they merit no censure when uttered on a laughing lip, and in an homonymous world are in some sort useful, since they do serve to distinguish one Jack from his fellow. Remember me, therefore, as Sir Thomas Browne."

"Are you a Sir? Oh, sorry!" He had heard of these gentlemen drivers. "It *is* good of you about the ticket. But if you go on at this rate, however does your bus pay?"

"It does not pay. It was not intended to pay. Many are the faults of my equipage; it is compounded too curiously of foreign woods; its cushions tickle erudition rather than promote repose; and my horses are nourished not on the evergreen pastures of the moment, but on the dried bents and clovers of Latinity. But that it pays!— that error at all events was never intended and never attained."

"Sorry again," said the boy rather hopelessly. Sir Thomas looked sad, fearing that, even for a moment, he had been the cause of sadness. He invited the boy to come up and sit beside him on the box, and together they journeyed on through the fog, which was now changing from yellow to white. There were no houses by the road; so it must be either Putney Heath or Wimbledon Common.

"Have you been a driver always?"

"I was a physician once."

"But why did you stop? Weren't you good?"

"As a healer of bodies I had scant success, and several score of my patients preceded me. But as a healer of the spirit I have succeeded beyond my hopes and my deserts. For though my draughts were not better nor subtler than those of other men, yet, by reason of the cunning goblets wherein I offered them, the queasy soul was oft-times tempted to sip and be refreshed."

"The queasy soul," he murmured; "if the sun sets with trees in front of it, and you suddenly come strange all over, is that a queasy soul?"

"Have you felt that?"

"Why yes."

After a pause he told the boy a little, a very little, about the journey's end. But they did not chatter much, for the boy, when he liked a person, would as soon sit silent in his company as speak, and this, he discovered, was also the mind of Sir Thomas Browne and of many others with whom he was to be acquainted. He heard, however, about the young man Shelley, who was now quite a famous person, with a carriage of his own, and about some of the other drivers who are in the service of the Company. Meanwhile the light grew stronger, though the fog did not disperse. It was now more like mist than fog, and at times would travel quickly across them, as if it was part of a cloud. They had been ascending, too, in a most puzzling way; for over two hours the horses had been pulling against the collar, and even if it were Richmond Hill they ought to have been at the top long ago. Perhaps it was Epsom, or even the North Downs; yet the air seemed keener than that which blows on either. And as to the name of their destination, Sir Thomas Browne was silent.

Crash!

"Thunder, by Jove!" said the boy, "and not so far off either. Listen to the echoes! It's more like mountains."

He thought, not very vividly, of his father and mother. He saw them sitting down to sausages and listening to the storm. He saw his own empty place. Then there would be questions, alarms, theories, jokes, consolations. They would expect him back at lunch. To lunch he would not come, nor to tea, but he would be in for dinner, and so his day's truancy would be over. If he had had his purse he would have bought them presents—not that he should have known what to get them.

Crash!

The peal and the lightning came together. The cloud quivered as if it were alive, and torn streamers of mist rushed past. "Are you afraid?" asked Sir Thomas Browne.

"What is there to be afraid of? Is it much farther?"

The horses of the omnibus stopped just as a ball of fire burst up and exploded with a ringing noise that was deafening but clear, like the noise of a blacksmith's forge. All the cloud was shattered.

"Oh, listen, Sir Thomas Browne! No, I mean look; we shall get a view at last. No, I mean listen; that sounds like a rainbow!"

The noise had died into the faintest murmur, beneath which another murmur grew, spreading stealthily, steadily, in a curve that widened but did not vary. And in widening curves a rainbow was spreading from the horses' feet into the dissolving mists.

"But how beautiful! What colours! Where will it stop? It is more like the rainbows you can tread on. More like dreams."

The colour and the sound grew together. The rainbow spanned an enormous gulf. Clouds rushed under it and were pierced by it, and still it grew, reaching forward, conquering the darkness, until it touched something that seemed more solid than a cloud.

The boy stood up. "What is that out there?" he called. "What does it rest on, out at that other end?"

In the morning sunshine a precipice shone forth beyond the gulf. A precipice—or was it a castle? The horses moved. They set their feet upon the rainbow.

"Oh, look!" the boy shouted. "Oh, listen! Those caves —or are they gateways? Oh, look between those cliffs at those ledges. I see people! I see trees!"

"Look also below," whispered Sir Thomas. "Neglect not the diviner Acheron."

The boy looked below, past the flames of the rainbow that licked against their wheels. The gulf also had cleared, and in its depths there flowed an everlasting river. One sunbeam entered and struck a green pool, and as they passed over he saw three maidens rise to the surface of the pool, singing, and playing with something that glistened like a ring.

"You down in the water—" he called.

They answered, "You up on the bridge—" There was a burst of music. "You up on the bridge, good luck to you. Truth in the depth, truth on the height."

"You down in the water, what are you doing?"

Sir Thomas Browne replied: "They sport in the mancipiary possession of their gold"; and the omnibus arrived.

III

The boy was in disgrace. He sat locked up in the nursery of Agathox Lodge, learning poetry for a punishment. His father had said, "My boy! I can pardon anything but untruthfulness," and had caned him, saying at each stroke, "There is *no* omnibus, *no* driver, *no* bridge, *no* mountain; you are a *truant*, a *guttersnipe*, a *liar*." His father could be very stern at times. His mother had begged him to say he was sorry. But he could not say that. It was the greatest day of his life, in spite of the caning and the poetry at the end of it.

He had returned punctually at sunset—driven not by Sir Thomas Browne, but by a maiden lady who was full of quiet fun. They had talked of omnibuses and also of barouche landaus. How far away her gentle voice seemed now! Yet it was scarcely three hours since he had left her up the alley.

His mother called through the door. "Dear, you are to come down and to bring your poetry with you."

He came down, and found that Mr. Bons was in the smoking-room with his father. It had been a dinner party.

"Here is the great traveller!" said his father grimly. "Here is the young gentleman who drives in an omnibus over rainbows, while young ladies sing to him." Pleased with his wit, he laughed.

"After all," said Mr. Bons, smiling, "there is something a little like it in Wagner. It is odd how, in quite illiterate minds, you will find glimmers of Artistic Truth. The case interests me. Let me plead for the culprit. We have all romanced in our time, haven't we?"

"Hear how kind Mr. Bons is," said his mother, while his father said, "Very well. Let him say his Poem, and that will do. He is going away to my sister on Tuesday, and she will cure him of this alley-slopering." (Laughter.) "Say your Poem."

The boy began. " 'Standing aloof in giant ignorance.' "

His father laughed again—roared. "One for you, my son! 'Standing aloof in giant ignorance'! I never knew these poets talked sense. Just describes you. Here, Bons, you go in for poetry. Put him through it, will you, while I fetch up the whisky?"

"Yes, give me the Keats," said Mr. Bons. "Let him say his Keats to me."

So for a few moments the wise man and the ignorant boy were left alone in the smoking-room.

" 'Standing aloof in giant ignorance, of thee I dream and of the Cyclades, as one who sits ashore and longs perchance to visit—' "

"Quite right. To visit what?"

" 'To visit dolphin coral in deep seas,' " said the boy, and burst into tears.

"Come, come! why do you cry?"

"Because—because all these words that only rhymed before, now that I've come back they're me."

Mr. Bons laid the Keats down. The case was more

interesting than he had expected. *"You?"* he exclaimed. "This sonnet, *you?"*

"Yes—and look further on: 'Aye, on the shores of darkness there is light, and precipices show untrodden green.' It *is* so, sir. All these things are true."

"I never doubted it," said Mr. Bons, with closed eyes.

"You—then you believe me? You believe in the omnibus and the driver and the storm and that return ticket I got for nothing and—"

"Tut, tut! No more of your yarns, my boy. I meant that I have never doubted the essential truth of Poetry. Some day, when you have read more, you will understand what I mean."

"But Mr. Bons, it is so. There *is* light upon the shores of darkness. I have seen it coming, light and a wind."

"Nonsense," said Mr. Bons.

"If I had stopped! They tempted me. They told me to give up my ticket—for you cannot come back if you lose your ticket. They called from the river for it, and indeed I was tempted, for I have never been so happy as among those precipices. But I thought of my mother and father, and that I must fetch them. Yet they will not come, though the road starts opposite our house. It has all happened as the people up there warned me, and Mr. Bons has disbelieved me like every one else. I have been caned. I shall never see that mountain again."

"What's that about me?" said Mr. Bons, sitting up in his chair very suddenly.

"I told them about you, and how clever you were, and how many books you had, and they said, 'Mr. Bons will certainly disbelieve you.'"

"Stuff and nonsense, my young friend. You grow impertinent. I—well—I will settle the matter. Not a word to your father. I will cure you. To-morrow evening

I will myself call here to take you for a walk, and at sunset we will go up this alley opposite and hunt for your omnibus, you silly little boy."

His face grew serious, for the boy was not disconcerted, but leapt about the room singing, "Joy! joy! I told them you would believe me. We will drive together over the rainbow. I told them that you would come." After all, could there be anything in the story? Wagner? Keats? Shelley? Sir Thomas Browne? Certainly the case was interesting.

And on the morrow evening, though it was pouring with rain, Mr. Bons did not omit to call at Agathox Lodge.

The boy was ready, bubbling with excitement, and skipping about in a way that rather vexed the President of the Literary Society. They took a turn down Buckingham Park Road, and then—having seen that no one was watching them—slipped up the alley. Naturally enough (for the sun was setting) they ran straight against the omnibus.

"Good heavens!" exclaimed Mr. Bons. "Good gracious heavens!"

It was not the omnibus in which the boy had driven first, nor yet that in which he had returned. There were three horses—black, grey, and white, the grey being the finest. The driver, who turned round at the mention of goodness and of heaven, was a sallow man with terrifying jaws and sunken eyes. Mr. Bons, on seeing him, gave a cry as if of recognition, and began to tremble violently.

The boy jumped in.

"Is it possible?" cried Mr. Bons. "Is the impossible possible?"

"Sir; come in, sir. It is such a fine omnibus. Oh, here is his name—Dan someone."

Mr. Bons sprang in too. A blast of wind immediately slammed the omnibus door, and the shock jerked down all the omnibus blinds, which were very weak on their springs.

"Dan . . . Show me. Good gracious heavens! we're moving."

"Hooray!" said the boy.

Mr. Bons became flustered. He had not intended to be kidnapped. He could not find the door-handle, nor push up the blinds. The omnibus was quite dark, and by the time he had struck a match, night had come on outside also. They were moving rapidly.

"A strange, a memorable adventure," he said, surveying the interior of the omnibus, which was large, roomy, and constructed with extreme regularity, every part exactly answering to every other part. Over the door (the handle of which was outside) was written '*Lasciate ogni baldanza voi che entrate*'—at least, that was what was written, but Mr. Bons said that it was Lashy arty something, and that *baldanza* was a mistake for *speranza*. His voice sounded as if he was in church. Meanwhile, the boy called to the cadaverous driver for two return tickets. They were handed in without a word. Mr. Bons covered his face with his hand and again trembled. "Do you know who that is!" he whispered, when the little window had shut upon them. "It is the impossible."

"Well, I don't like him as much as Sir Thomas Browne, though I shouldn't be surprised if he had even more in him."

"More in him?" He stamped irritably. "By accident you have made the greatest discovery of the century, and all you can say is that there is more in this man. Do you remember those vellum books in my library, stamped with red lilies? This—sit still, I bring you stupendous news!—*this is the man who wrote them.*"

The boy sat quite still. "I wonder if we shall see Mrs. Gamp?" he asked, after a civil pause.

"Mrs. — ?"

"Mrs. Gamp and Mrs. Harris. I like Mrs. Harris. I came upon them quite suddenly, Mrs. Gamp's bandboxes have moved over the rainbow so badly. All the bottoms have fallen out, and two of the pippins off her bedstead tumbled into the stream."

"Out there sits the man who wrote my vellum books!" thundered Mr. Bons, "and you talk to me of Dickens and of Mrs. Gamp?"

"I know Mrs. Gamp so well, "he apologized. "I could not help being glad to see her. I recognized her voice. She was telling Mrs. Harris about Mrs. Prig."

"Did you spend the whole day in her elevating company?"

"Oh, no. I raced. I met a man who took me out beyond to a race-course. You run, and there are dolphins out at sea."

"Indeed. Do you remember the man's name?"

"Achilles. No; he was later. Tom Jones."

Mr. Bons sighed heavily. "Well, my lad, you have made a miserable mess of it. Think of a cultured person with your opportunities! A cultured person would have known all these characters and known what to have said to each. He would not have wasted his time with a Mrs. Gamp or a Tom Jones. The creations of Homer, of Shakespeare, and of Him who drives us now, would alone have contented him. He would not have raced. He would have asked intelligent questions."

"But, Mr. Bons," said the boy humbly, "you will be a cultured person. I told them so."

"True, true, and I beg you not to disgrace me when we arrive. No gossiping. No running. Keep close to my side, and never speak to these Immortals unless they speak to you. Yes, and give me the return tickets. You will be losing them."

The boy surrendered the tickets but felt a little sore. After all, he had found the way to this place. It was hard first to be disbelieved and then to be lectured. Meanwhile, the rain had stopped, and moonlight crept into the omnibus through the cracks in the blinds.

"But how is there to be a rainbow?" cried the boy.

"You distract me," snapped Mr. Bons. "I wish to meditate on beauty. I wish to goodness I was with a reverent and sympathetic person."

The lad bit his lip. He made a hundred good resolutions. He would imitate Mr. Bons all the visit. He would not laugh, or run, or sing, or do any of the vulgar things that must have disgusted his new friends last time. He would be very careful to pronounce their names properly, and to remember who knew whom. Achilles did not know Tom Jones—at least, so Mr. Bons said. The Duchess of Malfi was older than Mrs. Gamp—at least, so Mr. Bons said. He would be self-conscious, reticent, and prim. He would never say he liked anyone. Yet, when the blind flew up at a chance touch of his head, all these good resolutions went to the winds, for the omnibus had reached the summit of a moonlit hill, and there was the chasm, and there, across it, stood the old precipices, dreaming, with their feet in the everlasting river. He exclaimed, "The mountain! Listen to the new tune in the water! Look at the camp fires in the ravines," and Mr. Bons, after a hasty glance, retorted, "Water? Camp fires? Ridiculous rubbish. Hold your tongue. There is nothing at all."

Yet, under his eyes, a rainbow formed, compounded not of sunlight and storm, but of moonlight and the spray of the river. The three horses put their feet upon it. He thought it the finest rainbow he had seen, but did not dare to say so, since Mr. Bons said that nothing was there. He leant out—the window had opened—and sang the tune that rose from the sleeping waters.

"The prelude to Rhinegold?" said Mr. Bons suddenly. "Who taught you these *leit motifs?*" He, too, looked out of the window. Then he behaved very oddly. He gave a choking cry, and fell back on the omnibus floor. He writhed and kicked. His face was green.

"Does the bridge make you dizzy?" the boy asked.

"Dizzy!" gasped Mr. Bons. "I want to go back. Tell the driver."

But the driver shook his head.

"We are nearly there," said the boy. "They are asleep. Shall I call? They will be so pleased to see you, for I have prepared them."

Mr. Bons moaned. They moved over the lunar rainbow, which ever and ever broke away behind their wheels. How still the night was! Who would be sentry at the Gate?

"I am coming," he shouted, again forgetting the hundred resolutions. "I am returning—I, the boy."

"The boy is returning," cried a voice to other voices, who repeated, "The boy is returning."

"I am bringing Mr. Bons with me."

Silence.

"I should have said Mr. Bons is bringing me with him."

Profound silence.

"Who stands sentry?"

"Achilles."

And on the rocky causeway, close to the springing of the rainbow bridge, he saw a young man who carried a wonderful shield.

"Mr. Bons, it is Achilles, armed."

"I want to go back," said Mr. Bons.

The last fragment of the rainbow melted, the wheels sang upon the living rock, the door of the omnibus burst open. Out leapt the boy—he could not resist—and sprang to meet the warrior, who, stooping suddenly, caught him on his shield.

"Achilles!" he cried, "let me get down, for I am ignorant and vulgar, and I must wait for that Mr. Bons of whom I told you yesterday."

But Achilles raised him aloft. He crouched on the wonderful shield, on heroes and burning cities, on vineyards graven in gold, on every dear passion, every joy, on the entire image of the Mountain that he had discovered, encircled, like it, with an everlasting stream. "No, no," he protested, "I am not worthy. It is Mr. Bons who must be up here."

But Mr. Bons was whimpering, and Achilles trumpeted and cried, "Stand upright upon my shield!"

"Sir, I did not mean to stand! something made me stand. Sir, why do you delay? Here is only the great Achilles, whom you knew."

Mr. Bons screamed, "I see no one. I see nothing. I want to go back." Then he cried to the driver, "Save me! Let me stop in your chariot. I have honoured you. I have quoted you. I have bound you in vellum. Take me back to my world."

The driver replied, "I am the means and not the end. I am the food and not the life. Stand by yourself, as that boy has stood. I cannot save you. For poetry is a spirit; and they that would worship it must worship in spirit and in truth."

Mr. Bons—he could not resist—crawled out of the beautiful omnibus. His face appeared, gaping horribly.

His hands followed, one gripping the step, the other beating the air. Now his shoulders emerged, his chest, his stomach. With a shriek of "I see London," he fell—fell against the hard, moonlit rock, fell into it as if it were water, fell through it, vanished, and was seen by the boy no more.

"Where have you fallen to, Mr. Bons? Here is a procession arriving to honour you with music and torches. Here come the men and women whose names you know. The mountain is awake, over the racecourse the sea is awaking those dolphins, and it is all for you. They want you—"

There was the touch of fresh leaves on his forehead. Someone had crowned him.

ΤΕΛΟΣ

From the *Kingston Gazette, Surbiton Times,* and *Raynes Park Observer.*

The body of Mr. Septimus Bons has been found in a shockingly mutilated condition in the vicinity of the Bermondsey gas-works. The deceased's pockets contained a sovereign-purse, a silver cigar-case, a bijou pronouncing dictionary, and a couple of omnibus tickets. The unfortunate gentleman had apparently been hurled from a considerable height. Foul play is suspected, and a thorough investigation is pending by the authorities.

NOTES

JOHN PUDNEY (b. 1909) is poet, novelist and short-story writer. Several books of his poems have been published, including *Dispersal Point* and *Almanack of Hope,* and he became especially well-known during the 1939–45 war as a writer of what one might call 'Air Force Poems'; for he served in the R.A.F. and found in his military experiences much subject-matter for poetry.

In prose he has written, among other works, *And Lastly the Fireworks, Jacobson's Ladder, Estuary* and the many short stories of which *Uncle Arthur* is but the best and which were published in selection under the title, *It Breathed Down My Neck.*

Like E. M. Forster's *The Celestial Omnibus, Uncle Arthur* is a moral tale: it is, in part at least, allegorical: the elephant represents something larger even than itself. Little Lily was the child of parents whose lives were so conditioned by 'possessions' and the opinions of neighbours and acquaintances that neither their own lives nor—more important—hers were really worth living. But there was one possession about which the opinions of other people were dreaded: a skeleton in the cupboard, a terrible family secret whose preservation took to itself a great deal of time and energy: little Lily's Uncle Arthur, gaol-bird. And so, in order that her parents might be released from their false way of life, and in order that little Lily might herself be set free from her mother's destructive 'vigilance,' the skeleton emerged from the cupboard in such a form, such an elephantine form, that there was no hiding it. Lily was thrilled; and ultimately her parents' minds were opened and set free. Uncle Arthur, the black sheep, had played the white man—but it was little Lily who forced his hand, and she really did see an elephant coming down the garden. Unless ye become like one of these little ones. . . .

AMBROSE BIERCE, who was born in Ohio in 1842, fought in the Union Army during the American Civil War. How he died is not known: he disappeared after going to Mexico in 1913 to fight in the civil war there. Many of his macabre short stories are about war and soldiers, the best and most famous of them being those collected first under the title, *Tales of Soldiers and Civilians,* and later under the title, *In the Midst of Life.* The book was published in 1891.

From its sudden, laconic opening to its even more sudden and laconic close, *A Horseman in the Sky* is a model of the art of short-story writing. Throughout the atmosphere is tense—every moment of the tale is charged with uncertainty—and the ending comes only when it must. Bierce springs his surprise on us from the start, but we are not surprised until the end; and in the interval we are told only just as much and as little as we need to know. Note, for example, how Druse's biographical background is sketched to our complete satisfaction in the two short paragraphs, "The sleeping sentinel . . . disturb her." Note, too, the swift transference of our attention from point to point. And it all happened—Carter Druse killed his father—but it is too terrible in the telling ever to be what we normally know as 'true.'

H. G. WELLS (1866–1946) turned from salesmanship and, later, teaching to writing, in 1893, after which year an enormous amount of literature originated from his mercurial mind: ranging from *The Outline of History*, through novels and short stories, to a hundred-and-one forms of journalism, pamphleteering and politico-scientific propaganda. It is as a tale-teller that he lives on: as the author of social novels like *Love and Mr. Lewisham, Kipps, Tono-Bungay, The History of Mr. Polly* and *The Bulpington of Blup*; such unusual stories as *The Invisible Man* and *The War in the Air*; and the many scores of fantastic short stories of which *The Truth about Pyecraft* is at once the most amusing and the least disturbing. *Wellsian* is a twentieth-century addition to the English vocabulary. It means all that is contained in such adjectives as visionary, futuristic, prophetic, fantastic. The story about poor old Pyecraft is certainly funny; it is an excellent short story; it is fantastic; who knows but that it may yet prove to have been prophetic?

ERIC LINKLATER (b. 1899), whose reputation as an original novelist was assured by *Poet's Pub* (1929), *Juan in America* and *Juan in China*, has achieved further and different fame in recent years as a writer of dramatic imaginary conversations—*The Raft, Socrates Asks Why* and *Crisis in Heaven*—and as one of the authors of the official accounts of the 1939–45 campaigns—e.g. *The Defence of Calais*. But he is one of the most versatile writers of our time, and his new book of short stories, *Sealskin Trousers*, has reminded the public of what *The Dancers* had proved, that he is among our best short-story writers.

The Dancers, like *Uncle Arthur*, is a moral tale. Mr. Pomfret, family and friends, were not famous until they disappeared, but the world was far from the truth in its explanations of their disappearance. The fancy-less world of stocking-suspenders cannot be expected to offer such an explanation as Otto Samways gave to Mr. Pinto. And Mr. Pomfret and his wife needed Joan, in love and bewitched, to put on the right records to charm up the little brown men and make him caper in the middle and his wife move "as lightly as any of them" (except Joan herself). But—and this is the point—Joan, like little Lily and the boy at Agathox Lodge, did exist, and "none of the Pomfrets had any wish to be found." Like Lily's parents, they had escaped into happiness. But Otto had to come back to our fancy-less world of stocking-suspenders for some more needles.

RICHARD MIDDLETON (1882–1911) is known by only three books, one of poems, *Poems and Songs,* and two of prose stories, *The Ghost Ship and Other Stories* and *The Day Before Yesterday,* all posthumously published in 1912. Little of his work is read now, but the poem, 'On a Dead Child,' and the story in this book have already given him at least their own limited immortality.

The atmosphere of *The Ghost Ship* is wholly that of the freak-ish, superstitious, poetic countryside. It is a folk-lore atmosphere—and what is folk-lore but a collection of short stories? The action of the tale is set in a region of the earth's surface and of the human mind where happen things so fantastic and so real that "all the London yarns" do not contain anything like them. No explana-tions are possible of these events, none is desired ; and if any reader of this admirable little story is foolhardy enough to doubt the truth of its final paragraph, let him go to Fairfield and find out how wrong he can be.

LORD DUNSANY (b. 1878) is one of those Irishmen who seem to be able to write with equal felicity anything that is to be written. One thinks of Goldsmith or Yeats in the connexion. No doubt if you're Irish. . . . And because he is Irish he writes fantastically, be it in prose or verse, drama or criticism. The full-length play, *If,* and the one-act *A Night at an Inn,* have placed him among the important dramatists of our century, and the series of short stories whose central character is Jorkens, the 'old wanderer,' have won wide popularity and critical appreciation.

How Jembu Played for Cambridge, one of this series, is 'a long story' for a club, no doubt, but it is just the right length for a short story. It is all absurd and Jorkens, all my eye and Lord Dunsany, yet truth is often stranger than fiction, and there is a something sinister in this story which leaves us in no uncertainty whether or not Jembu did play for Cambridge, and leaves Mungo safe from all those impertinent ones who might dare to question him on the rules of cricket.

A. J. ALAN is the pseudonym of a man whose true identity is, though we are assured that he is dead these several years, still a mystery to all but those who knew him personally and had been admitted to the secret. He is, also, unique among the writers repre-sented in this book, in that he has no reputation whatsoever as a writer. *Wottie,* indeed, has appeared in print in England only once before, and the text here published is a copy of the actual type-script used for the original broadcast.

Two collections of Alan's stories have been published, *Good Evening, Everyone* and *A. J. Alan's Second Book,* but neither of these contains *Wottie,* which is, at any rate in the opinion of the present writer, the best tale ever told by him and was chosen by the BBC for recorded rebroadcast during its jubilee celebrations in 1947.

Those who did not already know it, then, know now that A. J. Alan was a broadcaster and not a writer. He composed his own tales, and told them in a sophisticated, 'blasé' manner quite unparalleled before or since. During the late twenties and thirties he was, without question, the most famous and popular broadcaster of all.

Wottie is thus a tale to be told rather than read silently to oneself. It is full of colloquialisms and schoolboy slang; its whole style is oral and not written. But what a good story it is, and how well Alan understood the short-story technique! He leads us right up, or down, the garden path to Blane's Hill Quarry, and no-one dares to ask what did, after all, happen to Wottie. The two boys went back next day and saw that it was only a sheep's body.

A. J. Alan and Wottie will never even be mentioned in any history of English literature: the present writer is proud to have done this little to ensure that they nevertheless do not yet join the forever forgotten.

W. W. JACOBS (1863–1944) was born in Wapping, where his father was a wharfman and which became the setting of many, perhaps most, of the numerous short stories which he wrote. His first collection, *Many Cargoes*, was published in 1896; *The Lady of the Barge* appeared in 1902, *Deep Waters* in 1919. Our story is from *Captains All* (1905). He also wrote many one-act plays. A large proportion of his work is realistically comic, but by far the best known single composition is his horrific and moving story, *The Monkey's Paw*.

Over The Side, whose extreme economy of vocabulary and information is paralleled in this book only by that of *A Horseman in the Sky*, has a lesson to teach no less important than those of *Uncle Arthur* and *The Dancers*, even if it does teach it in a sinister, even morbid way. Jem Dadd was spiteful and morose and liked to frighten his fellows with 'the supernatural.' He was not popular. And then he died, and a stranger came over the side to take his place and sleep in his bunk. And when it was his turn to die, the crew became compassionate. On Jem Dad reincarnate? But this dying stranger seemed to have a wife and four children. Or did he mean something else by his sign? What were the two words he uttered? Silly questions. We have been on one of fancy's boats. Let us count our blessings—and be compassionate.

E. M. FORSTER was born in 1879. He is best known as a novelist and is, indeed, ranked by all discerning critics among the few lastingly significant writers of fiction so far in our century. His best books are *Howards End* (1910) and *A Passage to India* (1924), both novels, *The Celestial Omnibus and Other Stories* (1911), and *Abinger Harvest* (1936), essays.

The moral of *The Celestial Omnibus* is not wholly dissimilar to that of *Uncle Arthur*. For Lily's parents had to be liberated from fear—i.e., a recoiling from and deliberate ignoring of reality; and the boy at Agathox Lodge had to have proved to him and to prove that his parents and Mr. Bons (a 'bookful blockhead ignorantly read') were also criminally mistaken in their fear and wilful ignorance of reality: not, this time, the reality of a family black sheep, family pride and the neighbours, but the reality of literature, and particularly of poetry. Little Lily and the boy at Agathox Lodge had both to triumph, and both did: they always must if life is to be worth living and is to be glorious. Mr. Bons might be President of the Literary Society and know all the dead paraphernalia of literary history and criticism, but it was the boy for whom literature was alive. Mr. Bons worshipped Dante from afar, scholastically and coldly; the boy recognized Mrs. Gamp's voice.

Some individual notes:—

Shelley (Percy Bysshe, 1792–1822), the poet, was sent down from Oxford in 1811 for writing and circulating the pamphlet, "The Necessity of Atheism."

Sir Thomas Browne (1605–82) is famous for his peculiar style, which is characterized by a classical vocabulary and syntax, made fun of in the story. His best works were *Religio Medici* and *Urn Burial*.

John Keats, the poet, lived from 1795 to 1821: Shelley wrote the elegy on his death, *Adonais*.

Mrs. Gamp appears in Dickens's *Martin Chuzzlewit*.

Tom Jones is the hero of Fielding's novel, published in 1749.

The Duchess of Malfi is the heroine of the tragedy by John Webster (1580?–1625?).

"Das Rheingold" is one of Wagner's operas.

The line, referred to in the story, from Dante Alighieri's *Inferno*, is the famous "Lasciate ogni speranza voi che entrate": "All hope abandon, ye who enter here." Dante lived from 1265 to 1321.

GEORGE ALLEN & UNWIN LTD
London: 40 Museum Street, W.C.1

Auckland: 24 Wyndham Street
Bombay: 15 Graham Road, Ballard Estate, Bombay 1
Calcutta: 17 Chittaranjan Avenue, Calcutta 13
Cape Town: 109 Long Street
Karachi: Metherson's Estate, Wood Street, Karachi 2
Mexico : Villalongin, 32 - 10. Piso, Mexico 5, D.F.
New Delhi: 13-14 Ajmeri Gate Extension, New Delhi 1
São Paulo: Avenida 9 de Julho 1138-Ap. 51
Singapore, South-East Asia and Far East: 36c Prinsep Street
Sydney, N.S.W.: Bradbury House, 55 York Street
Toronto: 91 Wellington Street West

The
Psalms
of David in Metre

According to
the Version approved by

The Church of Scotland

and appointed to be
used in worship

Trinitarian Bible Society

Tyndale House, Dorset Road, London, SW19 3NN, England

ISBN 1-86228-096-7

Printed and bound in Great Britain by Bath Press
10m/11/02

Psalm 1

1 THAT man hath perfect blessedness
   who walketh not astray
In counsel of ungodly men,
   nor stands in sinners' way,
Nor sitteth in the scorner's chair:
2   But placeth his delight
Upon God's law, and meditates
   on his law day and night.

3   He shall be like a tree that grows
   near planted by a river,
Which in his season yields his fruit,
   and his leaf fadeth never:
And all he doth shall prosper well.
4   The wicked are not so;
But like they are unto the chaff,
   which wind drives to and fro.

5   In judgment therefore shall not stand
   such as ungodly are;
Nor in th' assembly of the just
   shall wicked men appear.
6 For why? the way of godly men
   unto the Lord is known:
Whereas the way of wicked men
   shall quite be overthrown.

Psalm 2

1 WHY rage the heathen? and vain things
   why do the people mind?
2 Kings of the earth do set themselves,
   and princes are combin'd,

To plot against the Lord, and his
    Anointed, saying thus,
3   Let us asunder break their bands,
    and cast their cords from us.

4   He that in heaven sits shall laugh;
    the Lord shall scorn them all.
5   Then shall he speak to them in wrath,
    in rage he vex them shall.
6   Yet, notwithstanding, I have him
    to be my King appointed;
And over Sion, my holy hill,
    I have him King anointed.

7   The sure decree I will declare;
    the Lord hath said to me,
Thou art mine only Son; this day
    I have begotten thee.
8   Ask of me, and for heritage
    the heathen I'll make thine;
And, for possession, I to thee
    will give earth's utmost line.

9   Thou shalt, as with a weighty rod
    of iron, break them all;
And, as a potter's sherd, thou shalt
    them dash in pieces small.
10 Now therefore, kings, be wise; be taught,
    ye judges of the earth:
11 Serve God in fear, and see that ye
    join trembling with your mirth.

12 Kiss ye the Son, lest in his ire
    ye perish from the way,

If once his wrath begin to burn:
　bless'd all that on him stay.

Psalm 3

A Psalm of David, when he fled from Absalom his son.

1　O LORD, how are my foes increas'd?
　　against me many rise.
2　Many say of my soul, For him
　　in God no succour lies.
3　Yet thou my shield and glory art,
　　th' uplifter of mine head.
4　I cry'd, and, from his holy hill,
　　the Lord me answer made.

5　I laid me down and slept; I wak'd,
　　for God sustained me.
6　I will not fear though thousands ten
　　set round against me be.
7　Arise, O Lord; save me, my God;
　　for thou my foes hast stroke
All on the cheek-bone, and the teeth
　　of wicked men hast broke.

8　Salvation doth appertain
　　unto the Lord alone:
Thy blessing, Lord, for evermore
　　thy people is upon.

Psalm 4

To the chief Musician on Neginoth, A Psalm of David.

1　GIVE ear unto me when I call,
　　God of my righteousness;
Have mercy, hear my pray'r; thou hast
　　enlarg'd me in distress.

2   O ye the sons of men! how long
      will ye love vanities?
   How long my glory turn to shame,
      and will ye follow lies?

3   But know, that for himself the Lord
      the godly man doth chuse:
   The Lord, when I on him do call,
      to hear will not refuse.
4   Fear, and sin not; talk with your heart
      on bed, and silent be.
5   Off'rings present of righteousness,
      and in the Lord trust ye.

6   O who will shew us any good?
      is that which many say:
   But of thy countenance the light,
      Lord, lift on us alway.
7   Upon my heart, bestow'd by thee,
      more gladness I have found
   Than they, ev'n then, when corn and wine
      did most with them abound.

8   I will both lay me down in peace,
      and quiet sleep will take;
   Because thou only me to dwell
      in safety, Lord, dost make.

Psalm 5

To the chief Musician upon Nehiloth, A Psalm of David.

1   GIVE ear unto my words, O Lord,
      my meditation weigh.
2   Hear my loud cry, my King, my God;
      for I to thee will pray.

3   Lord, thou shalt early hear my voice:
        I early will direct
    My pray'r to thee; and, looking up,
        an answer will expect.

4   For thou art not a God that doth
        in wickedness delight;
    Neither shall evil dwell with thee,
5   Nor fools stand in thy sight.
    All that ill-doers are thou hat'st;
6   Cutt'st off that liars be:
    The bloody and deceitful man
        abhorred is by thee.

7   But I into thy house will come
        in thine abundant grace;
    And I will worship in thy fear
        toward thy holy place.
8   Because of those mine enemies,
        Lord, in thy righteousness
    Do thou me lead; do thou thy way
        make straight before my face.

9   For in their mouth there is no truth,
        their inward part is ill;
    Their throat's an open sepulchre,
        their tongue doth flatter still.
10 O God, destroy them; let them be
        by their own counsel quell'd:
    Them for their many sins cast out,
        for they 'gainst thee rebell'd.

11 But let all joy that trust in thee,
        and still make shouting noise;

For them thou sav'st: let all that love
    thy name in thee rejoice.
12 For, Lord, unto the righteous man
    thou wilt thy blessing yield:
With favour thou wilt compass him
    about, as with a shield.

Psalm 6

To the chief Musician on Neginoth upon Sheminith,
A Psalm of David.

1 LORD, in thy wrath rebuke me not;
    Nor in thy hot rage chasten me.
2 Lord, pity me, for I am weak:
    Heal me, for my bones vexed be.
3 My soul is also vexed sore;
    But, Lord, how long stay wilt thou make?
4 Return, O Lord, my soul set free;
    O save me, for thy mercies' sake.

5 Because those that deceased are
    Of thee shall no remembrance have;
And who is he that will to thee
    Give praises lying in the grave?
6 I with my groaning weary am,
    I also all the night my bed
Have caused for to swim; and I
    With tears my couch have watered.

7 Mine eye, consum'd with grief, grows old,
    Because of all mine enemies.
8 Hence from me, wicked workers all;
    For God hath heard my weeping cries.
9 God hath my supplication heard,
    My pray'r received graciously.

10 Sham'd and sore vex'd be all my foes,
    Sham'd and back turned suddenly.

Another of the same

1 IN thy great indignation,
    O Lord, rebuke me not;
Nor on me lay thy chast'ning hand,
    in thy displeasure hot.
2 Lord, I am weak, therefore on me
    have mercy, and me spare:
Heal me, O Lord, because thou know'st
    my bones much vexed are.

3 My soul is vexed sore: but, Lord,
    how long stay wilt thou make?
4 Return, Lord, free my soul; and save
    me, for thy mercies' sake.
5 Because of thee in death there shall
    no more remembrance be:
Of those that in the grave do lie,
    who shall give thanks to thee?

6 I with my groaning weary am,
    and all the night my bed
I caused for to swim; with tears
    my couch I watered.
7 By reason of my vexing grief
    mine eye consumed is;
It waxeth old, because of all
    that be mine enemies.

8 But now, depart from me all ye
    that work iniquity:
For why? the Lord hath heard my voice,
    when I did mourn and cry.

9 Unto my supplication
    the Lord did hearing give:
When I to him my prayer make,
    the Lord will it receive.

10 Let all be sham'd and troubled sore,
    That en'mies are to me;
Let them turn back, and suddenly
    ashamed let them be.

Psalm 7

*Shiggaion of David, which he sang unto the Lord,
concerning the words of Cush the Benjamite.*

1 O LORD my God, in thee do I
    my confidence repose:
Save and deliver me from all
    my persecuting foes;
2 Lest that the enemy my soul
    should, like a lion, tear,
In pieces rending it, while there
    is no deliverer.

3 O Lord my God, if it be so
    that I committed this;
If it be so that in my hands
    iniquity there is:
4 If I rewarded ill to him
    that was at peace with me;
(Yea, ev'n the man that without cause
    my foe was I did free;)

5 Then let the foe pursue and take
    my soul, and my life thrust
Down to the earth, and let him lay
    mine honour in the dust.

6 Rise in thy wrath, Lord, raise thyself,
       for my foes raging be;
   And, to the judgment which thou hast
       commanded, wake for me.

7 So shall th' assembly of thy folk
       about encompass thee:
   Thou, therefore, for their sakes, return
       unto thy place on high.
8 The Lord he shall the people judge;
       my judge, JEHOVAH, be,
   After my righteousness, and mine
       integrity in me.

9 O let the wicked's malice end;
       but stablish stedfastly
   The righteous: for the righteous God
       the hearts and reins doth try.
10 In God, who saves th' upright in heart,
       is my defence and stay.
11 God just men judgeth, God is wroth
       with ill men ev'ry day.

12 If he do not return again,
       then he his sword will whet;
   His bow he hath already bent,
       and hath it ready set:
13 He also hath for him prepar'd
       the instruments of death;
   Against the persecutors he
       his shafts ordained hath.

14 Behold, he with iniquity
       doth travail, as in birth;

A mischief he conceived hath,
 and falsehood shall bring forth.
15 He made a pit and digg'd it deep,
 another there to take;
But he is fall'n into the ditch
 which he himself did make.

16 Upon his own head his mischief
 shall be returned home;
His vi'lent dealing also down
 on his own pate shall come.
17 According to his righteousness
 the Lord I'll magnify;
And will sing praise unto the name
 of God that is most high.

Psalm 8

*To the chief Musician upon Gittith,
A Psalm of David.*

1 HOW excellent in all the earth,
 Lord, our Lord, is thy name!
Who hast thy glory far advanc'd
 above the starry frame.
2 From infants' and from sucklings' mouth
 thou didest strength ordain,
For thy foes' cause, that so thou might'st
 th' avenging foe restrain.

3 When I look up unto the heav'ns,
 which thine own fingers fram'd,
Unto the moon, and to the stars,
 which were by thee ordain'd;
4 Then say I, What is man, that he
 remember'd is by thee?

Or what the son of man, that thou
   so kind to him should'st be?

5 For thou a little lower hast
    him than the angels made;
  With glory and with dignity
    thou crowned hast his head.

6 Of thy hands' works thou mad'st him lord,
    all under's feet didst lay;

7 All sheep and oxen, yea, and beasts
    that in the field do stray;

8 Fowls of the air, fish of the sea,
    all that pass through the same.

9 How excellent in all the earth,
    Lord, our Lord, is thy name!

Psalm 9

To the chief Musician upon Muth-labben,
A Psalm of David.

1 LORD, thee I'll praise with all my heart,
    thy wonders all proclaim.

2 In thee, most High, I'll greatly joy,
    and sing unto thy name.

3 When back my foes were turn'd, they fell,
    and perish'd at thy sight:

4 For thou maintain'dst my right and cause;
    on throne sat'st judging right.

5 The heathen thou rebuked hast,
    the wicked overthrown;
  Thou hast put out their names, that they
    may never more be known.

6 O en'my! now destructions have
    an end perpetual:

Thou cities raz'd; perish'd with them
  is their memorial.

7 God shall endure for aye; he doth
    for judgment set his throne;
8 In righteousness to judge the world,
    justice to give each one.
9 God also will a refuge be
    for those that are oppress'd;
  A refuge will he be in times
    of trouble to distress'd.

10 And they that know thy name, in thee
    their confidence will place:
  For thou hast not forsaken them
    that truly seek thy face.
11 O sing ye praises to the Lord
    that dwells in Sion hill;
  And all the nations among
    his deeds record ye still.

12 When he enquireth after blood,
    he then rememb'reth them:
  The humble folk he not forgets
    that call upon his name.
13 Lord, pity me; behold the grief
    which I from foes sustain;
  Ev'n thou, who from the gates of death
    dost raise me up again;

14 That I, in Sion's daughters' gates,
    may all thy praise advance;
  And that I may rejoice always
    in thy deliverance.

15 The heathen are sunk in the pit
    which they themselves prepar'd;
And in the net which they have hid
    their own feet fast are snar'd.

16 The Lord is by the judgment known
    which he himself hath wrought:
The sinners' hands do make the snares
    wherewith themselves are caught.
17 They who are wicked into hell
    each one shall turned be;
And all the nations that forget
    to seek the Lord most high.

18 For they that needy are shall not
    forgotten be alway;
The expectation of the poor
    shall not be lost for aye.
19 Arise, Lord, let not man prevail;
    judge heathen in thy sight:
20 That they may know themselves but men,
    the nations, Lord, affright.

Psalm 10

1 WHEREFORE is it that thou, O Lord,
    dost stand from us afar?
And wherefore hidest thou thyself
    when times so troublous are?
2 The wicked in his loftiness
    doth persecute the poor:
In these devices they have fram'd
    let them be taken sure.

3 The wicked of his heart's desire
      doth talk with boasting great;
   He blesseth him that's covetous,
      whom yet the Lord doth hate.
4 The wicked, through his pride of face,
      on God he doth not call;
   And in the counsels of his heart
      the Lord is not at all.

5 His ways they always grievous are;
      thy judgments from his sight
   Removed are: at all his foes
      he puffeth with despite.
6 Within his heart he thus hath said,
      I shall not moved be;
   And no adversity at all
      shall ever come to me.

7 His mouth with cursing, fraud, deceit,
      is fill'd abundantly;
   And underneath his tongue there is
      mischief and vanity.
8 He closely sits in villages;
      he slays the innocent:
   Against the poor that pass him by
      his cruel eyes are bent.

9 He, lion-like, lurks in his den;
      he waits the poor to take;
   And when he draws him in his net,
      his prey he doth him make.
10 Himself he humbleth very low,
      he croucheth down withal,
   That so a multitude of poor
      may by his strong ones fall.

11 He thus hath said within his heart,
  The Lord hath quite forgot;
 He hides his countenance, and he
  for ever sees it not.
12 O Lord, do thou arise; O God,
  lift up thine hand on high:
 Put not the meek afflicted ones
  out of thy memory.

13 Why is it that the wicked man
  thus doth the Lord despise?
 Because that God will it require
  he in his heart denies.
14 Thou hast it seen; for their mischief
  and spite thou wilt repay:
 The poor commits himself to thee;
  thou art the orphan's stay.

15 The arm break of the wicked man,
  and of the evil one;
 Do thou seek out his wickedness,
  until thou findest none.
16 The Lord is king through ages all,
  ev'n to eternity;
 The heathen people from his land
  are perish'd utterly.

17 O Lord, of those that humble are
  thou the desire didst hear;
 Thou wilt prepare their heart, and thou
  to hear wilt bend thine ear;
18 To judge the fatherless, and those
  that are oppressed sore;
 That man, that is but sprung of earth,
  may them oppress no more.

Psalm 11

To the chief Musician, A Psalm of David.

1   I IN the Lord do put my trust;
      how is it then that ye
    Say to my soul, Flee, as a bird,
      unto your mountain high?
2   For, lo, the wicked bend their bow,
      their shafts on string they fit,
    That those who upright are in heart
      they privily may hit.

3   If the foundations be destroy'd,
      what hath the righteous done?
4   God in his holy temple is,
      in heaven is his throne:
    His eyes do see, his eyelids try
5   men's sons. The just he proves:
    But his soul hates the wicked man,
      and him that vi'lence loves.

6   Snares, fire and brimstone, furious storms,
      on sinners he shall rain:
    This, as the portion of their cup,
      doth unto them pertain.
7   Because the Lord most righteous doth
      in righteousness delight;
    And with a pleasant countenance
      beholdeth the upright.

Psalm 12

To the chief Musician upon Sheminith, A Psalm of David.

1   HELP, Lord, because the godly man
      doth daily fade away;

And from among the sons of men
   the faithful do decay.
2 Unto his neighbour ev'ry one
   doth utter vanity:
They with a double heart do speak,
   and lips of flattery.

3 God shall cut off all flatt'ring lips,
   tongues that speak proudly thus,
4 We'll with our tongue prevail, our lips
   are ours: who's lord o'er us?
5 For poor oppress'd, and for the sighs
   of needy, rise will I,
Saith God, and him in safety set
   from such as him defy.

6 The words of God are words most pure;
   they be like silver try'd
In earthen furnace, seven times
   that hath been purify'd.
7 Lord, thou shalt them preserve and keep
   for ever from this race.
8 On each side walk the wicked, when
   vile men are high in place.

Psalm 13

To the chief Musician, A Psalm of David.

1 HOW long wilt thou forget me, Lord?
   shall it for ever be?
O how long shall it be that thou
   wilt hide thy face from me?
2 How long take counsel in my soul,
   still sad in heart, shall I?

How long exalted over me
   shall be mine enemy?

3 O Lord my God, consider well,
   and answer to me make:
Mine eyes enlighten, lest the sleep
   of death me overtake:
4 Lest that mine enemy should say,
   Against him I prevail'd;
And those that trouble me rejoice,
   when I am mov'd and fail'd.

5 But I have all my confidence
   thy mercy set upon;
My heart within me shall rejoice
   in thy salvation.
6 I will unto the Lord my God
   sing praises cheerfully,
Because he hath his bounty shown
   to me abundantly.

Psalm 14

To the chief Musician, A Psalm of David.

1 THAT there is not a God, the fool
   doth in his heart conclude:
They are corrupt, their works are vile;
   not one of them doth good.
2 Upon men's sons the Lord from heav'n
   did cast his eyes abroad,
To see if any understood,
   and did seek after God.

3 They altogether filthy are,
   they all aside are gone;

And there is none that doeth good,
    yea, sure there is not one.
4 These workers of iniquity
    do they not know at all,
That they my people eat as bread,
    and on God do not call?

5 There fear'd they much; for God is with
    the whole race of the just.
6 You shame the counsel of the poor,
    because God is his trust.
7 Let Isr'el's help from Sion come:
    when back the Lord shall bring
His captives, Jacob shall rejoice,
    and Israel shall sing.

Psalm 15

A Psalm of David.

1 WITHIN thy tabernacle, Lord,
    who shall abide with thee?
And in thy high and holy hill
    who shall a dweller be?
2 The man that walketh uprightly,
    and worketh righteousness,
And as he thinketh in his heart,
    so doth he truth express.

3 Who doth not slander with his tongue,
    nor to his friend doth hurt;
Nor yet against his neighbour doth
    take up an ill report.
4 In whose eyes vile men are despis'd;
    but those that God do fear

He honoureth; and changeth not,
    though to his hurt he swear.

5   His coin puts not to usury,
      nor take reward will he
Against the guiltless. Who doth thus
    shall never moved be.

Psalm 16

Michtam of David.

1   L ORD, keep me; for I trust in thee.
2   To God thus was my speech,
Thou art my Lord; and unto thee
    my goodness doth not reach:
3   To saints on earth, to th' excellent,
    where my delight's all plac'd.
4   Their sorrows shall be multiply'd
    to other gods that haste:

Of their drink-offerings of blood
    I will no off'ring make;
Yea, neither I their very names
    up in my lips will take.
5   God is of mine inheritance
    and cup the portion;
The lot that fallen is to me
    thou dost maintain alone.

6   Unto me happily the lines
    in pleasant places fell;
Yea, the inheritance I got
    in beauty doth excel.
7   I bless the Lord, because he doth
    by counsel me conduct;

And in the seasons of the night
   my reins do me instruct.

8 Before me still the Lord I set:
   sith it is so that he
Doth ever stand at my right hand,
   I shall not moved be.
9 Because of this my heart is glad,
   and joy shall be exprest
Ev'n by my glory; and my flesh
   in confidence shall rest.

10 Because my soul in grave to dwell
   shall not be left by thee;
Nor wilt thou give thine Holy One
   corruption to see.
11 Thou wilt me shew the path of life:
   of joys there is full store
Before thy face; at thy right hand
   are pleasures evermore.

Psalm 17

A Prayer of David.

1 LORD, hear the right, attend my cry,
   unto my pray'r give heed,
That doth not in hypocrisy
   from feigned lips proceed.
2 And from before thy presence forth
   my sentence do thou send:
Toward these things that equal are
   do thou thine eyes intend.

3 Thou prov'dst mine heart, thou visit'dst me
   by night, thou didst me try,

Yet nothing found'st; for that my mouth
 shall not sin, purpos'd I.
4 As for men's works, I, by the word
  that from thy lips doth flow,
Did me preserve out of the paths
 wherein destroyers go.

5 Hold up my goings, Lord, me guide
  in those thy paths divine,
So that my footsteps may not slide
 out of those ways of thine.
6 I called have on thee, O God,
  because thou wilt me hear:
That thou may'st hearken to my speech,
 to me incline thine ear.

7 Thy wondrous loving-kindness show,
  thou that, by thy right hand,
Sav'st them that trust in thee from those
 that up against them stand.
8 As th' apple of the eye me keep;
  in thy wings' shade me close
9 From lewd oppressors, compassing
 me round, as deadly foes.

10 In their own fat they are inclos'd;
  their mouth speaks loftily.
11 Our steps they compass'd; and to ground
  down bowing set their eye.
12 He like unto a lion is
  that's greedy of his prey,
Or lion young, which lurking doth
 in secret places stay.

13 Arise, and disappoint my foe,
    and cast him down, O Lord:
My soul save from the wicked man,
    the man which is thy sword.
14 From men, which are thy hand, O Lord,
    from worldly men me save,
Which only in this present life
    their part and portion have.

Whose belly with thy treasure hid
    thou fill'st: they children have
In plenty; of their goods the rest
    they to their children leave.
15 But as for me, I thine own face
    in righteousness will see;
And with thy likeness, when I wake,
    I satisfy'd shall be.

Psalm 18

*To the chief Musician, A Psalm of David, the servant of the Lord,
who spake unto the Lord the words of this song in the day
that the Lord delivered him from the hand of all his enemies,
and from the hand of Saul: And he said,*

1 THEE will I love, O Lord, my strength.
2   My fortress is the Lord,
My rock, and he that doth to me
    deliverance afford:
My God, my strength, whom I will trust,
    a buckler unto me,
The horn of my salvation,
    and my high tow'r, is he.

3 Upon the Lord, who worthy is
    of praises, will I cry;

And then shall I preserved be
  safe from mine enemy.
4 Floods of ill men affrighted me,
  death's pangs about me went;
5 Hell's sorrows me environed;
  death's snares did me prevent.

6 In my distress I call'd on God,
  cry to my God did I;
He from his temple heard my voice,
  to his ears came my cry.
7 Th' earth, as affrighted, then did shake,
  trembling upon it seiz'd:
The hills' foundations moved were,
  because he was displeas'd.

8 Up from his nostrils came a smoke,
  and from his mouth there came
Devouring fire, and coals by it
  were turned into flame.
9 He also bowed down the heav'ns,
  and thence he did descend;
And thickest clouds of darkness did
  under his feet attend.

10 And he upon a cherub rode,
  and thereon he did fly;
Yea, on the swift wings of the wind
  his flight was from on high.
11 He darkness made his secret place:
  about him, for his tent,
Dark waters were, and thickest clouds
  of th' airy firmament.

12 And at the brightness of that light,
    which was before his eye,
  His thick clouds pass'd away, hailstones
    and coals of fire did fly.
13 The Lord God also in the heav'ns
    did thunder in his ire;
  And there the Highest gave his voice,
    hailstones and coals of fire.

14 Yea, he his arrows sent abroad,
    and them he scattered;
  His lightnings also he shot out,
    and them discomfited.
15 The waters' channels then were seen,
    the world's foundations vast
  At thy rebuke discover'd were,
    and at thy nostrils' blast.

16 And from above the Lord sent down,
    and took me from below;
  From many waters he me drew,
    which would me overflow.
17 He me reliev'd from my strong foes,
    and such as did me hate;
  Because he saw that they for me
    too strong were, and too great.

18 They me prevented in the day
    of my calamity;
  But even then the Lord himself
    a stay was unto me.
19 He to a place where liberty
    and room was hath me brought;

Because he took delight in me,
  he my deliv'rance wrought.

20 According to my righteousness
    he did me recompense,
  He me repaid according to
    my hands' pure innocence.
21 For I God's ways kept, from my God
    did not turn wickedly.
22 His judgments were before me, I
    his laws put not from me.

23 Sincere before him was my heart,
    with him upright was I;
  And watchfully I kept myself
    from mine iniquity.
24 After my righteousness the Lord
    hath recompensed me,
  After the cleanness of my hands
    appearing in his eye.

25 Thou gracious to the gracious art,
    to upright men upright:
26 Pure to the pure, froward thou kyth'st
    unto the froward wight.
27 For thou wilt the afflicted save
    in grief that low do lie:
  But wilt bring down the countenance
    of them whose looks are high.

28 The Lord will light my candle so,
    that it shall shine full bright:
  The Lord my God will also make
    my darkness to be light.

29 By thee through troops of men I break,
　　and them discomfit all;
　And, by my God assisting me,
　　I overleap a wall.

30 As for God, perfect is his way:
　　the Lord his word is try'd;
　He is a buckler to all those
　　who do in him confide.
31 Who but the Lord is God? but he
　　who is a rock and stay?
32 'Tis God that girdeth me with strength,
　　and perfect makes my way.

33 He made my feet swift as the hinds,
　　set me on my high places.
34 Mine hands to war he taught, mine arms
　　brake bows of steel in pieces.
35 The shield of thy salvation
　　thou didst on me bestow:
　Thy right hand held me up, and great
　　thy kindness made me grow.

36 And in my way my steps thou hast
　　enlarged under me,
　That I go safely, and my feet
　　are kept from sliding free.
37 Mine en'mies I pursued have,
　　and did them overtake;
　Nor did I turn again till I
　　an end of them did make.

38 I wounded them, they could not rise;
　　they at my feet did fall.

39 Thou girdedst me with strength for war;
  my foes thou brought'st down all:
40 And thou hast giv'n to me the necks
  of all mine enemies;
  That I might them destroy and slay,
  who did against me rise.

41 They cried out, but there was none
  that would or could them save;
  Yea, they did cry unto the Lord,
  but he no answer gave.
42 Then did I beat them small as dust
  before the wind that flies;
  And I did cast them out like dirt
  upon the street that lies.

43 Thou mad'st me free from people's strife,
  and heathen's head to be:
  A people whom I have not known
  shall service do to me.
44 At hearing they shall me obey,
  to me they shall submit.
45 Strangers for fear shall fade away,
  who in close places sit.

46 God lives, bless'd be my Rock; the God
  of my health praised be.
47 God doth avenge me, and subdues
  the people under me.
48 He saves me from mine enemies;
  yea, thou hast lifted me
  Above my foes; and from the man
  of vi'lence set me free.

49 Therefore to thee will I give thanks
  the heathen folk among;
 And to thy name, O Lord, I will
  sing praises in a song.
50 He great deliv'rance gives his king:
  he mercy doth extend
 To David, his anointed one,
  and his seed without end.

Psalm 19

To the chief Musician, A Psalm of David.

1 THE heav'ns God's glory do declare,
  the skies his hand-works preach:
2 Day utters speech to day, and night
  to night doth knowledge teach.
3 There is no speech nor tongue to which
  their voice doth not extend:
4 Their line is gone through all the earth,
  their words to the world's end.

 In them he set the sun a tent;
5 Who, bridegroom-like, forth goes
 From's chamber, as a strong man doth
  to run his race rejoice.
6 From heav'n's end is his going forth,
  circling to th' end again;
 And there is nothing from his heat
  that hidden doth remain.

7 God's law is perfect, and converts
  the soul in sin that lies:
 God's testimony is most sure,
  and makes the simple wise.

8 The statutes of the Lord are right,
    and do rejoice the heart:
  The Lord's command is pure, and doth
    light to the eyes impart.

9 Unspotted is the fear of God,
    and doth endure for ever:
  The judgments of the Lord are true
    and righteous altogether.
10 They more than gold, yea, much fine gold,
    to be desired are:
  Than honey, honey from the comb
    that droppeth, sweeter far.

11 Moreover, they thy servant warn
    how he his life should frame:
  A great reward provided is
    for them that keep the same.
12 Who can his errors understand?
    O cleanse thou me within
13 From secret faults. Thy servant keep
    from all presumptuous sin:

  And do not suffer them to have
    dominion over me:
  Then, righteous and innocent,
    I from much sin shall be.
14 The words which from my mouth proceed,
    the thoughts sent from my heart,
  Accept, O Lord, for thou my strength
    and my Redeemer art.

Psalm 20

To the chief Musician, A Psalm of David.

1   JEHOVAH hear thee in the day
        when trouble he doth send:
     And let the name of Jacob's God
        thee from all ill defend.
2   O let him help send from above,
        out of his sanctuary:
     From Sion, his own holy hill,
        let him give strength to thee.

3   Let him remember all thy gifts,
        accept thy sacrifice:
4   Grant thee thine heart's wish, and fulfil
        thy thoughts and counsel wise.
5   In thy salvation we will joy;
        in our God's name we will
     Display our banners: and the Lord
        thy prayers all fulfil.

6   Now know I God his king doth save:
        he from his holy heav'n
     Will hear him, with the saving strength
        by his own right hand giv'n.
7   In chariots some put confidence,
        some horses trust upon:
     But we remember will the name
        of our Lord God alone.

8   We rise, and upright stand, when they
        are bowed down, and fall.
9   Deliver, Lord; and let the King
        us hear, when we do call.

Psalm 21

To the chief Musician, A Psalm of David.

1 THE king in thy great strength, O Lord,
   shall very joyful be:
In thy salvation rejoice
   how veh'mently shall he!
2 Thou hast bestowed upon him
   all that his heart would have;
And thou from him didst not withhold
   whate'er his lips did crave.

3 For thou with blessings him prevent'st
   of goodness manifold;
And thou hast set upon his head
   a crown of purest gold.
4 When he desired life of thee,
   thou life to him didst give;
Ev'n such a length of days, that he
   for evermore should live.

5 In that salvation wrought by thee
   his glory is made great;
Honour and comely majesty
   thou hast upon him set.
6 Because that thou for evermore
   most blessed hast him made;
And thou hast with thy countenance
   made him exceeding glad.

7 Because the king upon the Lord
   his confidence doth lay;
And through the grace of the most High
   shall not be mov'd away.

8   Thine hand shall all those men find out
      that en'mies are to thee;
  Ev'n thy right hand shall find out those
      of thee that haters be.

9   Like fiery ov'n thou shalt them make,
      when kindled is thine ire;
  God shall them swallow in his wrath,
      devour them shall the fire.
10 Their fruit from earth thou shalt destroy,
      their seed men from among:
11 For they beyond their might 'gainst thee
      did plot mischief and wrong.

12 Thou therefore shalt make them turn back,
      when thou thy shafts shalt place
  Upon thy strings, made ready all
      to fly against their face.
13 In thy great pow'r and strength, O Lord,
      be thou exalted high;
  So shall we sing with joyful hearts,
      thy power praise shall we.

Psalm 22

To the chief Musician upon Aijeleth Shahar, A Psalm of David.

1   MY God, my God, why hast thou me
      forsaken? why so far
  Art thou from helping me, and from
      my words that roaring are?
2   All day, my God, to thee I cry,
      yet am not heard by thee;
  And in the season of the night
      I cannot silent be.

3 But thou art holy, thou that dost
      inhabit Isr'el's praise.
4 Our fathers hop'd in thee, they hop'd,
      and thou didst them release.
5 When unto thee they sent their cry,
      to them deliv'rance came:
Because they put their trust in thee,
      they were not put to shame.

6 But as for me, a worm I am,
      and as no man am priz'd:
Reproach of men I am, and by
      the people am despis'd.
7 All that me see laugh me to scorn;
      shoot out the lip do they;
They nod and shake their heads at me,
      and, mocking, thus do say,

8 This man did trust in God, that he
      would free him by his might:
Let him deliver him, sith he
      had in him such delight.
9 But thou art he out of the womb
      that didst me safely take;
When I was on my mother's breasts
      thou me to hope didst make.

10 And I was cast upon thy care,
      ev'n from the womb till now;
And from my mother's belly, Lord,
      my God and guide art thou.
11 Be not far off, for grief is near,
      and none to help is found.

12 Bulls many compass me, strong bulls
    of Bashan me surround.

13 Their mouths they open'd wide on me,
    upon me gape did they,
    Like to a lion ravening
    and roaring for his prey.
14 Like water I'm pour'd out, my bones
    all out of joint do part:
    Amidst my bowels, as the wax,
    so melted is my heart.

15 My strength is like a potsherd dry'd;
    my tongue it cleaveth fast
    Unto my jaws; and to the dust
    of death thou brought me hast.
16 For dogs have compass'd me about:
    the wicked, that did meet
    In their assembly, me inclos'd;
    they pierc'd my hands and feet.

17 I all my bones may tell; they do
    upon me look and stare.
18 Upon my vesture lots they cast,
    and clothes among them share.
19 But be not far, O Lord, my strength;
    haste to give help to me.
20 From sword my soul, from pow'r of dogs
    my darling set thou free.

21 Out of the roaring lion's mouth
    do thou me shield and save:
    For from the horns of unicorns
    an ear to me thou gave.

22 I will shew forth thy name unto
    those that my brethren are;
Amidst the congregation
    thy praise I will declare.

23 Praise ye the Lord, who do him fear;
    him glorify all ye
The seed of Jacob; fear him all
    that Isr'el's children be.
24 For he despis'd not nor abhorr'd
    th' afflicted's misery;
Nor from him hid his face, but heard
    when he to him did cry.

25 Within the congregation great
    my praise shall be of thee;
My vows before them that him fear
    shall be perform'd by me.
26 The meek shall eat, and shall be fill'd;
    they also praise shall give
Unto the Lord that do him seek:
    your heart shall ever live.

27 All ends of th' earth remember shall,
    and turn the Lord unto;
All kindreds of the nations
    to him shall homage do:
28 Because the kingdom to the Lord
    doth appertain as his;
Likewise among the nations
    the Governor he is.

29 Earth's fat ones eat, and worship shall:
    all who to dust descend

Shall bow to him; none of them can
his soul from death defend.
30 A seed shall service do to him;
unto the Lord it shall
Be for a generation
reckon'd in ages all.

31 They shall come, and they shall declare
his truth and righteousness
Unto a people yet unborn,
and that he hath done this.

Psalm 23

A Psalm of David.

1 THE Lord's my shepherd, I'll not want.
2 He makes me down to lie
In pastures green: he leadeth me
the quiet waters by.
3 My soul he doth restore again;
and me to walk doth make
Within the paths of righteousness,
ev'n for his own name's sake.

4 Yea, though I walk in death's dark vale,
yet will I fear none ill:
For thou art with me; and thy rod
and staff me comfort still.
5 My table thou hast furnished
in presence of my foes;
My head thou dost with oil anoint,
and my cup overflows.

6 Goodness and mercy all my life
shall surely follow me:

And in God's house for evermore
my dwelling-place shall be.

Psalm 24

A Psalm of David.

1 THE earth belongs unto the Lord,
and all that it contains;
The world that is inhabited,
and all that there remains.

2 For the foundations thereof
he on the seas did lay,
And he hath it established
upon the floods to stay.

3 Who is the man that shall ascend
into the hill of God?
Or who within his holy place
shall have a firm abode?

4 Whose hands are clean, whose heart is pure,
and unto vanity
Who hath not lifted up his soul,
nor sworn deceitfully.

5 He from th' Eternal shall receive
the blessing him upon,
And righteousness, ev'n from the God
of his salvation.

6 This is the generation
that after him enquire,
O Jacob, who do seek thy face
with their whole heart's desire.

7 Ye gates, lift up your heads on high;
ye doors that last for aye,

Be lifted up, that so the King
    of glory enter may.
8   But who of glory is the King?
    The mighty Lord is this;
    Ev'n that same Lord, that great in might
    and strong in battle is.

9   Ye gates, lift up your heads; ye doors,
    doors that do last for aye,
    Be lifted up, that so the King
    of glory enter may.
10 But who is he that is the King
    of glory? who is this?
    The Lord of hosts, and none but he,
    the King of glory is.

Psalm 25

A Psalm of David.

1   TO thee I lift my soul:
2   O Lord, I trust in thee:
    My God, let me not be asham'd,
    nor foes triumph o'er me.
3   Let none that wait on thee
    be put to shame at all;
    But those that without cause transgress,
    let shame upon them fall.

4   Shew me thy ways, O Lord;
    thy paths, O teach thou me:
5   And do thou lead me in thy truth,
    therein my teacher be:
    For thou art God that dost
    to me salvation send,

And I upon thee all the day
   expecting do attend.

6   Thy tender mercies, Lord,
     I pray thee to remember,
   And loving-kindnesses; for they
     have been of old for ever.
7   My sins and faults of youth
     do thou, O Lord, forget:
   After thy mercy think on me,
     and for thy goodness great.

8   God good and upright is:
     the way he'll sinners show.
9   The meek in judgment he will guide,
     and make his path to know.
10 The whole paths of the Lord
     are truth and mercy sure,
   To those that do his cov'nant keep,
     and testimonies pure.

11 Now, for thine own name's sake,
     O Lord, I thee entreat
   To pardon mine iniquity;
     for it is very great.
12 What man is he that fears
     the Lord, and doth him serve?
   Him shall he teach the way that he
     shall choose, and still observe.

13 His soul shall dwell at ease;
     and his posterity
   Shall flourish still, and of the earth
     inheritors shall be.

14 With those that fear him is
  the secret of the Lord;
 The knowledge of his covenant
  he will to them afford.

15 Mine eyes upon the Lord
  continually are set;
 For he it is that shall bring forth
  my feet out of the net.
16 Turn unto me thy face,
  and to me mercy show;
 Because that I am desolate,
  and am brought very low.

17 My heart's griefs are increas'd:
  me from distress relieve.
18 See mine affliction and my pain,
  and all my sins forgive.
19 Consider thou my foes,
  because they many are;
 And it a cruel hatred is
  which they against me bear.

20 O do thou keep my soul,
  do thou deliver me:
 And let me never be asham'd,
  because I trust in thee.
21 Let uprightness and truth
  keep me, who thee attend.
22 Redemption, Lord, to Israel
  from all his troubles send.

Another of the same

1 TO thee I lift my soul, O Lord:
2   My God, I trust in thee:
  Let me not be asham'd; let not
    my foes triumph o'er me.
3 Yea, let thou none ashamed be
    that do on thee attend:
  Ashamed let them be, O Lord,
    who without cause offend.

4 Thy ways, Lord, shew; teach me thy paths:
5   Lead me in truth, teach me:
  For of my safety thou art God;
    all day I wait on thee.
6 Thy mercies, that most tender are,
    do thou, O Lord, remember,
  And loving-kindnesses; for they
    have been of old for ever.

7 Let not the errors of my youth,
    nor sins, remember'd be:
  In mercy, for thy goodness' sake,
    O Lord, remember me.
8 The Lord is good and gracious,
    he upright is also:
  He therefore sinners will instruct
    in ways that they should go.

9 The meek and lowly he will guide
    in judgment just alway:
  To meek and poor afflicted ones
    he'll clearly teach his way.
10 The whole paths of the Lord our God
    are truth and mercy sure,

To such as keep his covenant,
  and testimonies pure.

11 Now, for thine own name's sake, O Lord,
    I humbly thee entreat
To pardon mine iniquity;
    for it is very great.
12 What man fears God? him shall he teach
    the way that he shall chuse.
13 His soul shall dwell at ease; his seed
    the earth, as heirs, shall use.

14 The secret of the Lord is with
    such as do fear his name;
And he his holy covenant
    will manifest to them.
15 Towards the Lord my waiting eyes
    continually are set;
For he it is that shall bring forth
    my feet out of the net.

16 O turn thee unto me, O God,
    have mercy me upon;
Because I solitary am,
    and in affliction.
17 Enlarg'd the griefs are of mine heart;
    me from distress relieve.
18 See mine affliction and my pain,
    and all my sins forgive.

19 Consider thou mine enemies,
    because they many are;
And it a cruel hatred is
    which they against me bear.

20 O do thou keep my soul; O God,
  do thou deliver me:
Let me not be asham'd; for I
  do put my trust in thee.

21 O let integrity and truth
  keep me, who thee attend.
22 Redemption, Lord, to Israel
  from all his troubles send.

Psalm 26

A Psalm of David.

1 JUDGE me, O Lord, for I have walk'd
  in mine integrity:
 I trusted also in the Lord;
  slide therefore shall not I.
2 Examine me, and do me prove;
  try heart and reins, O God:
3 For thy love is before mine eyes,
  thy truth's paths I have trode.

4 With persons vain I have not sat,
  nor with dissemblers gone:
5 Th' assembly of ill men I hate;
  to sit with such I shun.
6 Mine hands in innocence, O Lord,
  I'll wash and purify;
So to thine holy altar go,
  and compass it will I:

7 That I, with voice of thanksgiving,
  may publish and declare,

And tell of all thy mighty works,
    that great and wondrous are.
8   The habitation of thy house,
    Lord, I have loved well;
Yea, in that place I do delight
    where doth thine honour dwell.

9   With sinners gather not my soul,
    and such as blood would spill:
10 Whose hands mischievous plots, right hand
    corrupting bribes do fill.
11 But as for me, I will walk on
    in mine integrity:
Do thou redeem me, and, O Lord,
    be merciful to me.

12 My foot upon an even place
    doth stand with stedfastness:
Within the congregations
    th' Eternal I will bless.

Psalm 27

A Psalm of David.

1   THE Lord's my light and saving health,
    who shall make me dismay'd?
My life's strength is the Lord, of whom
    then shall I be afraid?
2   When as mine enemies and foes,
    most wicked persons all,
To eat my flesh against me rose,
    they stumbled and did fall.

3   Against me though an host encamp,
    my heart yet fearless is:

Though war against me rise, I will
   be confident in this.
4 One thing I of the Lord desir'd,
   and will seek to obtain,
That all days of my life I may
   within God's house remain;

That I the beauty of the Lord
   behold may and admire,
And that I in his holy place
   may rev'rently enquire.
5 For he in his pavilion shall
   me hide in evil days;
In secret of his tent me hide,
   and on a rock me raise.

6 And now, ev'n at this present time,
   mine head shall lifted be
Above all those that are my foes,
   and round encompass me:
Therefore unto his tabernacle
   I'll sacrifices bring
Of joyfulness; I'll sing, yea, I
   to God will praises sing.

7 O Lord, give ear unto my voice,
   when I do cry to thee;
Upon me also mercy have,
   and do thou answer me.
8 When thou didst say, Seek ye my face,
   then unto thee reply
Thus did my heart, Above all things
   thy face, Lord, seek will I.

9 Far from me hide not thou thy face;
    put not away from thee
Thy servant in thy wrath: thou hast
    an helper been to me.
O God of my salvation,
    leave me not, nor forsake:
10 Though me my parents both should leave,
    the Lord will me up take.

11 O Lord, instruct me in thy way,
    to me a leader be
In a plain path, because of those
    that hatred bear to me.
12 Give me not to mine en'mies' will;
    for witnesses that lie
Against me risen are, and such
    as breathe out cruelty.

13 I fainted had, unless that I
    believed had to see
The Lord's own goodness in the land
    of them that living be.
14 Wait on the Lord, and be thou strong,
    and he shall strength afford
Unto thine heart; yea, do thou wait,
    I say, upon the Lord.

Psalm 28

A Psalm of David.

1 TO thee I'll cry, O Lord, my rock;
    hold not thy peace to me;
Lest like those that to pit descend
    I by thy silence be.

2   The voice hear of my humble pray'rs,
      when unto thee I cry;
    When to thine holy oracle
      I lift mine hands on high.

3   With ill men draw me not away
      that work iniquity;
    That speak peace to their friends, while in
      their hearts doth mischief lie.

4   Give them according to their deeds
      and ills endeavoured:
    And as their handy-works deserve,
      to them be rendered.

5   God shall not build, but them destroy,
      who would not understand
    The Lord's own works, nor did regard
      the doing of his hand.

6   For ever blessed be the Lord,
      for graciously he heard
    The voice of my petitions,
      and prayers did regard.

7   The Lord's my strength and shield; my heart
      upon him did rely;
    And I am helped: hence my heart
      doth joy exceedingly,
    And with my song I will him praise.

8   Their strength is God alone:
    He also is the saving strength
      of his anointed one.

9   O thine own people do thou save,
      bless thine inheritance;

Them also do thou feed, and them
for evermore advance.

Psalm 29

A Psalm of David.

1 GIVE ye unto the Lord, ye sons
that of the mighty be,
All strength and glory to the Lord
with cheerfulness give ye.
2 Unto the Lord the glory give
that to his name is due;
And in the beauty of holiness
unto JEHOVAH bow.

3 The Lord's voice on the waters is;
the God of majesty
Doth thunder, and on multitudes
of waters sitteth he.
4 A pow'rful voice it is that comes
out from the Lord most high;
The voice of that great Lord is full
of glorious majesty.

5 The voice of the Eternal doth
asunder cedars tear;
Yea, God the Lord doth cedars break
that Lebanon doth bear.
6 He makes them like a calf to skip,
ev'n that great Lebanon,
And, like to a young unicorn,
the mountain Sirion.

7 God's voice divides the flames of fire;
8 The desert it doth shake:

The Lord doth make the wilderness
    of Kadesh all to quake.
9 God's voice doth make the hinds to calve,
    it makes the forest bare:
And in his temple ev'ry one
    his glory doth declare.

10 The Lord sits on the floods; the Lord
    sits King, and ever shall.
11 The Lord will give his people strength,
    and with peace bless them all.

Psalm 30

A Psalm and Song at the dedication of the house of David.

1 LORD, I will thee extol, for thou
    hast lifted me on high,
And over me thou to rejoice
    mad'st not mine enemy.
2 O thou who art the Lord my God,
    I in distress to thee,
With loud cries lifted up my voice,
    and thou hast healed me.

3 O Lord, my soul thou hast brought up,
    and rescu'd from the grave;
That I to pit should not go down,
    alive thou didst me save.
4 O ye that are his holy ones,
    sing praise unto the Lord;
And give unto him thanks, when ye
    his holiness record.

5 For but a moment lasts his wrath;
    life in his favour lies:

Weeping may for a night endure,
    at morn doth joy arise.
6   In my prosperity I said,
    that nothing shall me move.
7   O Lord, thou hast my mountain made
    to stand strong by thy love:

But when that thou, O gracious God,
    didst hide thy face from me,
Then quickly was my prosp'rous state
    turn'd into misery.
8   Wherefore unto the Lord my cry
    I caused to ascend:
My humble supplication
    I to the Lord did send.

9   What profit is there in my blood,
    when I go down to pit?
Shall unto thee the dust give praise?
    thy truth declare shall it?
10 Hear, Lord, have mercy; help me, Lord:
11   Thou turned hast my sadness
To dancing; yea, my sackcloth loos'd,
    and girded me with gladness;

12 That sing thy praise my glory may,
    and never silent be.
O Lord my God, for evermore
    I will give thanks to thee.

Psalm 31

To the chief Musician, A Psalm of David.

1   IN thee, O Lord, I put my trust,
    sham'd let me never be;

According to thy righteousness
  do thou deliver me.
2 Bow down thine ear to me, with speed
  send me deliverance:
To save me, my strong rock be thou,
  and my house of defence.

3 Because thou art my rock, and thee
  I for my fortress take;
Therefore do thou me lead and guide,
  ev'n for thine own name's sake.
4 And sith thou art my strength, therefore
  pull me out of the net,
Which they in subtilty for me
  so privily have set.

5 Into thine hands I do commit
  my sp'rit: for thou art he,
O thou, JEHOVAH, God of truth,
  that hast redeemed me.
6 Those that do lying vanities
  regard, I have abhorr'd:
But as for me, my confidence
  is fixed on the Lord.

7 I'll in thy mercy gladly joy:
  for thou my miseries
Consider'd hast; thou hast my soul
  known in adversities:
8 And thou hast not inclosed me
  within the en'my's hand;
And by thee have my feet been made
  in a large room to stand.

9 O Lord, upon me mercy have,
    for trouble is on me:
Mine eye, my belly, and my soul,
    with grief consumed be.
10 Because my life with grief is spent,
    my years with sighs and groans:
My strength doth fail; and for my sin
    consumed are my bones.

11 I was a scorn to all my foes,
    and to my friends a fear;
And specially reproach'd of those
    that were my neighbours near:
When they me saw they from me fled.
12   Ev'n so I am forgot,
As men are out of mind when dead:
    I'm like a broken pot.

13 For slanders I of many heard;
    fear compass'd me, while they
Against me did consult, and plot
    to take my life away.
14 But as for me, O Lord, my trust
    upon thee I did lay;
And I to thee, Thou art my God,
    did confidently say.

15 My times are wholly in thine hand:
    do thou deliver me
From their hands that mine enemies
    and persecutors be.
16 Thy countenance to shine do thou
    upon thy servant make:

Unto me give salvation,
 for thy great mercies' sake.

17 Let me not be asham'd, O Lord,
 for on thee call'd I have:
Let wicked men be sham'd, let them
 be silent in the grave.
18 To silence put the lying lips,
 that grievous things do say,
And hard reports, in pride and scorn,
 on righteous men do lay.

19 How great's the goodness thou for them
 that fear thee keep'st in store,
And wrought'st for them that trust in thee
 the sons of men before!
20 In secret of thy presence thou
 shalt hide them from man's pride:
From strife of tongues thou closely shalt,
 as in a tent, them hide.

21 All praise and thanks be to the Lord;
 for he hath magnify'd
His wondrous love to me within
 a city fortify'd.
22 For from thine eyes cut off I am,
 I in my haste had said;
My voice yet heard'st thou, when to thee
 with cries my moan I made.

23 O love the Lord, all ye his saints;
 because the Lord doth guard
The faithful, and he plenteously
 proud doers doth reward.

24 Be of good courage, and he strength
    unto your heart shall send,
All ye whose hope and confidence
    doth on the Lord depend.

Psalm 32

A Psalm of David, Maschil.

1 O BLESSED is the man to whom
    is freely pardoned
All the transgression he hath done,
    whose sin is covered.

2 Bless'd is the man to whom the Lord
    imputeth not his sin,
And in whose sp'rit there is no guile,
    nor fraud is found therein.

3 When as I did refrain my speech,
    and silent was my tongue,
My bones then waxed old, because
    I roared all day long.

4 For upon me both day and night
    thine hand did heavy lie,
So that my moisture turned is
    in summer's drought thereby.

5 I thereupon have unto thee
    my sin acknowledged,
And likewise mine iniquity
    I have not covered:
I will confess unto the Lord
    my trespasses, said I;
And of my sin thou freely didst
    forgive th' iniquity.

6   For this shall ev'ry godly one
        his prayer make to thee;
    In such a time he shall thee seek,
        as found thou mayest be.
    Surely, when floods of waters great
        do swell up to the brim,
    They shall not overwhelm his soul,
        nor once come near to him.

7   Thou art my hiding-place, thou shalt
        from trouble keep me free:
    Thou with songs of deliverance
        about shalt compass me.
8   I will instruct thee, and thee teach
        the way that thou shalt go;
    And, with mine eye upon thee set,
        I will direction show.

9   Then be not like the horse or mule,
        which do not understand;
    Whose mouth, lest they come near to thee,
        a bridle must command.
10 Unto the man that wicked is
        his sorrows shall abound;
    But him that trusteth in the Lord
        mercy shall compass round.

11 Ye righteous, in the Lord be glad,
        in him do ye rejoice:
    All ye that upright are in heart,
        for joy lift up your voice.

Psalm 33

1 YE righteous, in the Lord rejoice;
     it comely is and right,
  That upright men, with thankful voice,
     should praise the Lord of might.
2 Praise God with harp, and unto him
     sing with the psaltery;
  Upon a ten-string'd instrument
     make ye sweet melody.

3 A new song to him sing, and play
     with loud noise skilfully;
4 For right is God's word, all his works
     are done in verity.
5 To judgment and to righteousness
     a love he beareth still;
  The loving-kindness of the Lord
     the earth throughout doth fill.

6 The heavens by the word of God
     did their beginning take;
  And by the breathing of his mouth
     he all their hosts did make.
7 The waters of the seas he brings
     together as an heap;
  And in storehouses, as it were,
     he layeth up the deep.

8 Let earth, and all that live therein,
     with rev'rence fear the Lord;
  Let all the world's inhabitants
     dread him with one accord.
9 For he did speak the word, and done
     it was without delay;

Established it firmly stood,
   whatever he did say.

10 God doth the counsel bring to nought
   which heathen folk do take;
And what the people do devise
   of none effect doth make.
11 O but the counsel of the Lord
   doth stand for ever sure;
And of his heart the purposes
   from age to age endure.

12 That nation blessed is, whose God
   JEHOVAH is, and those
A blessed people are, whom for
   his heritage he chose.
13 The Lord from heav'n sees and beholds
   all sons of men full well:
14 He views all from his dwelling-place
   that in the earth do dwell.

15 He forms their hearts alike, and all
   their doings he observes.
16 Great hosts save not a king, much strength
   no mighty man preserves.
17 An horse for preservation
   is a deceitful thing;
And by the greatness of his strength
   can no deliv'rance bring.

18 Behold, on those that do him fear
   the Lord doth set his eye;
Ev'n those who on his mercy do
   with confidence rely.

19 From death to free their soul, in dearth
      life unto them to yield.
20 Our soul doth wait upon the Lord;
      he is our help and shield.

21 Sith in his holy name we trust,
      our heart shall joyful be.
22 Lord, let thy mercy be on us,
      as we do hope in thee.

Psalm 34

*A Psalm of David, when he changed his behaviour before
Abimelech; who drove him away, and he departed.*

1 GOD will I bless all times; his praise
      my mouth shall still express.
2 My soul shall boast in God: the meek
      shall hear with joyfulness.
3 Extol the Lord with me, let us
      exalt his name together.
4 I sought the Lord, he heard, and did
      me from all fears deliver.

5 They look'd to him, and lighten'd were:
      not shamed were their faces.
6 This poor man cry'd, God heard, and sav'd
      him from all his distresses.
7 The angel of the Lord encamps,
      and round encompasseth
   All those about that do him fear,
      and them delivereth.

8 O taste and see that God is good:
      who trusts in him is bless'd.

9 Fear God his saints: none that him fear
    shall be with want oppress'd.
10 The lions young may hungry be,
    and they may lack their food:
    But they that truly seek the Lord
    shall not lack any good.

11 O children, hither do ye come,
    and unto me give ear;
    I shall you teach to understand
    how ye the Lord should fear.
12 What man is he that life desires,
    to see good would live long?
13 Thy lips refrain from speaking guile,
    and from ill words thy tongue.

14 Depart from ill, do good, seek peace,
    pursue it earnestly.
15 God's eyes are on the just; his ears
    are open to their cry.
16 The face of God is set against
    those that do wickedly,
    That he may quite out from the earth
    cut off their memory.

17 The righteous cry unto the Lord,
    he unto them gives ear;
    And they out of their troubles all
    by him deliver'd are.
18 The Lord is ever nigh to them
    that be of broken sp'rit;
    To them he safety doth afford
    that are in heart contrite.

19 The troubles that afflict the just
    in number many be;
    But yet at length out of them all
    the Lord doth set him free.
20 He carefully his bones doth keep,
    whatever can befall;
    That not so much as one of them
    can broken be at all.

21 Ill shall the wicked slay; laid waste
    shall be who hate the just.
22 The Lord redeems his servants' souls;
    none perish that him trust.

Psalm 35

A Psalm of David.

1 PLEAD, Lord, with those that plead; and
        fight
    with those that fight with me.
2 Of shield and buckler take thou hold,
    stand up mine help to be.
3 Draw also out the spear, and do
    against them stop the way
    That me pursue: unto my soul,
    I'm thy salvation, say.

4 Let them confounded be and sham'd
    that for my soul have sought:
    Who plot my hurt turn'd back be they,
    and to confusion brought.
5 Let them be like unto the chaff
    that flies before the wind;
    And let the angel of the Lord
    pursue them hard behind.

6 With darkness cover thou their way,
  and let it slipp'ry prove;
And let the angel of the Lord
  pursue them from above.
7 For without cause have they for me
  their net hid in a pit,
They also have without a cause
  for my soul digged it.

8 Let ruin seize him unawares;
  his net he hid withal
Himself let catch; and in the same
  destruction let him fall.
9 My soul in God shall joy; and glad
  in his salvation be:
10 And all my bones shall say, O Lord,
  who is like unto thee,

Which dost the poor set free from him
  that is for him too strong;
The poor and needy from the man
  that spoils and does him wrong?
11 False witnesses rose; to my charge
  things I not knew they laid.
12 They, to the spoiling of my soul,
  me ill for good repaid.

13 But as for me, when they were sick,
  in sackcloth sad I mourn'd:
My humbled soul did fast, my pray'r
  into my bosom turn'd.
14 Myself I did behave as he
  had been my friend or brother;

I heavily bow'd down, as one
    that mourneth for his mother.

15 But in my trouble they rejoic'd,
    gath'ring themselves together;
Yea, abjects vile together did
    themselves against me gather:
I knew it not; they did me tear,
    and quiet would not be.
16 With mocking hypocrites, at feasts
    they gnash'd their teeth at me.

17 How long, Lord, look'st thou on? from those
    destructions they intend
Rescue my soul, from lions young
    my darling do defend.
18 I will give thanks to thee, O Lord,
    within th' assembly great;
And where much people gather'd are
    thy praises forth will set.

19 Let not my wrongful enemies
    proudly rejoice o'er me;
Nor who me hate without a cause,
    let them wink with the eye.
20 For peace they do not speak at all;
    but crafty plots prepare
Against all those within the land
    that meek and quiet are.

21 With mouths set wide, they 'gainst me said,
    Ha, ha! our eye doth see.
22 Lord, thou hast seen, hold not thy peace;
    Lord, be not far from me.

23 Stir up thyself; wake, that thou may'st
    judgment to me afford,
  Ev'n to my cause, O thou that art
    my only God and Lord.

24 O Lord my God, do thou me judge
    after thy righteousness;
  And let them not their joy 'gainst me
    triumphantly express:
25 Nor let them say within their hearts,
    Ah, we would have it thus;
  Nor suffer them to say, that he
    is swallow'd up by us.

26 Sham'd and confounded be they all
    that at my hurt are glad;
  Let those against me that do boast
    with shame and scorn be clad.
27 Let them that love my righteous cause
    be glad, shout, and not cease
  To say, The Lord be magnify'd,
    who loves his servant's peace.

28 Thy righteousness shall also be
    declared by my tongue;
  The praises that belong to thee
    speak shall it all day long.

Psalm 36

To the chief Musician, A Psalm of David the servant of the Lord.

1 THE wicked man's transgression
    within my heart thus says,
  Undoubtedly the fear of God
    is not before his eyes.

2 Because himself he flattereth
   in his own blinded eye,
Until the hatefulness be found
   of his iniquity.

3 Words from his mouth proceeding are,
   fraud and iniquity:
He to be wise, and to do good,
   hath left off utterly.
4 He mischief, lying on his bed,
   most cunningly doth plot:
He sets himself in ways not good,
   ill he abhorreth not.

5 Thy mercy, Lord, is in the heav'ns;
   thy truth doth reach the clouds:
6 Thy justice is like mountains great;
   thy judgments deep as floods:
Lord, thou preservest man and beast.
7   How precious is thy grace!
Therefore in shadow of thy wings
   men's sons their trust shall place.

8 They with the fatness of thy house
   shall be well satisfy'd;
From rivers of thy pleasures thou
   wilt drink to them provide.
9 Because of life the fountain pure
   remains alone with thee;
And in that purest light of thine
   we clearly light shall see.

10 Thy loving-kindness unto them
   continue that thee know;

And still on men upright in heart
   thy righteousness bestow.
11 Let not the foot of cruel pride
   come, and against me stand;
And let me not removed be,
   Lord, by the wicked's hand.

12 There fallen are they, and ruined,
   that work iniquities:
Cast down they are, and never shall
   be able to arise.

Psalm 37

A Psalm of David.

1 FOR evil-doers fret thou not
   thyself unquietly;
Nor do thou envy bear to those
   that work iniquity.
2 For, even like unto the grass,
   soon be cut down shall they;
And, like the green and tender herb,
   they wither shall away.

3 Set thou thy trust upon the Lord,
   and be thou doing good;
And so thou in the land shalt dwell,
   and verily have food.
4 Delight thyself in God; he'll give
   thine heart's desire to thee.
5 Thy way to God commit, him trust,
   it bring to pass shall he.

6 And, like unto the light, he shall
   thy righteousness display;

And he thy judgment shall bring forth
  like noon-tide of the day.
7 Rest in the Lord, and patiently
  wait for him: do not fret
For him who, prosp'ring in his way,
  success in sin doth get.

8 Do thou from anger cease, and wrath
  see thou forsake also:
Fret not thyself in any wise,
  that evil thou should'st do.
9 For those that evil doers are
  shall be cut off and fall:
But those that wait upon the Lord
  the earth inherit shall.

10 For yet a little while, and then
  the wicked shall not be;
His place thou shalt consider well,
  but it thou shalt not see.
11 But by inheritance the earth
  the meek ones shall possess:
They also shall delight themselves
  in an abundant peace.

12 The wicked plots against the just,
  and at him whets his teeth:
13 The Lord shall laugh at him, because
  his day he coming seeth.
14 The wicked have drawn out the sword,
  and bent their bow, to slay
The poor and needy, and to kill
  men of an upright way.

15 But their own sword, which they have
          drawn,
      shall enter their own heart:
  Their bows which they have bent shall
          break,
      and into pieces part.
16 A little that a just man hath
      is more and better far
  Than is the wealth of many such
      as lewd and wicked are.

17 For sinners' arms shall broken be;
      but God the just sustains.
18 God knows the just man's days, and still
      their heritage remains.
19 They shall not be asham'd when they
      the evil time do see;
  And when the days of famine are,
      they satisfy'd shall be.

20 But wicked men, and foes of God,
      as fat of lambs, decay;
  They shall consume, yea, into smoke
      they shall consume away.
21 The wicked borrows, but the same
      again he doth not pay;
  Whereas the righteous mercy shews,
      and gives his own away.

22 For such as blessed be of him
      the earth inherit shall;
  And they that cursed are of him
      shall be destroyed all.

23 A good man's footsteps by the Lord
    are ordered aright;
And in the way wherein he walks
    he greatly doth delight.

24 Although he fall, yet shall he not
    be cast down utterly;
Because the Lord with his own hand
    upholds him mightily.
25 I have been young, and now am old,
    yet have I never seen
The just man left, nor that his seed
    for bread have beggars been.

26 He's ever merciful, and lends:
    his seed is bless'd therefore.
27 Depart from evil, and do good,
    and dwell for evermore.
28 For God loves judgment, and his saints
    leaves not in any case;
They are kept ever: but cut off
    shall be the sinner's race.

29 The just inherit shall the land,
    and ever in it dwell:
30 The just man's mouth doth wisdom speak;
    his tongue doth judgment tell.
31 In's heart the law is of his God,
    his steps slide not away.
32 The wicked man doth watch the just,
    and seeketh him to slay.

33 Yet him the Lord will not forsake,
    nor leave him in his hands:

The righteous will he not condemn,
  when he in judgment stands.
34 Wait on the Lord, and keep his way,
  and thee exalt shall he
Th' earth to inherit; when cut off
  the wicked thou shalt see.

35 I saw the wicked great in pow'r,
  spread like a green bay-tree:
36 He pass'd, yea, was not; him I sought,
  but found he could not be.
37 Mark thou the perfect, and behold
  the man of uprightness;
Because that surely of this man
  the latter end is peace.

38 But those men that transgressors are
  shall be destroy'd together;
The latter end of wicked men
  shall be cut off for ever.
39 But the salvation of the just
  is from the Lord above;
He in the time of their distress
  their stay and strength doth prove.

40 The Lord shall help, and them deliver:
  he shall them free and save
From wicked men; because in him
  their confidence they have.

Psalm 38

A Psalm of David, to bring to remembrance.

1 IN thy great indignation,
  O Lord, rebuke me not;

Nor on me lay thy chast'ning hand,
    in thy displeasure hot.
2 For in me fast thine arrows stick,
    thine hand doth press me sore:
3 And in my flesh there is no health,
    nor soundness any more.

This grief I have, because thy wrath
    is forth against me gone;
And in my bones there is no rest,
    for sin that I have done.
4 Because gone up above mine head
    my great transgressions be;
And, as a weighty burden, they
    too heavy are for me.

5 My wounds do stink, and are corrupt;
    my folly makes it so.
6 I troubled am, and much bow'd down;
    all day I mourning go.
7 For a disease that loathsome is
    so fills my loins with pain,
That in my weak and weary flesh
    no soundness doth remain.

8 So feeble and infirm am I,
    and broken am so sore,
That, through disquiet of my heart,
    I have been made to roar.
9 O Lord, all that I do desire
    is still before thine eye;
And of my heart the secret groans
    not hidden are from thee.

10 My heart doth pant incessantly,
   my strength doth quite decay;
  As for mine eyes, their wonted light
   is from me gone away.
11 My lovers and my friends do stand
   at distance from my sore;
  And those do stand aloof that were
   kinsmen and kind before.

12 Yea, they that seek my life lay snares:
   who seek to do me wrong
  Speak things mischievous, and deceits
   imagine all day long.
13 But, as one deaf, that heareth not,
   I suffer'd all to pass;
  I as a dumb man did become,
   whose mouth not open'd was:

14 As one that hears not, in whose mouth
   are no reproofs at all.
15 For, Lord, I hope in thee; my God,
   thou'lt hear me when I call.
16 For I said, Hear me, lest they should
   rejoice o'er me with pride;
  And o'er me magnify themselves,
   when as my foot doth slide.

17 For I am near to halt, my grief
   is still before mine eye:
18 For I'll declare my sin, and grieve
   for mine iniquity.
19 But yet mine en'mies lively are,
   and strong are they beside;

And they that hate me wrongfully
 are greatly multiply'd.

20 And they for good that render ill,
 as en'mies me withstood;
Yea, ev'n for this, because that I
 do follow what is good.
21 Forsake me not, O Lord; my God,
 far from me never be.
22 O Lord, thou my salvation art,
 haste to give help to me.

Psalm 39

*To the chief Musician, even to Jeduthun,
A Psalm of David.*

1 I SAID, I will look to my ways,
 lest with my tongue I sin:
In sight of wicked men my mouth
 with bridle I'll keep in.
2 With silence I as dumb became,
 I did myself restrain
From speaking good; but then the more
 increased was my pain.

3 My heart within me waxed hot;
 and, while I musing was,
The fire did burn; and from my tongue
 these words I did let pass:
4 Mine end, and measure of my days,
 O Lord, unto me show
What is the same; that I thereby
 my frailty well may know.

5   Lo, thou my days an handbreadth mad'st;
   mine age is in thine eye
As nothing: sure each man at best
   is wholly vanity.
6   Sure each man walks in a vain show;
   they vex themselves in vain:
He heaps up wealth, and doth not know
   to whom it shall pertain.

7   And now, O Lord, what wait I for?
   my hope is fix'd on thee.
8   Free me from all my trespasses,
   the fool's scorn make not me.
9   Dumb was I, op'ning not my mouth,
   because this work was thine.
10 Thy stroke take from me; by the blow
   of thine hand I do pine.

11 When with rebukes thou dost correct
   man for iniquity,
Thou wastes his beauty like a moth:
   sure each man's vanity.
12 Attend my cry, Lord, at my tears
   and pray'rs not silent be:
I sojourn as my fathers all,
   and stranger am with thee.

13 O spare thou me, that I my strength
   recover may again,
Before from hence I do depart,
   and here no more remain.

Psalm 40

To the chief Musician, A Psalm of David.

1 I WAITED for the Lord my God,
   and patiently did bear;
  At length to me he did incline
   my voice and cry to hear.
2 He took me from a fearful pit,
   and from the miry clay,
  And on a rock he set my feet,
   establishing my way.

3 He put a new song in my mouth,
   our God to magnify:
  Many shall see it, and shall fear,
   and on the Lord rely.
4 O blessed is the man whose trust
   upon the Lord relies;
  Respecting not the proud, nor such
   as turn aside to lies.

5 O Lord my God, full many are
   the wonders thou hast done;
  Thy gracious thoughts to us-ward far
   above all thoughts are gone:
  In order none can reckon them
   to thee: if them declare,
  And speak of them I would, they more
   than can be number'd are.

6 No sacrifice nor offering
   didst thou at all desire;
  Mine ears thou bor'd: sin-off'ring thou
   and burnt didst not require:

7   Then to the Lord these were my words,
      I come, behold and see;
Within the volume of the book
      it written is of me:

8   To do thy will I take delight,
      O thou my God that art;
Yea, that most holy law of thine
      I have within my heart.
9   Within the congregation great
      I righteousness did preach:
Lo, thou dost know, O Lord, that I
      refrained not my speech.

10 I never did within my heart
      conceal thy righteousness;
I thy salvation have declar'd,
      and shown thy faithfulness:
Thy kindness, which most loving is,
      concealed have not I,
Nor from the congregation great
      have hid thy verity.

11 Thy tender mercies, Lord, from me
      O do thou not restrain:
Thy loving-kindness, and thy truth,
      let them me still maintain.
12 For ills past reck'ning compass me,
      and mine iniquities
Such hold upon me taken have,
      I cannot lift mine eyes:

They more than hairs are on mine head,
      thence is my heart dismay'd.

13 Be pleased, Lord, to rescue me;
    Lord, hasten to mine aid.
14 Sham'd and confounded be they all
    that seek my soul to kill;
    Yea, let them backward driven be,
    and sham'd, that wish me ill.

15 For a reward of this their shame
    confounded let them be,
    That in this manner scoffing say,
    Aha, aha! to me.
16 In thee let all be glad, and joy,
    who seeking thee abide;
    Who thy salvation love, say still,
    The Lord be magnify'd.

17 I'm poor and needy, yet the Lord
    of me a care doth take:
    Thou art my help and saviour,
    my God, no tarrying make.

Psalm 41

To the chief Musician, A Psalm of David.

1 BLESSED is he that wisely doth
    the poor man's case consider;
    For when the time of trouble is,
    the Lord will him deliver.
2 God will him keep, yea, save alive;
    on earth he bless'd shall live;
    And to his enemies' desire
    thou wilt him not up give.

3 God will give strength when he on bed
    of languishing doth mourn;

And in his sickness sore, O Lord,
    thou all his bed wilt turn.
4 I said, O Lord, do thou extend
    thy mercy unto me;
O do thou heal my soul; for why?
    I have offended thee.

5 Those that to me are enemies,
    of me do evil say,
When shall he die, that so his name
    may perish quite away?
6 To see me if he comes, he speaks
    vain words: but then his heart
Heaps mischief to it, which he tells,
    when forth he doth depart.

7 My haters jointly whispering,
    'gainst me my hurt devise.
8 Mischief, say they, cleaves fast to him;
    he li'th, and shall not rise.
9 Yea, ev'n mine own familiar friend,
    on whom I did rely,
Who ate my bread, ev'n he his heel
    against me lifted high.

10 But, Lord, be merciful to me,
    and up again me raise,
That I may justly them requite
    according to their ways.
11 By this I know that certainly
    I favour'd am by thee;
Because my hateful enemy
    triumphs not over me.

12 But as for me, thou me uphold'st
    in mine integrity;
And me before thy countenance
    thou sett'st continually.
13 The Lord, the God of Israel,
    be bless'd for ever then,
From age to age eternally.
    Amen, yea, and amen.

Psalm 42

To the chief Musician, Maschil, for the sons of Korah.

1 LIKE as the hart for water-brooks
    in thirst doth pant and bray;
So pants my longing soul, O God,
    that come to thee I may.
2 My soul for God, the living God,
    doth thirst: when shall I near
Unto thy countenance approach,
    and in God's sight appear?

3 My tears have unto me been meat,
    both in the night and day,
While unto me continually,
    Where is thy God? they say.
4 My soul is poured out in me,
    when this I think upon;
Because that with the multitude
    I heretofore had gone:

With them into God's house I went
    with voice of joy and praise;
Yea, with the multitude that kept
    the solemn holy days.

5 O why art thou cast down, my soul?
    why in me so dismay'd?
  Trust God, for I shall praise him yet,
    his count'nance is mine aid.

6 My God, my soul's cast down in me;
    thee therefore mind I will
  From Jordan's land, the Hermonites,
    and ev'n from Mizar hill.
7 At the noise of thy water-spouts
    deep unto deep doth call;
  Thy breaking waves pass over me,
    yea, and thy billows all.

8 His loving-kindness yet the Lord
    command will in the day,
  His song's with me by night; to God,
    by whom I live, I'll pray:
9 And I will say to God my rock,
    Why me forgett'st thou so?
  Why, for my foes' oppression,
    thus mourning do I go?

10 'Tis as a sword within my bones,
    when my foes me upbraid;
  Ev'n when by them, Where is thy God?
    'tis daily to me said.
11 O why art thou cast down, my soul?
    why, thus with grief opprest,
  Art thou disquieted in me?
    in God still hope and rest:

  For yet I know I shall him praise,
    who graciously to me

The health is of my countenance,
yea, mine own God is he.

Psalm 43

1 JUDGE me, O God, and plead my cause
against th' ungodly nation;
From the unjust and crafty man,
O be thou my salvation.

2 For thou the God art of my strength;
why thrusts thou me thee fro'?
For th' enemy's oppression
why do I mourning go?

3 O send thy light forth and thy truth;
let them be guides to me,
And bring me to thine holy hill,
ev'n where thy dwellings be.

4 Then will I to God's altar go,
to God my chiefest joy:
Yea, God, my God, thy name to praise
my harp I will employ.

5 Why art thou then cast down, my soul?
what should discourage thee?
And why with vexing thoughts art thou
disquieted in me?
Still trust in God; for him to praise
good cause I yet shall have:
He of my count'nance is the health,
my God that doth me save.

Psalm 44

To the chief Musician for the sons of Korah, Maschil.

1 O GOD, we with our ears have heard,
　　our fathers have us told,
What works thou in their days hadst done,
　　ev'n in the days of old.
2 Thy hand did drive the heathen out,
　　and plant them in their place;
Thou didst afflict the nations,
　　but them thou didst increase.

3 For neither got their sword the land,
　　nor did their arm them save;
But thy right hand, arm, countenance;
　　for thou them favour gave.
4 Thou art my King: for Jacob, Lord,
　　deliv'rances command.
5 Through thee we shall push down our foes,
　　that do against us stand:

We, through thy name, shall tread down
　　　　those
　　that ris'n against us have.
6 For in my bow I shall not trust,
　　nor shall my sword me save.
7 But from our foes thou hast us sav'd,
　　our haters put to shame.
8 In God we all the day do boast,
　　and ever praise thy name.

9 But now we are cast off by thee,
　　and us thou putt'st to shame;
And when our armies do go forth,
　　thou go'st not with the same.

10 Thou mak'st us from the enemy,
    faint-hearted, to turn back;
   And they who hate us for themselves
    our spoils away do take.

11 Like sheep for meat thou gavest us;
    'mong heathen cast we be.
12 Thou didst for nought thy people sell;
    their price enrich'd not thee.
13 Thou mak'st us a reproach to be
    unto our neighbours near;
   Derision and a scorn to them
    that round about us are.

14 A by-word also thou dost us
    among the heathen make;
   The people, in contempt and spite,
    at us their heads do shake.
15 Before me my confusion
    continually abides;
   And of my bashful countenance
    the shame me ever hides:

16 For voice of him that doth reproach,
    and speaketh blasphemy;
   By reason of th' avenging foe,
    and cruel enemy.
17 All this is come on us, yet we
    have not forgotten thee;
   Nor falsely in thy covenant
    behav'd ourselves have we.

18 Back from thy way our heart not turn'd;
    our steps no straying made;

19 Though us thou brak'st in dragons' place,
    and cover'dst with death's shade.
20 If we God's name forgot, or stretch'd
    to a strange god our hands,
21 Shall not God search this out? for he
    heart's secrets understands.

22 Yea, for thy sake we're kill'd all day,
    counted as slaughter-sheep.
23 Rise, Lord, cast us not ever off;
    awake, why dost thou sleep?
24 O wherefore hidest thou thy face?
    forgett'st our cause distress'd,
25 And our oppression? For our soul
    is to the dust down press'd:

    Our belly also on the earth
    fast cleaving, hold doth take.
26 Rise for our help, and us redeem,
    ev'n for thy mercies' sake.

Psalm 45

To the chief Musician upon Shoshannim,
for the sons of Korah, Maschil, A Song of loves.

1 MY heart brings forth a goodly thing;
    my words that I indite
Concern the King: my tongue's a pen
    of one that swift doth write.
2 Thou fairer art than sons of men:
    into thy lips is store
Of grace infus'd; God therefore thee
    hath bless'd for evermore.

3 O thou that art the mighty One,
    thy sword gird on thy thigh;

Ev'n with thy glory excellent,
   and with thy majesty.
4 For meekness, truth, and righteousness,
   in state ride prosp'rously;
And thy right hand shall thee instruct
   in things that fearful be.

5 Thine arrows sharply pierce the heart
   of th' en'mies of the King;
And under thy subjection
   the people down do bring.
6 For ever and for ever is,
   O God, thy throne of might;
The sceptre of thy kingdom is
   a sceptre that is right.

7 Thou lovest right, and hatest ill;
   for God, thy God, most high,
Above thy fellows hath with th' oil
   of joy anointed thee.
8 Of aloes, myrrh, and cassia,
   a smell thy garments had,
Out of the iv'ry palaces,
   whereby they made thee glad.

9 Among thy women honourable
   kings' daughters were at hand:
Upon thy right hand did the queen
   in gold of Ophir stand.
10 O daughter, hearken and regard,
   and do thine ear incline;
Likewise forget thy father's house,
   and people that are thine.

11 Then of the King desir'd shall be
   thy beauty veh'mently:
   Because he is thy Lord, do thou
   him worship rev'rently.
12 The daughter there of Tyre shall be
   with gifts and off'rings great:
   Those of the people that are rich
   thy favour shall entreat.

13 Behold, the daughter of the King
   all glorious is within;
   And with embroideries of gold
   her garments wrought have been.
14 She shall be brought unto the King
   in robes with needle wrought;
   Her fellow-virgins following
   shall unto thee be brought.

15 They shall be brought with gladness great,
   and mirth on ev'ry side,
   Into the palace of the King,
   and there they shall abide.
16 Instead of those thy fathers dear,
   thy children thou may'st take,
   And in all places of the earth
   them noble princes make.

17 Thy name remember'd I will make
   through ages all to be:
   The people therefore evermore
   shall praises give to thee.

Another of the same

1 MY heart inditing is
   good matter in a song:

I speak the things that I have made,
   which to the King belong:
My tongue shall be as quick,
   his honour to indite,
As is the pen of any scribe
   that useth fast to write.

2 Thou'rt fairest of all men;
   grace in thy lips doth flow:
And therefore blessings evermore
   on thee doth God bestow.

3 Thy sword gird on thy thigh,
   thou that art most of might:
Appear in dreadful majesty,
   and in thy glory bright.

4 For meekness, truth, and right,
   ride prosp'rously in state;
And thy right hand shall teach to thee
   things terrible and great.

5 Thy shafts shall pierce their hearts
   that foes are to the King;
Whereby into subjection
   the people thou shalt bring.

6 Thy royal seat, O Lord,
   for ever shall remain:
The sceptre of thy kingdom doth
   all righteousness maintain.

7 Thou lov'st right, and hat'st ill;
   for God, thy God, most high,
Above thy fellows hath with th' oil
   of joy anointed thee.

8 Of myrrh and spices sweet
   a smell thy garments had,

Out of the iv'ry palaces,
    whereby they made thee glad.
9 And in thy glorious train
    kings' daughters waiting stand;
And thy fair queen, in Ophir gold,
    doth stand at thy right hand.

10 O daughter, take good heed,
    incline, and give good ear;
Thou must forget thy kindred all,
    and father's house most dear.
11 Thy beauty to the King
    shall then delightful be:
And do thou humbly worship him,
    because thy Lord is he.

12 The daughter then of Tyre
    there with a gift shall be,
And all the wealthy of the land
    shall make their suit to thee.
13 The daughter of the King
    all glorious is within;
And with embroideries of gold
    her garments wrought have been.

14 She cometh to the King
    in robes with needle wrought;
The virgins that do follow her
    shall unto thee be brought.
15 They shall be brought with joy,
    and mirth on ev'ry side,
Into the palace of the King,
    and there they shall abide.

16 And in thy fathers' stead,
    thy children thou may'st take,
And in all places of the earth
    them noble princes make.
17 I will shew forth thy name
    to generations all:
Therefore the people evermore
    to thee give praises shall.

Psalm 46

*To the chief Musician for the sons of Korah,
A Song upon Alamoth.*

1 GOD is our refuge and our strength,
    in straits a present aid;
2 Therefore, although the earth remove,
    we will not be afraid:
Though hills amidst the seas be cast;
3   Though waters roaring make,
And troubled be; yea though the hills
    by swelling seas do shake.

4 A river is, whose streams do glad
    the city of our God;
The holy place, wherein the Lord
    most high hath his abode.
5 God in the midst of her doth dwell;
    nothing shall her remove:
The Lord to her an helper will,
    and that right early, prove.

6 The heathen rag'd tumultuously,
    the kingdoms moved were:
The Lord God uttered his voice,
    the earth did melt for fear.

7 The Lord of hosts upon our side
    doth constantly remain:
  The God of Jacob's our refuge,
    us safely to maintain.

8 Come, and behold what wondrous works
    have by the Lord been wrought;
  Come, see what desolations
    he on the earth hath brought.
9 Unto the ends of all the earth
    wars into peace he turns:
  The bow he breaks, the spear he cuts,
    in fire the chariot burns.

10 Be still, and know that I am God;
    among the heathen I
  Will be exalted; I on earth
    will be exalted high.
11 Our God, who is the Lord of hosts,
    is still upon our side;
  The God of Jacob our refuge
    for ever will abide.

Psalm 47

To the chief Musician, A Psalm for the sons of Korah.

1 ALL people, clap your hands; to God
    with voice of triumph shout:
2 For dreadful is the Lord most high,
    great King the earth throughout.
3 The heathen people under us
    he surely shall subdue;
  And he shall make the nations
    under our feet to bow.

4 The lot of our inheritance
    chuse out for us shall he,

Of Jacob, whom he loved well,
ev'n the excellency.

5 God is with shouts gone up, the Lord
with trumpets sounding high.

6 Sing praise to God, sing praise, sing praise,
praise to our King sing ye.

7 For God is King of all the earth;
with knowledge praise express.

8 God rules the nations: God sits on
his throne of holiness.

9 The princes of the people are
assembled willingly;
Ev'n of the God of Abraham
they who the people be.

For why? the shields that do defend
the earth are only his:
They to the Lord belong; yea, he
exalted greatly is.

Psalm 48

A Song and Psalm for the sons of Korah.

1 GREAT is the Lord, and greatly he
is to be praised still,
Within the city of our God,
upon his holy hill.

2 Mount Sion stands most beautiful,
the joy of all the land;
The city of the mighty King
on her north side doth stand.

3 The Lord within her palaces
is for a refuge known.

4   For, lo, the kings that gather'd were
      together, by have gone.
5   But when they did behold the same,
      they, wond'ring, would not stay;
  But, being troubled at the sight,
      they thence did haste away.

6   Great terror there took hold on them;
      they were possess'd with fear;
  Their grief came like a woman's pain,
      when she a child doth bear.
7   Thou Tarshish ships with east wind
      break'st:
8   As we have heard it told,
  So, in the city of the Lord,
      our eyes did it behold;

  In our God's city, which his hand
      for ever stablish will.
9   We of thy loving-kindness thought,
      Lord, in thy temple still.
10 O Lord, according to thy name,
      through all the earth's thy praise;
  And thy right hand, O Lord, is full
      of righteousness always.

11 Because thy judgments are made known,
      let Sion mount rejoice;
  Of Judah let the daughters all
      send forth a cheerful voice.
12 Walk about Sion, and go round;
      the high tow'rs thereof tell:
13 Consider ye her palaces,
      and mark her bulwarks well;

That ye may tell posterity.
14   For this God doth abide
Our God for evermore; he will
   ev'n unto death us guide.

Psalm 49

To the chief Musician, A Psalm for the sons of Korah.

1   HEAR this, all people, and give ear,
    all in the world that dwell;
2 Both low and high, both rich and poor.
3   My mouth shall wisdom tell:
My heart shall knowledge meditate.
4   I will incline mine ear
To parables, and on the harp
   my sayings dark declare.

5 Amidst those days that evil be,
   why should I, fearing, doubt?
When of my heels th' iniquity
   shall compass me about.
6 Whoe'er they be that in their wealth
   their confidence do pitch,
And boast themselves, because they are
   become exceeding rich:

7 Yet none of these his brother can
   redeem by any way;
Nor can he unto God for him
   sufficient ransom pay,
8 (Their soul's redemption precious is,
   and it can never be,)
9 That still he should for ever live,
   and not corruption see.

10 For why? he seeth that wise men die,
    and brutish fools also
  Do perish; and their wealth, when dead,
    to others they let go.
11 Their inward thought is, that their house
    and dwelling-places shall
  Stand through all ages; they their lands
    by their own names do call.

12 But yet in honour shall not man
    abide continually;
  But passing hence, may be compar'd
    unto the beasts that die.
13 Thus brutish folly plainly is
    their wisdom and their way;
  Yet their posterity approve
    what they do fondly say.

14 Like sheep they in the grave are laid,
    and death shall them devour;
  And in the morning upright men
    shall over them have pow'r:
  Their beauty from their dwelling shall
    consume within the grave.
15 But from hell's hand God will me free,
    for he shall me receive.

16 Be thou not then afraid when one
    enriched thou dost see,
  Nor when the glory of his house
    advanced is on high:
17 For he shall carry nothing hence
    when death his days doth end;

Nor shall his glory after him
    into the grave descend.

18 Although he his own soul did bless
    whilst he on earth did live;
(And when thou to thyself dost well,
    men will thee praises give;)
19 He to his fathers' race shall go,
    they never shall see light.
20 Man honour'd wanting knowledge is
    like beasts that perish quite.

Psalm 50

A Psalm of Asaph.

1 THE mighty God, the Lord,
    hath spoken, and did call
The earth, from rising of the sun,
    to where he hath his fall.
2 From out of Sion hill,
    which of excellency
And beauty the perfection is,
    God shined gloriously.

3 Our God shall surely come,
    keep silence shall not he:
Before him fire shall waste, great storms
    shall round about him be.
4 Unto the heavens clear
    he from above shall call,
And to the earth likewise, that he
    may judge his people all.

5 Together let my saints
    unto me gather'd be,

Those that by sacrifice have made
  a covenant with me.
6 And then the heavens shall
  his righteousness declare:
Because the Lord himself is he
  by whom men judged are.

7 My people Isr'el hear,
  speak will I from on high,
Against thee I will testify;
  God, ev'n thy God, am I.
8 I for thy sacrifice
  no blame will on thee lay,
Nor for burnt-off'rings, which to me
  thou offer'dst ev'ry day.

9 I'll take no calf nor goats
  from house or fold of thine:
10 For beasts of forests, cattle all
  on thousand hills, are mine.
11 The fowls on mountains high
  are all to me well known;
Wild beasts which in the fields do lie,
  ev'n they are all mine own.

12 Then, if I hungry were,
  I would not tell it thee;
Because the world, and fulness all
  thereof, belongs to me.
13 Will I eat flesh of bulls?
  or goats' blood drink will I?
14 Thanks offer thou to God, and pay
  thy vows to the most High.

15 And call upon me when
    in trouble thou shalt be;
I will deliver thee, and thou
    my name shalt glorify.
16 But to the wicked man
    God saith, My laws and truth
Should'st thou declare? how dar'st thou take
    my cov'nant in thy mouth?

17 Sith thou instruction hat'st,
    which should thy ways direct;
And sith my words behind thy back
    thou cast'st, and dost reject.
18 When thou a thief didst see,
    with him thou didst consent;
And with the vile adulterers
    partaker on thou went.

19 Thou giv'st thy mouth to ill,
    thy tongue deceit doth frame;
20 Thou sitt'st, and 'gainst thy brother
        speak'st,
    thy mother's son dost shame.
21 Because I silence kept,
    while thou these things hast wrought;
That I was altogether like
    thyself, hath been thy thought;

Yet I will thee reprove,
    and set before thine eyes,
In order ranked, thy misdeeds,
    and thine iniquities.
22 Now, ye that God forget,
    this carefully consider;

Lest I in pieces tear you all,
    and none can you deliver.

23 Whoso doth offer praise
    me glorifies; and I
Will shew him God's salvation,
    that orders right his way.

Another of the same

1 THE mighty God, the Lord, hath spoke,
    and call'd the earth upon,
Ev'n from the rising of the sun
    unto his going down.
2 From out of Sion, his own hill,
    where the perfection high
Of beauty is, from thence the Lord
    hath shined gloriously.

3 Our God shall come, and shall no more
    be silent, but speak out:
Before him fire shall waste, great storms
    shall compass him about.
4 He to the heavens from above,
    and to the earth below,
Shall call, that he his judgments may
    before his people show.

5 Let all my saints together be
    unto me gathered;
Those that by sacrifice with me
    a covenant have made.
6 And then the heavens shall declare
    his righteousness abroad:
Because the Lord himself doth come;
    none else is judge but God.

7 Hear, O my people, and I'll speak;
      O Israel by name,
   Against thee I will testify;
      God, ev'n thy God, I am.
8 I for thy sacrifices few
      reprove thee never will,
   Nor for burnt-off'rings to have been
      before me offer'd still.

9 I'll take no bullock nor he-goats
      from house nor folds of thine:
10 For beasts of forests, cattle all
      on thousand hills, are mine.
11 The fowls are all to me well known
      that mountains high do yield;
   And I do challenge as mine own
      the wild beasts of the field.

12 If I were hungry, I would not
      to thee for need complain;
   For earth, and all its fulness, doth
      to me of right pertain.
13 That I to eat the flesh of bulls
      take pleasure dost thou think?
   Or that I need, to quench my thirst,
      the blood of goats to drink?

14 Nay, rather unto me, thy God,
      thanksgiving offer thou:
   To the most High perform thy word,
      and fully pay thy vow:
15 And in the day of trouble great
      see that thou call on me;

I will deliver thee, and thou
   my name shalt glorify.

16 But God unto the wicked saith,
   Why should'st thou mention make
Of my commands? how dar'st thou in
   thy mouth my cov'nant take?
17 Sith it is so that thou dost hate
   all good instruction;
And sith thou cast'st behind thy back,
   and slight'st my words each one.

18 When thou a thief didst see, then straight
   thou join'dst with him in sin,
And with the vile adulterers
   thou hast partaker been.
19 Thy mouth to evil thou dost give,
   thy tongue deceit doth frame.
20 Thou sitt'st, and 'gainst thy brother speak'st,
   thy mother's son to shame.

21 These things thou wickedly hast done,
   and I have silent been:
Thou thought'st that I was like thyself,
   and did approve thy sin:
But I will sharply thee reprove,
   and I will order right
Thy sins and thy transgressions
   in presence of thy sight.

22 Consider this, and be afraid,
   ye that forget the Lord,
Lest I in pieces tear you all,
   when none can help afford.

23 Who off'reth praise me glorifies:
    I will shew God's salvation
To him that ordereth aright
    his life and conversation.

Psalm 51

To the chief Musician, A Psalm of David, when Nathan the
prophet came unto him, after he had gone in to Bathsheba.

1 AFTER thy loving-kindness, Lord,
    have mercy upon me:
For thy compassions great, blot out
    all mine iniquity.
2 Me cleanse from sin, and throughly wash
    from mine iniquity:
3 For my transgressions I confess;
    my sin I ever see.

4 'Gainst thee, thee only, have I sinn'd,
    in thy sight done this ill;
That when thou speak'st thou may'st be
          just,
    and clear in judging still.
5 Behold, I in iniquity
    was form'd the womb within;
My mother also me conceiv'd
    in guiltiness and sin.

6 Behold, thou in the inward parts
    with truth delighted art;
And wisdom thou shalt make me know
    within the hidden part.
7 Do thou with hyssop sprinkle me,
    I shall be cleansed so;

Yea, wash thou me, and then I shall
   be whiter than the snow.

8 Of gladness and of joyfulness
    make me to hear the voice;
  That so these very bones which thou
    hast broken may rejoice.
9 All mine iniquities blot out,
    thy face hide from my sin.
10 Create a clean heart, Lord, renew
    a right sp'rit me within.

11 Cast me not from thy sight, nor take
    thy Holy Sp'rit away.
12 Restore me thy salvation's joy;
    with thy free Sp'rit me stay.
13 Then will I teach thy ways unto
    those that transgressors be;
  And those that sinners are shall then
    be turned unto thee.

14 O God, of my salvation God,
    me from blood-guiltiness
  Set free; then shall my tongue aloud
    sing of thy righteousness.
15 My closed lips, O Lord, by thee
    let them be opened;
  Then shall thy praises by my mouth
    abroad be published.

16 For thou desir'st not sacrifice,
    else would I give it thee;
  Nor wilt thou with burnt-offering
    at all delighted be.

17 A broken spirit is to God
 a pleasing sacrifice:
A broken and a contrite heart,
 Lord, thou wilt not despise.

18 Shew kindness, and do good, O Lord,
 to Sion, thine own hill:
The walls of thy Jerusalem
 build up of thy good will.
19 Then righteous off'rings shall thee please,
 and off'rings burnt, which they
With whole burnt-off'rings, and with
   calves,
 shall on thine altar lay.

Psalm 52

*To the chief Musician, Maschil, A Psalm of David, when Doeg the
Edomite came and told Saul, and said unto him, David is come
to the house of Ahimelech.*

1 WHY dost thou boast, O mighty man,
 of mischief and of ill?
The goodness of Almighty God
 endureth ever still.
2 Thy tongue mischievous calumnies
 deviseth subtilely,
Like to a razor sharp to cut,
 working deceitfully.

3 Ill more than good, and more than truth
 thou lovest to speak wrong:
4 Thou lovest all-devouring words,
 O thou deceitful tongue.
5 So God shall thee destroy for aye,
 remove thee, pluck thee out

Quite from thy house, out of the land
  of life he shall thee root.

6 The righteous shall it see, and fear,
  and laugh at him they shall:
7 Lo, this the man is that did not
  make God his strength at all:
But he in his abundant wealth
  his confidence did place;
And he took strength unto himself
  from his own wickedness.

8 But I am in the house of God
  like to an olive green:
My confidence for ever hath
  upon God's mercy been.
9 And I for ever will thee praise,
  because thou hast done this:
I on thy name will wait; for good
  before thy saints it is.

Psalm 53

To the chief Musician upon Mahalath, Maschil,
A Psalm of David.

1 THAT there is not a God, the fool
  doth in his heart conclude:
They are corrupt, their works are vile,
  not one of them doth good.
2 The Lord upon the sons of men
  from heav'n did cast his eyes,
To see if any one there was
  that sought God, and was wise.

3 They altogether filthy are,
  they all are backward gone;

And there is none that doeth good,
    no, not so much as one.
4   These workers of iniquity,
    do they not know at all,
That they my people eat as bread,
    and on God do not call?

5   Ev'n there they were afraid, and stood
    with trembling, all dismay'd,
Whereas there was no cause at all
    why they should be afraid:
For God his bones that thee besieg'd
    hath scatter'd all abroad;
Thou hast confounded them, for they
    despised are of God.

6   Let Isr'el's help from Sion come:
    when back the Lord shall bring
His captives, Jacob shall rejoice,
    and Israel shall sing.

Psalm 54

*To the chief Musician on Neginoth, Maschil, A Psalm of David,
when the Ziphims came and said to Saul, Doth not David hide
himself with us?*

1   SAVE me, O God, by thy great name,
    and judge me by thy strength:
2   My prayer hear, O God; give ear
    unto my words at length.
3   For they that strangers are to me
    do up against me rise;
Oppressors seek my soul, and God
    set not before their eyes.

4   The Lord my God my helper is,
        lo, therefore I am bold:
    He taketh part with ev'ry one
        that doth my soul uphold.
5   Unto mine enemies he shall
        mischief and ill repay:
    O for thy truth's sake cut them off,
        and sweep them clean away.

6   I will a sacrifice to thee
        give with free willingness;
    Thy name, O Lord, because 'tis good,
        with praise I will confess.
7   For he hath me delivered
        from all adversities;
    And his desire mine eye hath seen
        upon mine enemies.

Psalm 55

To the chief Musician on Neginoth, Maschil,
A Psalm of David.

1   LORD, hear my pray'r, hide not thyself
        from my entreating voice:
2   Attend and hear me; in my plaint
        I mourn and make a noise.
3   Because of th' en'my's voice, and for
        lewd men's oppression great:
    On me they cast iniquity,
        and they in wrath me hate.

4   Sore pain'd within me is my heart:
        death's terrors on me fall.
5   On me comes trembling, fear and dread
        o'erwhelmed me withal.

6 O that I, like a dove, had wings,
    said I, then would I flee
Far hence, that I might find a place
    where I in rest might be.

7 Lo, then far off I wander would,
    and in the desert stay;
8 From windy storm and tempest I
    would haste to 'scape away.
9 O Lord, on them destruction bring,
    and do their tongues divide;
For in the city violence
    and strife I have espy'd.

10 They day and night upon the walls
    do go about it round:
There mischief is, and sorrow there
    in midst of it is found.
11 Abundant wickedness there is
    within her inward part;
And from her streets deceitfulness
    and guile do not depart.

12 He was no foe that me reproach'd,
    then that endure I could;
Nor hater that did 'gainst me boast,
    from him me hide I would.
13 But thou, man, who mine equal, guide,
    and mine acquaintance wast:
14 We join'd sweet counsels, to God's house
    in company we past.

15 Let death upon them seize, and down
    let them go quick to hell;

For wickedness doth much abound
    among them where they dwell.
16 I'll call on God: God will me save.
17   I'll pray, and make a noise
At ev'ning, morning, and at noon;
    and he shall hear my voice.

18 He hath my soul delivered,
    that it in peace might be
From battle that against me was;
    for many were with me.
19 The Lord shall hear, and them afflict,
    of old who hath abode:
Because they never changes have,
    therefore they fear not God.

20 'Gainst those that were at peace with him
    he hath put forth his hand:
The covenant that he had made,
    by breaking he profan'd.
21 More smooth than butter were his words,
    while in his heart was war;
His speeches were more soft than oil,
    and yet drawn swords they are.

22 Cast thou thy burden on the Lord,
    and he shall thee sustain;
Yea, he shall cause the righteous man
    unmoved to remain.
23 But thou, O Lord my God, those men
    in justice shalt o'erthrow,
And in destruction's dungeon dark
    at last shalt lay them low:

The bloody and deceitful men
  shall not live half their days:
But upon thee with confidence
  I will depend always.

Psalm 56

*To the chief Musician upon Jonath-elem-rechokim, Michtam of
David, when the Philistines took him in Gath.*

1 SHEW mercy, Lord, to me, for man
  would swallow me outright;
He me oppresseth, while he doth
  against me daily fight.
2 They daily would me swallow up
  that hate me spitefully;
For they be many that do fight
  against me, O most High.

3 When I'm afraid I'll trust in thee:
4   In God I'll praise his word;
I will not fear what flesh can do,
  my trust is in the Lord.
5 Each day they wrest my words; their
      thoughts
  'gainst me are all for ill.
6 They meet, they lurk, they mark my steps,
  waiting my soul to kill.

7 But shall they by iniquity
  escape thy judgments so?
O God, with indignation down
  do thou the people throw.
8 My wand'rings all what they have been
  thou know'st, their number took;

Into thy bottle put my tears:
   are they not in thy book?

9 My foes shall, when I cry, turn back;
    I know't, God is for me.
10 In God his word I'll praise; his word
    in God shall praised be.
11 In God I trust; I will not fear
    what man can do to me.
12 Thy vows upon me are, O God:
    I'll render praise to thee.

13 Wilt thou not, who from death me sav'd,
    my feet from falls keep free,
To walk before God in the light
    of those that living be?

Psalm 57

*To the chief Musician, Al-taschith, Michtam
of David, when he fled from Saul in the cave.*

1 **B**E merciful to me, O God;
    thy mercy unto me
Do thou extend; because my soul
    doth put her trust in thee:
Yea, in the shadow of thy wings
    my refuge I will place,
Until these sad calamities
    do wholly overpass.

2 My cry I will cause to ascend
    unto the Lord most high;
To God, who doth all things for me
    perform most perfectly.

3 From heav'n he shall send down, and me
   from his reproach defend
 That would devour me: God his truth
   and mercy forth shall send.

4 My soul among fierce lions is,
   I firebrands live among,
 Men's sons, whose teeth are spears and
                     darts,
   a sharp sword is their tongue.
5 Be thou exalted very high
   above the heav'ns, O God;
 Let thou thy glory be advanc'd
   o'er all the earth abroad.

6 My soul's bow'd down; for they a net
   have laid, my steps to snare:
 Into the pit which they have digg'd
   for me, they fallen are.
7 My heart is fix'd, my heart is fix'd,
   O God; I'll sing and praise.
8 My glory wake; wake psalt'ry, harp;
   myself I'll early raise.

9 I'll praise thee 'mong the people, Lord;
   'mong nations sing will I:
10 For great to heav'n thy mercy is,
   thy truth is to the sky.
11 O Lord, exalted be thy name
   above the heav'ns to stand:
 Do thou thy glory far advance
   above both sea and land.

Psalm 58

To the chief Musician, Al-taschith, Michtam of David.

1 DO ye, O congregation,
  indeed speak righteousness?
O ye that are the sons of men,
  judge ye with uprightness?

2 Yea, ev'n within your very hearts
  ye wickedness have done;
And ye the vi'lence of your hands
  do weigh the earth upon.

3 The wicked men estranged are,
  ev'n from the very womb;
They, speaking lies, do stray as soon
  as to the world they come.

4 Unto a serpent's poison like
  their poison doth appear;
Yea, they are like the adder deaf,
  that closely stops her ear;

5 That so she may not hear the voice
  of one that charm her would,
No, not though he most cunning were,
  and charm most wisely could.

6 Their teeth, O God, within their mouth
  break thou in pieces small;
The great teeth break thou out, O Lord,
  of these young lions all.

7 Let them like waters melt away,
  which downward still do flow:
In pieces cut his arrows all,
  when he shall bend his bow.

8 Like to a snail that melts away,
    let each of them be gone;
  Like woman's birth untimely, that
    they never see the sun.

9 He shall them take away before
    your pots the thorns can find,
  Both living, and in fury great,
    as with a stormy wind.

10 The righteous, when he vengeance sees,
    he shall be joyful then;
  The righteous one shall wash his feet
    in blood of wicked men.

11 So men shall say, The righteous man
    reward shall never miss:
  And verily upon the earth
    a God to judge there is.

Psalm 59

To the chief Musician, Al-taschith, Michtam of David;
when Saul sent, and they watched the house to kill him.

1 MY God, deliver me from those
    that are mine enemies;
  And do thou me defend from those
    that up against me rise.

2 Do thou deliver me from them
    that work iniquity;
  And give me safety from the men
    of bloody cruelty.

3 For, lo, they for my soul lay wait:
    the mighty do combine
  Against me, Lord; not for my fault,
    nor any sin of mine.

4 They run, and, without fault in me,
    themselves do ready make:
  Awake to meet me with thy help;
    and do thou notice take.

5 Awake therefore, Lord God of hosts,
    thou God of Israel,
  To visit heathen all: spare none
    that wickedly rebel.
6 At ev'ning they go to and fro;
    they make great noise and sound,
  Like to a dog, and often walk
    about the city round.

7 Behold, they belch out with their mouth,
    and in their lips are swords:
  For they do say thus, Who is he
    that now doth hear our words?
8 But thou, O Lord, shalt laugh at them,
    and all the heathen mock.
9 While he's in pow'r I'll wait on thee;
    for God is my high rock.

10 He of my mercy that is God
    betimes shall me prevent;
  Upon mine en'mies God shall let
    me see mine heart's content.
11 Them slay not, lest my folk forget;
    but scatter them abroad
  By thy strong pow'r; and bring them down,
    O thou our shield and God.

12 For their mouth's sin, and for the words
    that from their lips do fly,

Let them be taken in their pride;
    because they curse and lie.
13 In wrath consume them, them consume,
    that so they may not be:
And that in Jacob God doth rule
    to th' earth's ends let them see.

14 At ev'ning let thou them return,
    making great noise and sound,
Like to a dog, and often walk
    about the city round.
15 And let them wander up and down,
    in seeking food to eat;
And let them grudge when they shall not
    be satisfy'd with meat.

16 But of thy pow'r I'll sing aloud;
    at morn thy mercy praise:
For thou to me my refuge wast,
    and tow'r, in troublous days.
17 O God, thou art my strength, I will
    sing praises unto thee;
For God is my defence, a God
    of mercy unto me.

Psalm 60

To the chief Musician upon Shushan-eduth, Michtam of David, to teach; when he strove with Aram-naharaim, and with Aram-zobah, when Joab returned, and smote of Edom in the valley of salt twelve thousand.

1 O LORD, thou hast rejected us,
    and scatter'd us abroad;
Thou justly hast displeased been;
    return to us, O God.

2   The earth to tremble thou hast made;
     therein didst breaches make:
Do thou thereof the breaches heal,
     because the land doth shake.

3   Unto thy people thou hard things
     hast shew'd, and on them sent;
And thou hast caused us to drink
     wine of astonishment.

4   And yet a banner thou hast giv'n
     to them who thee do fear;
That it by them, because of truth,
     displayed may appear.

5   That thy beloved people may
     deliver'd be from thrall,
Save with the pow'r of thy right hand,
     and hear me when I call.

6   God in his holiness hath spoke;
     herein I will take pleasure:
Shechem I will divide, and forth
     will Succoth's valley measure.

7   Gilead I claim as mine by right;
     Manasseh mine shall be;
Ephraim is of mine head the strength;
     Judah gives laws for me;

8   Moab's my washing-pot; my shoe
     I'll over Edom throw;
And over Palestina's land
     I will in triumph go.

9   O who is he will bring me to
     the city fortify'd?

O who is he that to the land
of Edom will me guide?
10 O God, which hadest us cast off,
this thing wilt thou not do?
Ev'n thou, O God, which didest not
forth with our armies go?

11 Help us from trouble; for the help
is vain which man supplies.
12 Through God we'll do great acts; he shall
tread down our enemies.

Psalm 61

To the chief Musician upon Neginoth, A Psalm of David.

1 O GOD, give ear unto my cry;
unto my pray'r attend.
2 From th' utmost corner of the land
my cry to thee I'll send.
What time my heart is overwhelm'd,
and in perplexity,
Do thou me lead unto the Rock
that higher is than I.

3 For thou hast for my refuge been
a shelter by thy pow'r;
And for defence against my foes
thou hast been a strong tow'r.
4 Within thy tabernacle I
for ever will abide;
And under covert of thy wings
with confidence me hide.

5 For thou the vows that I did make,
O Lord my God, didst hear:

Thou hast giv'n me the heritage
    of those thy name that fear.
6 A life prolong'd for many days
    thou to the king shalt give;
Like many generations be
    the years which he shall live.

7 He in God's presence his abode
    for evermore shall have:
O do thou truth and mercy both
    prepare, that may him save.
8 And so will I perpetually
    sing praise unto thy name;
That having made my vows, I may
    each day perform the same.

Psalm 62

To the chief Musician, to Jeduthun, A Psalm of David.

1 MY soul with expectation
    depends on God indeed;
My strength and my salvation doth
    from him alone proceed.
2 He only my salvation is,
    and my strong rock is he:
He only is my sure defence;
    much mov'd I shall not be.

3 How long will ye against a man
    plot mischief? ye shall all
Be slain; ye as a tott'ring fence
    shall be, and bowing wall.
4 They only plot to cast him down
    from his excellency:

They joy in lies; with mouth they bless,
    but they curse inwardly.

5 My soul, wait thou with patience
    upon thy God alone;
On him dependeth all my hope
    and expectation.
6 He only my salvation is,
    and my strong rock is he;
He only is my sure defence:
    I shall not moved be.

7 In God my glory placed is,
    and my salvation sure;
In God the rock is of my strength,
    my refuge most secure.
8 Ye people, place your confidence
    in him continually;
Before him pour ye out your heart;
    God is our refuge high.

9 Surely mean men are vanity,
    and great men are a lie;
In balance laid, they wholly are
    more light than vanity.
10 Trust ye not in oppression,
    in robb'ry be not vain;
On wealth set not your hearts, when as
    increased is your gain.

11 God hath it spoken once to me,
    yea, this I heard again,
That power to Almighty God
    alone doth appertain.

12 Yea, mercy also unto thee
    belongs, O Lord, alone:
For thou according to his work
    rewardest ev'ry one.

Psalm 63

A Psalm of David, when he was in the wilderness of Judah.

1 LORD, thee my God, I'll early seek:
    my soul doth thirst for thee;
My flesh longs in a dry parch'd land,
    wherein no waters be:
2 That I thy power may behold,
    and brightness of thy face,
As I have seen thee heretofore
    within thy holy place.

3 Since better is thy love than life,
    my lips thee praise shall give.
4 I in thy name will lift my hands,
    and bless thee while I live.
5 Ev'n as with marrow and with fat
    my soul shall filled be;
Then shall my mouth with joyful lips
    sing praises unto thee:

6 When I do thee upon my bed
    remember with delight,
And when on thee I meditate
    in watches of the night.
7 In shadow of thy wings I'll joy;
    for thou mine help hast been.
8 My soul thee follows hard; and me
    thy right hand doth sustain.

9   Who seek my soul to spill shall sink
     down to earth's lowest room.
10 They by the sword shall be cut off,
     and foxes' prey become.
11 Yet shall the king in God rejoice,
     and each one glory shall
    That swear by him: but stopp'd shall be
     the mouth of liars all.

Psalm 64

To the chief Musician, A Psalm of David.

1   WHEN I to thee my prayer make,
     Lord, to my voice give ear;
   My life save from the enemy,
     of whom I stand in fear.
2   Me from their secret counsel hide
     who do live wickedly;
   From insurrection of those men
     that work iniquity:

3   Who do their tongues with malice whet,
     and make them cut like swords;
   In whose bent bows are arrows set,
     ev'n sharp and bitter words:
4   That they may at the perfect man
     in secret aim their shot;
   Yea, suddenly they dare at him
     to shoot, and fear it not.

5   In ill encourage they themselves,
     and their snares close do lay:
   Together conference they have;
     Who shall them see? they say.

6 They have search'd out iniquities,
    a perfect search they keep:
Of each of them the inward thought,
    and very heart, is deep.

7 God shall an arrow shoot at them,
    and wound them suddenly:
8 So their own tongue shall them confound;
    all who them see shall fly.
9 And on all men a fear shall fall,
    God's works they shall declare;
For they shall wisely notice take
    what these his doings are.

10 In God the righteous shall rejoice,
    and trust upon his might;
Yea, they shall greatly glory all
    in heart that are upright.

Psalm 65

To the chief Musician, A Psalm and Song of David.

1 PRAISE waits for thee in Sion, Lord:
    to thee vows paid shall be.
2 O thou that hearer art of pray'r,
    all flesh shall come to thee.
3 Iniquities, I must confess,
    prevail against me do:
But as for our transgressions,
    them purge away shalt thou.

4 Bless'd is the man whom thou dost chuse,
    and mak'st approach to thee,
That he within thy courts, O Lord,
    may still a dweller be:

We surely shall be satisfy'd
    with thy abundant grace,
And with the goodness of thy house,
    ev'n of thy holy place.

5   O God of our salvation,
        thou, in thy righteousness,
    By fearful works unto our pray'rs
        thine answer dost express:
    Therefore the ends of all the earth,
        and those afar that be
    Upon the sea, their confidence,
        O Lord, will place in thee.

6   Who, being girt with pow'r, sets fast
        by his great strength the hills.
7   Who noise of seas, noise of their waves,
        and people's tumult, stills.
8   Those in the utmost parts that dwell
        are at thy signs afraid:
    Th' outgoings of the morn and ev'n
        by thee are joyful made.

9   The earth thou visit'st, wat'ring it;
        thou mak'st it rich to grow
    With God's full flood; thou corn prepar'st,
        when thou provid'st it so.
10   Her rigs thou wat'rest plenteously,
        her furrows settelest:
    With show'rs thou dost her mollify,
        her spring by thee is blest.

11   So thou the year most lib'rally
        dost with thy goodness crown;

And all thy paths abundantly
 on us drop fatness down.
12 They drop upon the pastures wide,
 that do in deserts lie;
The little hills on ev'ry side
 rejoice right pleasantly.

13 With flocks the pastures clothed be,
 the vales with corn are clad;
And now they shout and sing to thee,
 for thou hast made them glad.

Psalm 66

To the chief Musician, A Song or Psalm.

1 ALL lands to God in joyful sounds,
 aloft your voices raise.
2 Sing forth the honour of his name,
 and glorious make his praise.
3 Say unto God, How terrible
 in all thy works art thou!
Through thy great pow'r thy foes to thee
 shall be constrain'd to bow.

4 All on the earth shall worship thee,
 they shall thy praise proclaim
In songs: they shall sing cheerfully
 unto thy holy name.
5 Come, and the works that God hath wrought
 with admiration see:
In's working to the sons of men
 most terrible is he.

6 Into dry land the sea he turn'd,
 and they a passage had;

Ev'n marching through the flood on foot,
   there we in him were glad.
7 He ruleth ever by his pow'r;
   his eyes the nations see:
O let not the rebellious ones
   lift up themselves on high.

8 Ye people, bless our God; aloud
   the voice speak of his praise:
9 Our soul in life who safe preserves,
   our foot from sliding stays.
10 For thou didst prove and try us, Lord,
   as men do silver try;
11 Brought'st us into the net, and mad'st
   bands on our loins to lie.

12 Thou hast caus'd men ride o'er our heads;
   and though that we did pass
Through fire and water, yet thou brought'st
   us to a wealthy place.
13 I'll bring burnt-off'rings to thy house;
   to thee my vows I'll pay,
14 Which my lips utter'd, my mouth spake,
   when trouble on me lay.

15 Burnt-sacrifices of fat rams
   with incense I will bring;
Of bullocks and of goats I will
   present an offering.
16 All that fear God, come, hear, I'll tell
   what he did for my soul.
17 I with my mouth unto him cry'd,
   my tongue did him extol.

18 If in my heart I sin regard,
   the Lord me will not hear:
19 But surely God me heard, and to
   my prayer's voice gave ear.
20 O let the Lord, our gracious God,
   for ever blessed be,
   Who turned not my pray'r from him,
   nor yet his grace from me.

Psalm 67

To the chief Musician on Neginoth, A Psalm or Song.

1 LORD, bless and pity us,
   shine on us with thy face:
2 That th' earth thy way, and nations all
   may know thy saving grace.
3 Let people praise thee, Lord;
   let people all thee praise.
4 O let the nations be glad,
   in songs their voices raise:

   Thou'lt justly people judge,
   on earth rule nations all.
5 Let people praise thee, Lord; let them
   praise thee, both great and small.
6 The earth her fruit shall yield,
   our God shall blessing send.
7 God shall us bless; men shall him fear
   unto earth's utmost end.

Another of the same

1 LORD, unto us be merciful,
   do thou us also bless;

And graciously cause shine on us
   the brightness of thy face:
2 That so thy way upon the earth
   to all men may be known;
Also among the nations all
   thy saving health be shown.

3 O let the people praise thee, Lord;
   let people all thee praise.
4 O let the nations be glad,
   and sing for joy always:
For rightly thou shalt people judge,
   and nations rule on earth.
5 Let people praise thee, Lord; let all
   the folk praise thee with mirth.

6 Then shall the earth yield her increase;
   God, our God, bless us shall.
7 God shall us bless; and of the earth
   the ends shall fear him all.

Psalm 68

To the chief Musician, A Psalm or Song of David.

1 LET God arise, and scattered
   let all his en'mies be;
And let all those that do him hate
   before his presence flee.
2 As smoke is driv'n, so drive thou them;
   as fire melts wax away,
Before God's face let wicked men
   so perish and decay.

3 But let the righteous be glad:
   let them before God's sight

Be very joyful; yea, let them
   rejoice with all their might.
4   To God sing, to his name sing praise;
   extol him with your voice,
That rides on heav'n, by his name JAH,
   before his face rejoice.

5   Because the Lord a father is
   unto the fatherless;
God is the widow's judge, within
   his place of holiness.
6   God doth the solitary set
   in fam'lies: and from bands
The chain'd doth free; but rebels do
   inhabit parched lands.

7   O God, what time thou didst go forth
   before thy people's face;
And when through the great wilderness
   thy glorious marching was;
8   Then at God's presence shook the earth,
   then drops from heaven fell;
This Sinai shook before the Lord,
   the God of Israel.

9   O God, thou to thine heritage
   didst send a plenteous rain,
Whereby thou, when it weary was,
   didst it refresh again.
10 Thy congregation then did make
   their habitation there:
Of thine own goodness for the poor,
   O God, thou didst prepare.

11 The Lord himself did give the word,
    the word abroad did spread;
Great was the company of them
    the same who published.
12 Kings of great armies foiled were,
    and forc'd to flee away;
And women, who remain'd at home,
    did distribute the prey.

13 Though ye have lien among the pots,
    like doves ye shall appear,
Whose wings with silver, and with gold
    whose feathers cover'd are.
14 When there th' Almighty scatter'd kings,
    like Salmon's snow 'twas white.
15 God's hill is like to Bashan hill,
    like Bashan hill for height.

16 Why do ye leap, ye mountains high?
    this is the hill where God
Desires to dwell; yea, God in it
    for aye will make abode.
17 God's chariots twenty thousand are,
    thousands of angels strong;
In's holy place God is, as in
    mount Sinai, them among.

18 Thou hast, O Lord, most glorious,
    ascended up on high;
And in triumph victorious led
    captive captivity:
Thou hast received gifts for men,
    for such as did rebel;

Yea, ev'n for them, that God the Lord
    in midst of them might dwell.

19 Bless'd be the Lord, who is to us
    of our salvation God;
Who daily with his benefits
    us plenteously doth load.
20 He of salvation is the God,
    who is our God most strong;
And unto God the Lord from death
    the issues do belong.

21 But surely God shall wound the head
    of those that are his foes;
The hairy scalp of him that still
    on in his trespass goes.
22 God said, My people I will bring
    again from Bashan hill;
Yea, from the sea's devouring depths
    them bring again I will;

23 That in the blood of enemies
    thy foot imbru'd may be,
And of thy dogs dipp'd in the same
    the tongues thou mayest see.
24 Thy goings they have seen, O God;
    the steps of majesty
Of my God, and my mighty King,
    within the sanctuary.

25 Before went singers, players next
    on instruments took way;
And them among the damsels were
    that did on timbrels play.

26 Within the congregations
    bless God with one accord:
From Isr'el's fountain do ye bless
    and praise the mighty Lord.

27 With their prince, little Benjamin,
    princes and council there
Of Judah were, there Zabulon's
    and Napht'li's princes were.
28 Thy God commands thy strength; make
        strong
    what thou wrought'st for us, Lord.
29 For thy house at Jerusalem
    kings shall thee gifts afford.

30 The spearmen's host, the multitude
    of bulls, which fiercely look,
Those calves which people have forth sent,
    O Lord our God, rebuke,
Till ev'ry one submit himself,
    and silver pieces bring:
The people that delight in war
    disperse, O God and King.

31 Those that be princes great shall then
    come out of Egypt lands;
And Ethiopia to God
    shall soon stretch out her hands.
32 O all ye kingdoms of the earth,
    sing praises to this King;
For he is Lord that ruleth all,
    unto him praises sing.

33 To him that rides on heav'ns of heav'ns,
    which he of old did found;

Lo, he sends out his voice, a voice
    in might that doth abound.
34 Strength unto God do ye ascribe;
    for his excellency
Is over Israel, his strength
    is in the clouds most high.

35 Thou'rt from thy temple dreadful, Lord;
    Isr'el's own God is he,
Who gives his people strength and pow'r:
    O let God blessed be.

Psalm 69

To the chief Musician upon Shoshannim, A Psalm of David.

1 SAVE me, O God, because the floods
    do so environ me,
That ev'n unto my very soul
    come in the waters be.
2 I downward in deep mire do sink,
    where standing there is none:
I am into deep waters come,
    where floods have o'er me gone.

3 I weary with my crying am,
    my throat is also dry'd;
Mine eyes do fail, while for my God
    I waiting do abide.
4 Those men that do without a cause
    bear hatred unto me,
Than are the hairs upon my head
    in number more they be:

They that would me destroy, and are
    mine en'mies wrongfully,

Are mighty: so what I took not,
    to render forc'd was I.
5 Lord, thou my folly know'st, my sins
    not cover'd are from thee.
6 Let none that wait on thee be sham'd,
    Lord God of hosts, for me.

O Lord, the God of Israel,
    let none, who search do make,
And seek thee, be at any time
    confounded for my sake.
7 For I have borne reproach for thee,
    my face is hid with shame.
8 To brethren strange, to mother's sons
    an alien I became.

9 Because the zeal did eat me up,
    which to thine house I bear;
And the reproaches cast at thee
    upon me fallen are.
10 My tears and fasts, t' afflict my soul,
    were turned to my shame.
11 When sackcloth I did wear, to them
    a proverb I became.

12 The men that in the gate do sit
    against me evil spake;
They also that vile drunkards were
    of me their song did make.
13 But, in an acceptable time,
    my pray'r, Lord, is to thee:
In truth of thy salvation, Lord,
    and mercy great, hear me.

14 Deliver me out of the mire,
   from sinking do me keep;
   Free me from those that do me hate,
   and from the waters deep.
15 Let not the flood on me prevail,
   whose water overflows;
   Nor deep me swallow, nor the pit
   her mouth upon me close.

16 Hear me, O Lord, because thy love
   and kindness is most good;
   Turn unto me, according to
   thy mercies' multitude.
17 Nor from thy servant hide thy face:
   I'm troubled, soon attend.
18 Draw near my soul, and it redeem;
   me from my foes defend.

19 To thee is my reproach well known,
   my shame, and my disgrace:
   Those that mine adversaries be
   are all before thy face.
20 Reproach hath broke my heart; I'm full
   of grief: I look'd for one
   To pity me, but none I found;
   comforters found I none.

21 They also bitter gall did give
   unto me for my meat:
   They gave me vinegar to drink,
   when as my thirst was great.
22 Before them let their table prove
   a snare; and do thou make

Their welfare and prosperity
   a trap themselves to take.

23 Let thou their eyes so darken'd be,
   that sight may them forsake;
And let their loins be made by thee
   continually to shake.
24 Thy fury pour thou out on them,
   and indignation;
And let thy wrathful anger, Lord,
   fast hold take them upon.

25 All waste and desolate let be
   their habitation;
And in their tabernacles all
   inhabitants be none.
26 Because him they do persecute,
   whom thou didst smite before;
They talk unto the grief of those
   whom thou hast wounded sore.

27 Add thou iniquity unto
   their former wickedness;
And do not let them come at all
   into thy righteousness.
28 Out of the book of life let them
   be raz'd and blotted quite;
Among the just and righteous
   let not their names be writ.

29 But now become exceeding poor
   and sorrowful am I:
By thy salvation, O my God,
   let me be set on high.

30 The name of God I with a song
     most cheerfully will praise;
   And I, in giving thanks to him,
     his name shall highly raise.

31 This to the Lord a sacrifice
     more gracious shall prove
   Than bullock, ox, or any beast
     that hath both horn and hoof.
32 When this the humble men shall see,
     it joy to them shall give:
   O all ye that do seek the Lord,
     your hearts shall ever live.

33 For God the poor hears, and will not
     his prisoners contemn.
34 Let heav'n, and earth, and seas, him praise,
     and all that move in them.
35 For God will Judah's cities build,
     and he will Sion save,
   That they may dwell therein, and it
     in sure possession have.

36 And they that are his servants' seed
     inherit shall the same;
   So shall they have their dwelling there
     that love his blessed name.

Psalm 70

*To the chief Musician, A Psalm of David, to bring to
remembrance.*

1 LORD, haste me to deliver;
   with speed, Lord, succour me.
2 Let them that for my soul do seek
   sham'd and confounded be:

Turn'd back be they, and sham'd,
    that in my hurt delight.
3 Turn'd back be they, Ha, ha! that say,
    their shaming to requite.

4 In thee let all be glad,
    and joy that seek for thee:
Let them who thy salvation love
    say still, God praised be.
5 I poor and needy am;
    come, Lord, and make no stay:
My help thou and deliv'rer art;
    O Lord, make no delay.

Another of the same

1 MAKE haste, O God, me to preserve;
    with speed, Lord, succour me.
2 Let them that for my soul do seek
    sham'd and confounded be:
Let them be turned back, and sham'd,
    that in my hurt delight.
3 Turn'd back be they, Ha, ha! that say,
    their shaming to requite.

4 O Lord, in thee let all be glad,
    and joy that seek for thee:
Let them who thy salvation love
    say still, God praised be.
5 But I both poor and needy am;
    come, Lord, and make no stay:
My help thou and deliv'rer art;
    O Lord, make no delay.

Psalm 71

1 O LORD, my hope and confidence
  is plac'd in thee alone;
Then let thy servant never be
    put to confusion.
2 And let me, in thy righteousness,
    from thee deliv'rance have:
Cause me escape, incline thine ear
    unto me, and me save.

3 Be thou my dwelling-rock, to which
    I ever may resort:
Thou gav'st commandment me to save,
    for thou'rt my rock and fort.
4 Free me, my God, from wicked hands,
    hands cruel and unjust:
5 For thou, O Lord God, art my hope,
    and from my youth my trust.

6 Thou from the womb didst hold me up;
    thou art the same that me
Out of my mother's bowels took;
    I ever will praise thee.
7 To many I a wonder am;
    but thou'rt my refuge strong.
8 Fill'd let my mouth be with thy praise
    and honour all day long.

9 O do not cast me off, when as
    old age doth overtake me;
And when my strength decayed is,
    then do not thou forsake me.
10 For those that are mine enemies
    against me speak with hate;

And they together counsel take
   that for my soul lay wait.

11 They said, God leaves him; him pursue
   and take: none will him save.
12 Be thou not far from me, my God:
   thy speedy help I crave.
13 Confound, consume them, that unto
   my soul are enemies:
Cloth'd be they with reproach and shame
   that do my hurt devise.

14 But I with expectation
   will hope continually;
And yet with praises more and more
   I will thee magnify.
15 Thy justice and salvation
   my mouth abroad shall show,
Ev'n all the day; for I thereof
   the numbers do not know.

16 And I will constantly go on
   in strength of God the Lord;
And thine own righteousness, ev'n thine
   alone, I will record.
17 For even from my youth, O God,
   by thee I have been taught;
And hitherto I have declar'd
   the wonders thou hast wrought.

18 And now, Lord, leave me not, when I
   old and gray-headed grow:
Till to this age thy strength and pow'r
   to all to come I show.

19 And thy most perfect righteousness,
  O Lord, is very high,
Who hast so great things done: O God,
  who is like unto thee?

20 Thou, Lord, who great adversities,
  and sore, to me didst show,
Shalt quicken, and bring me again
  from depths of earth below.
21 My greatness and my pow'r thou wilt
  increase, and far extend:
On ev'ry side against all grief
  thou wilt me comfort send.

22 Thee, ev'n thy truth, I'll also praise,
  my God, with psaltery:
Thou Holy One of Israel,
  with harp I'll sing to thee.
23 My lips shall much rejoice in thee,
  when I thy praises sound;
My soul, which thou redeemed hast,
  in joy shall much abound.

24 My tongue thy justice shall proclaim,
  continuing all day long;
For they confounded are, and sham'd,
  that seek to do me wrong.

Psalm 72

A Psalm for Solomon.

1 O LORD, thy judgments give the king,
  his son thy righteousness.
2 With right he shall thy people judge,
  thy poor with uprightness.

3   The lofty mountains shall bring forth
       unto the people peace;
    Likewise the little hills the same
       shall do by righteousness.

4   The people's poor ones he shall judge,
       the needy's children save;
    And those shall he in pieces break
       who them oppressed have.

5   They shall thee fear, while sun and moon
       do last, through ages all.

6   Like rain on mown grass he shall drop,
       or show'rs on earth that fall.

7   The just shall flourish in his days,
       and prosper in his reign:
    He shall, while doth the moon endure,
       abundant peace maintain.

8   His large and great dominion shall
       from sea to sea extend:
    It from the river shall reach forth
       unto earth's utmost end.

9   They in the wilderness that dwell
       bow down before him must;
    And they that are his enemies
       shall lick the very dust.

10 The kings of Tarshish, and the isles,
       to him shall presents bring;
    And unto him shall offer gifts
       Sheba's and Seba's king.

11 Yea, all the mighty kings on earth
       before him down shall fall;

And all the nations of the world
    do service to him shall.
12 For he the needy shall preserve,
    when he to him doth call;
The poor also, and him that hath
    no help of man at all.

13 The poor man and the indigent
    in mercy he shall spare;
He shall preserve alive the souls
    of those that needy are.
14 Both from deceit and violence
    their soul he shall set free;
And in his sight right precious
    and dear their blood shall be.

15 Yea, he shall live, and giv'n to him
    shall be of Sheba's gold:
For him still shall they pray, and he
    shall daily be extoll'd.
16 Of corn an handful in the earth
    on tops of mountains high,
With prosp'rous fruit shall shake, like trees
    on Lebanon that be.

The city shall be flourishing,
    her citizens abound
In number shall, like to the grass
    that grows upon the ground.
17 His name for ever shall endure;
    last like the sun it shall:
Men shall be bless'd in him, and bless'd
    all nations shall him call.

18 Now blessed be the Lord our God,
    the God of Israel,
  For he alone doth wondrous works,
    in glory that excel.
19 And blessed be his glorious name
    to all eternity:
  The whole earth let his glory fill.
    Amen, so let it be.

The prayers of David the son of Jesse are ended.

Psalm 73

A Psalm of Asaph.

1 YET God is good to Israel,
    to each pure-hearted one.
2 But as for me, my steps near slipp'd,
    my feet were almost gone.
3 For I envious was, and grudg'd
    the foolish folk to see,
  When I perceiv'd the wicked sort
    enjoy prosperity.

4 For still their strength continueth firm;
    their death of bands is free.
5 They are not toil'd like other men,
    nor plagu'd, as others be.
6 Therefore their pride, like to a chain,
    them compasseth about;
  And, as a garment, violence
    doth cover them throughout.

7 Their eyes stand out with fat; they have
    more than their hearts could wish.

8 They are corrupt; their talk of wrong
    both lewd and lofty is.
9 They set their mouth against the heav'ns
    in their blasphemous talk;
  And their reproaching tongue throughout
    the earth at large doth walk.

10 His people oftentimes for this
    look back, and turn about;
  Sith waters of so full a cup
    to these are poured out.
11 And thus they say, How can it be
    that God these things doth know?
  Or, Can there in the Highest be
    knowledge of things below?

12 Behold, these are the wicked ones,
    yet prosper at their will
  In worldly things; they do increase
    in wealth and riches still.
13 I verily have done in vain
    my heart to purify;
  To no effect in innocence
    washed my hands have I.

14 For daily, and all day throughout,
    great plagues I suffer'd have;
  Yea, ev'ry morning I of new
    did chastisement receive.
15 If in this manner foolishly
    to speak I would intend,
  Thy children's generation,
    behold, I should offend.

16 When I this thought to know, it was
    too hard a thing for me;
17 Till to God's sanctuary I went,
    then I their end did see.
18 Assuredly thou didst them set
    a slipp'ry place upon;
Them suddenly thou castedst down
    into destruction.

19 How in a moment suddenly
    to ruin brought are they!
With fearful terrors utterly
    they are consum'd away.
20 Ev'n like unto a dream, when one
    from sleeping doth arise;
So thou, O Lord, when thou awak'st,
    their image shalt despise.

21 Thus grieved was my heart in me,
    and me my reins opprest:
22 So rude was I, and ignorant,
    and in thy sight a beast.
23 Nevertheless continually,
    O Lord, I am with thee:
Thou dost me hold by my right hand,
    and still upholdest me.

24 Thou, with thy counsel, while I live,
    wilt me conduct and guide;
And to thy glory afterward
    receive me to abide.
25 Whom have I in the heavens high
    but thee, O Lord, alone?

And in the earth whom I desire
   besides thee there is none.

26 My flesh and heart doth faint and fail,
   but God doth fail me never:
For of my heart God is the strength
   and portion for ever.
27 For, lo, they that are far from thee
   for ever perish shall;
Them that a whoring from thee go
   thou hast destroyed all.

28 But surely it is good for me
   that I draw near to God:
In God I trust, that all thy works
   I may declare abroad.

Psalm 74

Maschil of Asaph.

1 O GOD, why hast thou cast us off?
   is it for evermore?
Against thy pasture-sheep why doth
   thine anger smoke so sore?
2 O call to thy rememberance
   thy congregation,
Which thou hast purchased of old;
   still think the same upon:

The rod of thine inheritance,
   which thou redeemed hast,
This Sion hill, wherein thou hadst
   thy dwelling in times past.
3 To these long desolations
   thy feet lift, do not tarry;

For all the ills thy foes have done
   within thy sanctuary.

4 Amidst thy congregations
   thine enemies do roar:
They ensigns they set up for signs
   of triumph thee before.
5 A man was famous, and was had
   in estimation,
According as he lifted up
   his axe thick trees upon.

6 But all at once with axes now
   and hammers they go to,
And down the carved work thereof
   they break, and quite undo.
7 They fired have thy sanctuary,
   and have defil'd the same,
By casting down unto the ground
   the place where dwelt thy name.

8 Thus said they in their hearts, Let us
   destroy them out of hand:
They burnt up all the synagogues
   of God within the land.
9 Our signs we do not now behold;
   there is not us among
A prophet more, nor any one
   that knows the time how long.

10 How long, Lord, shall the enemy
   thus in reproach exclaim?
And shall the adversary thus
   always blaspheme thy name?

11 Thy hand, ev'n thy right hand of might,
    why dost thou thus draw back?
O from thy bosom pluck it out
    for our deliv'rance' sake.

12 For certainly God is my King,
    ev'n from the times of old,
Working in midst of all the earth
    salvation manifold.

13 The sea, by thy great pow'r, to part
    asunder thou didst make;
And thou the dragons' heads, O Lord,
    within the waters brake.

14 The leviathan's head thou brak'st
    in pieces, and didst give
Him to be meat unto the folk
    in wilderness that live.

15 Thou clav'st the fountain and the flood,
    which did with streams abound:
Thou dry'dst the mighty waters up
    unto the very ground.

16 Thine only is the day, O Lord,
    thine also is the night;
And thou alone prepared hast
    the sun and shining light.

17 By thee the borders of the earth
    were settled ev'ry where:
The summer and the winter both
    by thee created were.

18 That th' enemy reproached hath,
    O keep it in record;

And that the foolish people have
    blasphem'd thy name, O Lord.
19 Unto the multitude do not
    thy turtle's soul deliver:
The congregation of thy poor
    do not forget for ever.

20 Unto thy cov'nant have respect;
    for earth's dark places be
Full of the habitations
    of horrid cruelty.
21 O let not those that be oppress'd
    return again with shame:
Let those that poor and needy are
    give praise unto thy name.

22 Do thou, O God, arise and plead
    the cause that is thine own:
Remember how thou art reproach'd
    still by the foolish one.
23 Do not forget the voice of those
    that are thine enemies:
Of those the tumult ever grows
    that do against thee rise.

Psalm 75

To the chief Musician, Al-taschith, A Psalm or Song of Asaph.

1 TO thee, O God, do we give thanks,
    we do give thanks to thee;
Because thy wondrous works declare
    thy great name near to be.
2 I purpose, when I shall receive
    the congregation,

That I shall judgment uprightly
   render to ev'ry one.

3   Dissolved is the land, with all
      that in the same do dwell;
But I the pillars thereof do
      bear up, and stablish well.
4   I to the foolish people said,
      Do not deal foolishly;
And unto those that wicked are,
      Lift not your horn on high.

5   Lift not your horn on high, nor speak
6   with stubborn neck. But know,
That not from east, nor west, nor south,
      promotion doth flow.
7   But God is judge; he puts down one,
      and sets another up.
8   For in the hand of God most high
      of red wine is a cup:

'Tis full of mixture, he pours forth,
      and makes the wicked all
Wring out the bitter dregs thereof;
      yea, and they drink them shall.
9   But I for ever will declare,
      I Jacob's God will praise.
10 All horns of lewd men I'll cut off;
      but just men's horns will raise.

Psalm 76

To the chief Musician on Neginoth, A Psalm or Song of Asaph.

1   IN Judah's land God is well known,
      his name's in Isr'el great:

2 In Salem is his tabernacle,
     in Sion is his seat.
3 There arrows of the bow he brake,
     the shield, the sword, the war.
4 More glorious thou than hills of prey,
     more excellent art far.

5 Those that were stout of heart are spoil'd,
     they slept their sleep outright;
   And none of those their hands did find,
     that were the men of might.
6 When thy rebuke, O Jacob's God,
     had forth against them past,
   Their horses and their chariots both
     were in a dead sleep cast.

7 Thou, Lord, ev'n thou art he that should
     be fear'd; and who is he
   That may stand up before thy sight,
     if once thou angry be?
8 From heav'n thou judgment caus'd be heard;
     the earth was still with fear,
9 When God to judgment rose, to save
     all meek on earth that were.

10 Surely the very wrath of man
     unto thy praise redounds:
   Thou to the remnant of his wrath
     wilt set restraining bounds.
11 Vow to the Lord your God, and pay:
     all ye that near him be,
   Bring gifts and presents unto him;
     for to be fear'd is he.

12 By him the sp'rits shall be cut off
    of those that princes are:
  Unto the kings that are on earth
    he fearful doth appear.

Psalm 77

To the chief Musician, to Jeduthun, A Psalm of Asaph.

1 UNTO the Lord I with my voice,
    I unto God did cry;
  Ev'n with my voice, and unto me
    his ear he did apply.
2 I in my trouble sought the Lord,
    my sore by night did run,
  And ceased not; my grieved soul
    did consolation shun.

3 I to remembrance God did call,
    yet trouble did remain;
  And overwhelm'd my spirit was,
    whilst I did sore complain.
4 Mine eyes, debarr'd from rest and sleep,
    thou makest still to wake;
  My trouble is so great that I
    unable am to speak.

5 The days of old to mind I call'd,
    and oft did think upon
  The times and ages that are past
    full many years agone.
6 By night my song I call to mind,
    and commune with my heart;
  My sp'rit did carefully enquire
    how I might ease my smart.

7 For ever will the Lord cast off,
    and gracious be no more?
8 For ever is his mercy gone?
    fails his word evermore?
9 Is't true that to be gracious
    the Lord forgotten hath?
  And that his tender mercies he
    hath shut up in his wrath?

10 Then did I say, That surely this
    is mine infirmity:
  I'll mind the years of the right hand
    of him that is most High.
11 Yea, I remember will the works
    performed by the Lord:
  The wonders done of old by thee
    I surely will record.

12 I also will of all thy works
    my meditation make;
  And of thy doings to discourse
    great pleasure I will take.
13 O God, thy way most holy is
    within thy sanctuary;
  And what God is so great in pow'r
    as is our God most high?

14 Thou art the God that wonders dost
    by thy right hand most strong:
  Thy mighty pow'r thou hast declar'd
    the nations among.
15 To thine own people with thine arm
    thou didst redemption bring;

To Jacob's sons, and to the tribes
  of Joseph that do spring.

16 The waters, Lord, perceived thee,
  the waters saw thee well;
And they for fear aside did flee;
  the depths on trembling fell.
17 The clouds in water forth were pour'd,
  sound loudly did the sky;
And swiftly through the world abroad
  thine arrows fierce did fly.

18 Thy thunder's voice alongst the heav'n
  a mighty noise did make;
By lightnings lighten'd was the world,
  th' earth tremble did and shake.
19 Thy way is in the sea, and in
  the waters great thy path;
Yet are thy footsteps hid, O Lord;
  none knowledge thereof hath.

20 Thy people thou didst safely lead,
  like to a flock of sheep;
By Moses' hand and Aaron's thou
  didst them conduct and keep.

Psalm 78

Maschil of Asaph.

1 ATTEND, my people, to my law;
  thereto give thou an ear;
The words that from my mouth proceed
  attentively do hear.
2 My mouth shall speak a parable,
  and sayings dark of old;

3 The same which we have heard and known,
    and us our fathers told.

4 We also will them not conceal
    from their posterity;
Them to the generation
    to come declare will we:
The praises of the Lord our God,
    and his almighty strength,
The wondrous works that he hath done,
    we will shew forth at length.

5 His testimony and his law
    in Isr'el he did place,
And charg'd our fathers it to show
    to their succeeding race;
6 That so the race which was to come
    might well them learn and know;
And sons unborn, who should arise,
    might to their sons them show:

7 That they might set their hope in God,
    and suffer not to fall
His mighty works out of their mind,
    but keep his precepts all:
8 And might not, like their fathers, be
    a stiff rebellious race;
A race not right in heart; with God
    whose sp'rit not stedfast was.

9 The sons of Ephraim, who nor bows
    nor other arms did lack,
When as the day of battle was,
    they faintly turned back.

10 They brake God's cov'nant, and refus'd
    in his commands to go;
11 His works and wonders they forgot,
    which he to them did show.

12 Things marvellous he brought to pass;
    their fathers them beheld
Within the land of Egypt done,
    yea, ev'n in Zoan's field.
13 By him divided was the sea,
    he caus'd them through to pass;
And made the waters so to stand,
    as like an heap it was.

14 With cloud by day, with light of fire
    all night, he did them guide.
15 In desert rocks he clave, and drink,
    as from great depths, supply'd.
16 He from the rock brought streams, like floods
    made waters to run down.
17 Yet sinning more, in desert they
    provok'd the highest One.

18 For in their heart they tempted God,
    and, speaking with mistrust,
They greedily did meat require
    to satisfy their lust.
19 Against the Lord himself they spake,
    and, murmuring, said thus,
A table in the wilderness
    can God prepare for us?

20 Behold, he smote the rock, and thence
    came streams and waters great;

But can he give his people bread?
   and send them flesh to eat?
21 The Lord did hear, and waxed wroth;
   so kindled was a flame
'Gainst Jacob, and 'gainst Israel
   up indignation came.

22 For they believ'd not God, nor trust
   in his salvation had;
23 Though clouds above he did command,
   and heav'n's doors open made,
24 And manna rain'd on them, and gave
   them corn of heav'n to eat.
25 Man angels' food did eat; to them
   he to the full sent meat.

26 And in the heaven he did cause
   an eastern wind to blow;
And by his power he let out
   the southern wind to go.
27 Then flesh as thick as dust he made
   to rain down them among;
And feather'd fowls, like as the sand
   which li'th the shore along.

28 At his command amidst their camp
   these show'rs of flesh down fell,
All round about the tabernacles
   and tents where they did dwell.
29 So they did eat abundantly,
   and had of meat their fill;
For he did give to them what was
   their own desire and will.

30 They from their lust had not estrang'd
    their heart and their desire;
  But while the meat was in their mouths,
    which they did so require,
31 God's wrath upon them came, and slew
    the fattest of them all;
  So that the choice of Israel,
    o'erthrown by death, did fall.

32 Yet, notwithstanding of all this,
    they sinned still the more;
  And though he had great wonders wrought,
    believ'd him not therefore:
33 Wherefore their days in vanity
    he did consume and waste;
  And by his wrath their wretched years
    away in trouble past.

34 But when he slew them, then they did
    to seek him shew desire;
  Yea, they return'd, and after God
    right early did enquire.
35 And that the Lord had been their Rock,
    they did remember then;
  Ev'n that the high almighty God
    had their Redeemer been.

36 Yet with their mouth they flatter'd him,
    and spake but feignedly;
  And they unto the God of truth
    with their false tongues did lie.
37 For though their words were good, their
                        heart
    with him was not sincere;

Unstedfast and perfidious
  they in his cov'nant were.

38 But, full of pity, he forgave
    their sin, them did not slay;
  Nor stirr'd up all his wrath, but oft
    his anger turn'd away.
39 For that they were but fading flesh
    to mind he did recall;
  A wind that passeth soon away,
    and not returns at all.

40 How often did they him provoke
    within the wilderness!
  And in the desert did him grieve
    with their rebelliousness!
41 Yea, turning back, they tempted God,
    and limits set upon
  Him, who in midst of Isr'el is
    the only Holy One.

42 They did not call to mind his pow'r,
    nor yet the day when he
  Deliver'd them out of the hand
    of their fierce enemy;
43 Nor how great signs in Egypt land
    he openly had wrought;
  What miracles in Zoan's field
    his hand to pass had brought.

44 How lakes and rivers ev'ry where
    he turned into blood;
  So that nor man nor beast could drink
    of standing lake or flood.

45 He brought among them swarms of flies,
    which did them sore annoy;
  And divers kinds of filthy frogs
    he sent them to destroy.

46 He to the caterpillar gave
    the fruits of all their soil;
  Their labours he deliver'd up
    unto the locusts' spoil.
47 Their vines with hail, their sycamores
    he with the frost did blast:
48 Their beasts to hail he gave; their flocks
    hot thunderbolts did waste.

49 Fierce burning wrath he on them cast,
    and indignation strong,
  And troubles sore, by sending forth
    ill angels them among.
50 He to his wrath made way; their soul
    from death he did not save;
  But over to the pestilence
    the lives of them he gave.

51 In Egypt land the first-born all
    he smote down ev'ry where;
  Among the tents of Ham, ev'n these
    chief of their strength that were.
52 But his own people, like to sheep,
    thence to go forth he made;
  And he, amidst the wilderness,
    them, as a flock, did lead.

53 And he them safely on did lead,
    so that they did not fear;

Whereas their en'mies by the sea
    quite overwhelmed were.
54 To borders of his sanctuary
    the Lord his people led,
Ev'n to the mount which his right hand
    for them had purchased.

55 The nations of Canaan,
    by his almighty hand,
Before their face he did expel
    out of their native land;
Which for inheritance to them
    by line he did divide,
And made the tribes of Israel
    within their tents abide.

56 Yet God most high they did provoke,
    and tempted ever still;
And to observe his testimonies
    did not incline their will:
57 But, like their fathers, turned back,
    and dealt unfaithfully:
Aside they turned, like a bow
    that shoots deceitfully.

58 For they to anger did provoke
    him with their places high;
And with their graven images
    mov'd him to jealousy.
59 When God heard this, he waxed wroth,
    and much loath'd Isr'el then:
60 So Shiloh's tent he left, the tent
    which he had plac'd with men.

61 And he his strength delivered
    into captivity;
  He left his glory in the hand
    of his proud enemy.
62 His people also he gave o'er
    unto the sword's fierce rage:
  So sore his wrath inflamed was
    against his heritage.

63 The fire consum'd their choice young men;
    their maids no marriage had;
64 And when their priests fell by the sword,
    their wives no mourning made.
65 But then the Lord arose, as one
    that doth from sleep awake;
  And like a giant that, by wine
    refresh'd, a shout doth make:

66 Upon his en'mies' hinder parts
    he made his stroke to fall;
  And so upon them he did put
    a shame perpetual.
67 Moreover, he the tabernacle
    of Joseph did refuse;
  The mighty tribe of Ephraim
    he would in no wise chuse:

68 But he did chuse Jehudah's tribe
    to be the rest above;
  And of mount Sion he made choice,
    which he so much did love.
69 And he his sanctuary built
    like to a palace high,

Like to the earth which he did found
    to perpetuity.

70 Of David, that his servant was,
    he also choice did make,
And even from the folds of sheep
    was pleased him to take:
71 From waiting on the ewes with young,
    he brought him forth to feed
Israel, his inheritance,
    his people, Jacob's seed.

72 So after the integrity
    he of his heart them fed;
And by the good skill of his hands
    them wisely governed.

Psalm 79

A Psalm of Asaph.

1 O GOD, the heathen enter'd have
    thine heritage; by them
Defiled is thy house: on heaps
    they laid Jerusalem.
2 The bodies of thy servants they
    have cast forth to be meat
To rav'nous fowls; thy dear saints' flesh
    they gave to beasts to eat.

3 Their blood about Jerusalem
    like water they have shed;
And there was none to bury them
    when they were slain and dead.
4 Unto our neighbours a reproach
    most base become are we;

A scorn and laughingstock to them
   that round about us be.

5   How long, Lord, shall thine anger last?
     wilt thou still keep the same?
   And shall thy fervent jealousy
     burn like unto a flame?
6   On heathen pour thy fury forth,
     that have thee never known,
   And on those kingdoms which thy name
     have never call'd upon.

7   For these are they who Jacob have
     devoured cruelly;
   And they his habitation
     have caused waste to lie.
8   Against us mind not former sins;
     thy tender mercies show;
   Let them prevent us speedily,
     for we're brought very low.

9   For thy name's glory help us, Lord,
     who hast our Saviour been:
   Deliver us; for thy name's sake,
     O purge away our sin.
10 Why say the heathen, Where's their God?
     let him to them be known;
   When those who shed thy servants' blood
     are in our sight o'erthrown.

11 O let the pris'ner's sighs ascend
     before thy sight on high;
   Preserve those in thy mighty pow'r
     that are design'd to die.

12 And to our neighbours' bosom cause
    it sev'nfold render'd be,
Ev'n the reproach wherewith they have,
    O Lord, reproached thee.

13 So we thy folk, and pasture-sheep,
    shall give thee thanks always;
And unto generations all
    we will shew forth thy praise.

Psalm 80

To the chief Musician upon Shoshannim-Eduth, A Psalm of
Asaph.

1 HEAR, Isr'el's Shepherd! like a flock
    thou that dost Joseph guide;
Shine forth, O thou that dost between
    the cherubims abide.
2 In Ephraim's, and Benjamin's,
    and in Manasseh's sight,
O come for our salvation;
    stir up thy strength and might.

3 Turn us again, O Lord our God,
    and upon us vouchsafe
To make thy countenance to shine,
    and so we shall be safe.
4 O Lord of hosts, almighty God,
    how long shall kindled be
Thy wrath against the prayer made
    by thine own folk to thee?

5 Thou tears of sorrow giv'st to them
    instead of bread to eat;
Yea, tears instead of drink thou giv'st
    to them in measure great.

6   Thou makest us a strife unto
      our neighbours round about;
  Our enemies among themselves
      at us do laugh and flout.

7   Turn us again, O God of hosts,
      and upon us vouchsafe
  To make thy countenance to shine,
      and so we shall be safe.

8   A vine from Egypt brought thou hast,
      by thine outstretched hand;
  And thou the heathen out didst cast,
      to plant it in their land.

9   Before it thou a room didst make,
      where it might grow and stand;
  Thou causedst it deep root to take,
      and it did fill the land.

10 The mountains vail'd were with its shade,
      as with a covering;
  Like goodly cedars were the boughs
      which out from it did spring.

11 Upon the one hand to the sea
      her boughs she did out send;
  On th' other side unto the flood
      her branches did extend.

12 Why hast thou then thus broken down,
      and ta'en her hedge away?
  So that all passengers do pluck,
      and make of her a prey.

13 The boar who from the forest comes
      doth waste it at his pleasure;

The wild beast of the field also
    devours it out of measure.
14 O God of hosts, we thee beseech,
    return now unto thine;
Look down from heav'n in love, behold,
    and visit this thy vine:

15 This vineyard, which thine own right hand
    hath planted us among;
And that same branch, which for thyself
    thou hast made to be strong.
16 Burnt up it is with flaming fire,
    it also is cut down:
They utterly are perished,
    when as thy face doth frown.

17 O let thy hand be still upon
    the Man of thy right hand,
The Son of man, whom for thyself
    thou madest strong to stand.
18 So henceforth we will not go back,
    nor turn from thee at all:
O do thou quicken us, and we
    upon thy name will call.

19 Turn us again, Lord God of hosts,
    and upon us vouchsafe
To make thy countenance to shine,
    and so we shall be safe.

Psalm 81

To the chief Musician upon Gittith, A Psalm of Asaph.

1   SING loud to God our strength; with joy
    to Jacob's God do sing.

2 Take up a psalm, the pleasant harp,
   timbrel and psalt'ry bring.
3 Blow trumpets at new-moon, what day
   our feast appointed is:
4 For charge to Isr'el, and a law
   of Jacob's God was this.

5 To Joseph this a testimony
   he made, when Egypt land
He travell'd through, where speech I heard
   I did not understand.
6 His shoulder I from burdens took,
   his hands from pots did free.
7 Thou didst in trouble on me call,
   and I deliver'd thee:

In secret place of thundering
   I did thee answer make;
And at the streams of Meribah
   of thee a proof did take.
8 O thou, my people, give an ear,
   I'll testify to thee;
To thee, O Isr'el, if thou wilt
   but hearken unto me.

9 In midst of thee there shall not be
   any strange god at all;
Nor unto any god unknown
   thou bowing down shalt fall.
10 I am the Lord thy God, which did
   from Egypt land thee guide;
I'll fill thy mouth abundantly,
   do thou it open wide.

11 But yet my people to my voice
   would not attentive be;
   And ev'n my chosen Israel
   he would have none of me.
12 So to the lust of their own hearts
   I them delivered;
   And then in counsels of their own
   they vainly wandered.

13 O that my people had me heard,
   Isr'el my ways had chose!
14 I had their en'mies soon subdu'd,
   my hand turn'd on their foes.
15 The haters of the Lord to him
   submission should have feign'd;
   But as for them, their time should have
   for evermore remain'd.

16 He should have also fed them with
   the finest of the wheat;
   Of honey from the rock thy fill
   I should have made thee eat.

Psalm 82

A Psalm of Asaph.

1 IN gods' assembly God doth stand;
   he judgeth gods among.
2 How long, accepting persons vile,
   will ye give judgment wrong?
3 Defend the poor and fatherless;
   to poor oppress'd do right.
4 The poor and needy ones set free;
   rid them from ill men's might.

5 They know not, nor will understand;
in darkness they walk on:
All the foundations of the earth
out of their course are gone.

6 I said that ye are gods, and are
sons of the Highest all:

7 But ye shall die like men, and as
one of the princes fall.

8 O God, do thou raise up thyself,
the earth to judgment call:
For thou, as thine inheritance,
shalt take the nations all.

Psalm 83

A Song or Psalm of Asaph.

1 KEEP not, O God, we thee entreat,
O keep not silence now:
Do thou not hold thy peace, O God,
and still no more be thou.

2 For, lo, thine enemies a noise
tumultuously have made;
And they that haters are of thee
have lifted up the head.

3 Against thy chosen people they
do crafty counsel take;
And they against thy hidden ones
do consultations make.

4 Come, let us cut them off, said they,
from being a nation,
That of the name of Isr'el may
no more be mention.

5 For with joint heart they plot, in league
    against thee they combine.
6 The tents of Edom, Ishm'elites,
    Moab's and Hagar's line;
7 Gebal, and Ammon, Amalek,
    Philistines, those of Tyre;
8 And Assur join'd with them, to help
    Lot's children they conspire.

9 Do to them as to Midian,
    Jabin at Kison strand;
10 And Sis'ra, which at En-dor fell,
    as dung to fat the land.
11 Like Oreb and like Zeeb make
    their noble men to fall;
    Like Zeba and Zalmunna like,
    make thou their princes all;

12 Who said, For our possession
    let us God's houses take.
13 My God, them like a wheel, as chaff
    before the wind, them make.
14 As fire consumes the wood, as flame
    doth mountains set on fire,
15 Chase and affright them with the storm
    and tempest of thine ire.

16 Their faces fill with shame, O Lord,
    that they may seek thy name.
17 Let them confounded be, and vex'd,
    and perish in their shame:
18 That men may know that thou, to whom
    alone doth appertain
    The name JEHOVAH, dost most high
    o'er all the earth remain.

Psalm 84

To the chief Musician upon Gittith, A Psalm for the sons of Korah.

1 HOW lovely is thy dwelling-place,
   O Lord of hosts, to me!
 The tabernacles of thy grace
   how pleasant, Lord, they be!
2 My thirsty soul longs veh'mently,
   yea faints, thy courts to see:
 My very heart and flesh cry out,
   O living God, for thee.

3 Behold, the sparrow findeth out
   an house wherein to rest;
 The swallow also for herself
   hath purchased a nest;
 Ev'n thine own altars, where she safe
   her young ones forth may bring,
 O thou almighty Lord of hosts,
   who art my God and King.

4 Bless'd are they in thy house that dwell,
   they ever give thee praise.
5 Bless'd is the man whose strength thou art,
   in whose heart are thy ways:
6 Who passing thorough Baca's vale,
   therein do dig up wells;
 Also the rain that falleth down
   the pools with water fills.

7 So they from strength unwearied go
   still forward unto strength,
 Until in Zion they appear
   before the Lord at length.

8 Lord God of hosts, my prayer hear;
   O Jacob's God, give ear.
9 See God our shield, look on the face
   of thine anointed dear.

10 For in thy courts one day excels
   a thousand; rather in
My God's house will I keep a door,
   than dwell in tents of sin.
11 For God the Lord's a sun and shield:
   he'll grace and glory give;
And will withhold no good from them
   that uprightly do live.

12 O thou that art the Lord of hosts,
   that man is truly blest,
Who by assured confidence
   on thee alone doth rest.

Psalm 85

To the chief Musician, A Psalm for the sons of Korah.

1 O LORD, thou hast been favourable
   to thy beloved land:
Jacob's captivity thou hast
   recall'd with mighty hand.
2 Thou pardoned thy people hast
   all their iniquities;
Thou all their trespasses and sins
   hast cover'd from thine eyes.

3 Thou took'st off all thine ire, and turn'dst
   from thy wrath's furiousness.
4 Turn us, God of our health, and cause
   thy wrath 'gainst us to cease.

5 Shall thy displeasure thus endure
    against us without end?
Wilt thou to generations all
    thine anger forth extend?

6 That in thee may thy people joy,
    wilt thou not us revive?
7 Shew us thy mercy, Lord, to us
    do thy salvation give.
8 I'll hear what God the Lord will speak:
    to his folk he'll speak peace,
And to his saints; but let them not
    return to foolishness.

9 To them that fear him surely near
    is his salvation;
That glory in our land may have
    her habitation.
10 Truth met with mercy, righteousness
    and peace kiss'd mutually:
11 Truth springs from earth, and righteousness
    looks down from heaven high.

12 Yea, what is good the Lord shall give;
    our land shall yield increase:
13 Justice, to set us in his steps,
    shall go before his face.

Psalm 86

A Prayer of David.

1 O LORD, do thou bow down thine ear,
    and hear me graciously;
Because I sore afflicted am,
    and am in poverty.

2   Because I'm holy, let my soul
     by thee preserved be:
  O thou my God, thy servant save,
     that puts his trust in thee.

3   Sith unto thee I daily cry,
     be merciful to me.
4   Rejoice thy servant's soul; for, Lord,
     I lift my soul to thee.
5   For thou art gracious, O Lord,
     and ready to forgive;
  And rich in mercy, all that call
     upon thee to relieve.

6   Hear, Lord, my pray'r; unto the voice
     of my request attend:
7   In troublous times I'll call on thee;
     for thou wilt answer send.
8   Lord, there is none among the gods
     that may with thee compare;
  And like the works which thou hast done,
     not any work is there.

9   All nations whom thou mad'st shall come
     and worship rev'rently
  Before thy face; and they, O Lord,
     thy name shall glorify.
10 Because thou art exceeding great,
     and works by thee are done
  Which are to be admir'd; and thou
     art God thyself alone.

11 Teach me thy way, and in thy truth,
     O Lord, then walk will I;

Unite my heart, that I thy name
  may fear continually.
12 O Lord my God, with all my heart
  to thee I will give praise;
And I the glory will ascribe
  unto thy name always:

13 Because thy mercy toward me
  in greatness doth excel;
And thou deliver'd hast my soul
  out from the lowest hell.
14 O God, the proud against me rise,
  and vi'lent men have met,
That for my soul have sought; and thee
  before them have not set.

15 But thou art full of pity, Lord,
  a God most gracious,
Long-suffering, and in thy truth
  and mercy plenteous.
16 O turn to me thy countenance,
  and mercy on me have;
Thy servant strengthen, and the son
  of thine own handmaid save.

17 Shew me a sign for good, that they
  which do me hate may see,
And be asham'd; because thou, Lord,
  didst help and comfort me.

Psalm 87

A Psalm or Song for the sons of Korah.

1 UPON the hills of holiness
  he his foundation sets.

2   God, more than Jacob's dwellings all,
      delights in Sion's gates.
3   Things glorious are said of thee,
      thou city of the Lord.
4   Rahab and Babel I, to those
      that know me, will record:

Behold ev'n Tyrus, and with it
      the land of Palestine,
And likewise Ethiopia;
      this man was born therein.
5   And it of Sion shall be said,
      This man and that man there
Was born; and he that is most High
      himself shall stablish her.

6   When God the people writes, he'll count
      that this man born was there.
7   There be that sing and play; and all
      my well-springs in thee are.

Psalm 88

*A Song or Psalm for the sons of Korah, to the chief Musician
upon Mahalath Leannoth, Maschil of Heman the Ezrahite.*

1   L ORD God, my Saviour, day and night
      before thee cry'd have I.
2   Before thee let my prayer come;
      give ear unto my cry.
3   For troubles great do fill my soul;
      my life draws nigh the grave.
4   I'm counted with those that go down
      to pit, and no strength have.

5   Ev'n free among the dead, like them
      that slain in grave do lie;

Cut off from thy hand, whom no more
    thou hast in memory.
6   Thou hast me laid in lowest pit,
    in deeps and darksome caves.
7   Thy wrath lies hard on me, thou hast
    me press'd with all thy waves.

8   Thou hast put far from me my friends,
    thou mad'st them to abhor me;
And I am so shut up, that I
    find no evasion for me.
9   By reason of affliction
    mine eye mourns dolefully:
To thee, Lord, do I call, and stretch
    my hands continually.

10 Wilt thou shew wonders to the dead?
    shall they rise, and thee bless?
11 Shall in the grave thy love be told?
    in death thy faithfulness?
12 Shall thy great wonders in the dark,
    or shall thy righteousness
Be known to any in the land
    of deep forgetfulness?

13 But, Lord, to thee I cry'd; my pray'r
    at morn prevent shall thee.
14 Why, Lord, dost thou cast off my soul,
    and hid'st thy face from me?
15 Distress'd am I, and from my youth
    I ready am to die;
Thy terrors I have borne, and am
    distracted fearfully.

16 The dreadful fierceness of thy wrath
    quite over me doth go:
Thy terrors great have cut me off,
    they did pursue me so.
17 For round about me ev'ry day,
    like water, they did roll;
And, gathering together, they
    have compassed my soul.

18 My friends thou hast put far from me,
    and him that did me love;
And those that mine acquaintance were
    to darkness didst remove.

Psalm 89

Maschil of Ethan the Ezrahite.

1 GOD'S mercies I will ever sing;
    and with my mouth I shall
Thy faithfulness make to be known
    to generations all.
2 For mercy shall be built, said I,
    for ever to endure;
Thy faithfulness, ev'n in the heav'ns,
    thou wilt establish sure.

3 I with my chosen One have made
    a cov'nant graciously;
And to my servant, whom I lov'd,
    to David sworn have I;
4 That I thy seed establish shall
    for ever to remain,
And will to generations all
    thy throne build and maintain.

5   The praises of thy wonders, Lord,
      the heavens shall express;
    And in the congregation
      of saints thy faithfulness.
6   For who in heaven with the Lord
      may once himself compare?
    Who is like God among the sons
      of those that mighty are?

7   Great fear in meeting of the saints
      is due unto the Lord;
    And he of all about him should
      with rev'rence be ador'd.
8   O thou that art the Lord of hosts,
      what Lord in mightiness
    Is like to thee? who compass'd round
      art with thy faithfulness.

9   Ev'n in the raging of the sea
      thou over it dost reign;
    And when the waves thereof do swell,
      thou stillest them again.
10 Rahab in pieces thou didst break,
      like one that slaughter'd is;
    And with thy mighty arm thou hast
      dispers'd thine enemies.

11 The heav'ns are thine, thou for thine own
      the earth dost also take;
    The world, and fulness of the same,
      thy pow'r did found and make.
12 The north and south from thee alone
      their first beginning had;

Both Tabor mount and Hermon hill
   shall in thy name be glad.

13 Thou hast an arm that's full of pow'r,
   thy hand is great in might;
And thy right hand exceedingly
   exalted is in height.
14 Justice and judgment of thy throne
   are made the dwelling-place;
Mercy, accompany'd with truth,
   shall go before thy face.

15 O greatly bless'd the people are
   the joyful sound that know;
In brightness of thy face, O Lord,
   they ever on shall go.
16 They in thy name shall all the day
   rejoice exceedingly;
And in thy righteousness shall they
   exalted be on high.

17 Because the glory of their strength
   doth only stand in thee;
And in thy favour shall our horn
   and pow'r exalted be.
18 For God is our defence; and he
   to us doth safety bring:
The Holy One of Israel
   is our almighty King.

19 In vision to thy Holy One
   thou saidst, I help upon
A strong one laid; out of the folk
   I rais'd a chosen one;

20 Ev'n David, I have found him out
    a servant unto me;
  And with my holy oil my King
    anointed him to be.

21 With whom my hand shall stablish'd be;
    mine arm shall make him strong.
22 On him the foe shall not exact,
    nor son of mischief wrong.
23 I will beat down before his face
    all his malicious foes;
  I will them greatly plague who do
    with hatred him oppose.

24 My mercy and my faithfulness
    with him yet still shall be;
  And in my name his horn and pow'r
    men shall exalted see.
25 His hand and pow'r shall reach afar,
    I'll set it in the sea;
  And his right hand established
    shall in the rivers be.

26 Thou art my Father, he shall cry,
    thou art my God alone;
  And he shall say, Thou art the Rock
    of my salvation.
27 I'll make him my first-born, more high
    than kings of any land.
28 My love I'll ever keep for him,
    my cov'nant fast shall stand.

29 His seed I by my pow'r will make
    for ever to endure;

And, as the days of heav'n, his throne
   shall stable be, and sure.
30 But if his children shall forsake
   my laws, and go astray,
And in my judgments shall not walk,
   but wander from my way:

31 If they my laws break, and do not
   keep my commandements;
32 I'll visit then their faults with rods,
   their sins with chastisements.
33 Yet I'll not take my love from him,
   nor false my promise make.
34 My cov'nant I'll not break, nor change
   what with my mouth I spake.

35 Once by my holiness I sware,
   to David I'll not lie;
36 His seed and throne shall, as the sun,
   before me last for aye.
37 It, like the moon, shall ever be
   establish'd stedfastly;
And like to that which in the heav'n
   doth witness faithfully.

38 But thou, displeased, hast cast off,
   thou didst abhor and loathe;
With him that thine anointed is
   thou hast been very wroth.
39 Thou hast thy servant's covenant
   made void, and quite cast by;
Thou hast profan'd his crown, while it
   cast on the ground doth lie.

40 Thou all his hedges hast broke down,
    his strong holds down hast torn.
41 He to all passers-by a spoil,
    to neighbours is a scorn.
42 Thou hast set up his foes' right hand;
    mad'st all his en'mies glad:
43 Turn'd his sword's edge, and him to stand
    in battle hast not made.

44 His glory thou hast made to cease,
    his throne to ground down cast;
45 Shorten'd his days of youth, and him
    with shame thou cover'd hast.
46 How long, Lord, wilt thou hide thyself?
    for ever, in thine ire?
And shall thine indignation
    burn like unto a fire?

47 Remember, Lord, how short a time
    I shall on earth remain:
O wherefore is it so that thou
    has made all men in vain?
48 What man is he that liveth here,
    and death shall never see?
Or from the power of the grave
    what man his soul shall free?

49 Thy former loving-kindnesses,
    O Lord, where be they now?
Those which in truth and faithfulness
    to David sworn hast thou?
50 Mind, Lord, thy servant's sad reproach;
    how I in bosom bear

The scornings of the people all,
 who strong and mighty are.

51 Wherewith thy raging enemies
  reproach'd, O Lord, think on;
 Wherewith they have reproach'd the steps
  of thine anointed one.
52 All blessing to the Lord our God
  let be ascribed then:
 For evermore so let it be.
  Amen, yea, and amen.

Psalm 90

A Prayer of Moses the man of God.

1 LORD, thou hast been our dwelling-place
 in generations all.
2 Before thou ever hadst brought forth
  the mountains great or small;
 Ere ever thou hadst form'd the earth,
  and all the world abroad;
 Ev'n thou from everlasting art
  to everlasting God.

3 Thou dost unto destruction
  man that is mortal turn;
 And unto them thou say'st, Again,
  ye sons of men, return.
4 Because a thousand years appear
  no more before thy sight
 Than yesterday, when it is past,
  or than a watch by night.

5 As with an overflowing flood
  thou carry'st them away:

They like a sleep are, like the grass
    that grows at morn are they.
6 At morn it flourishes and grows,
    cut down at ev'n doth fade.
7 For by thine anger we're consum'd,
    thy wrath makes us afraid.

8 Our sins thou and iniquities
    dost in thy presence place,
And sett'st our secret faults before
    the brightness of thy face.
9 For in thine anger all our days
    do pass on to an end;
And as a tale that hath been told,
    so we our years do spend.

10 Threescore and ten years do sum up
    our days and years, we see;
Or, if, by reason of more strength,
    in some fourscore they be:
Yet doth the strength of such old men
    but grief and labour prove;
For it is soon cut off, and we
    fly hence, and soon remove.

11 Who knows the power of thy wrath?
    according to thy fear
12 So is thy wrath: Lord, teach thou us
    our end in mind to bear;
And so to count our days, that we
    our hearts may still apply
To learn thy wisdom and thy truth,
    that we may live thereby.

13 Turn yet again to us, O Lord,
　　　how long thus shall it be?
　　Let it repent thee now for those
　　　that servants are to thee.
14 O with thy tender mercies, Lord,
　　　us early satisfy;
　　So we rejoice shall all our days,
　　　and still be glad in thee.

15 According as the days have been,
　　　wherein we grief have had,
　　And years wherein we ill have seen,
　　　so do thou make us glad.
16 O let thy work and pow'r appear
　　　thy servants' face before;
　　And shew unto their children dear
　　　thy glory evermore:

17 And let the beauty of the Lord
　　　our God be us upon:
　　Our handy-works establish thou,
　　　establish them each one.

Psalm 91

1 HE that doth in the secret place
　　　of the most High reside,
　　Under the shade of him that is
　　　th' Almighty shall abide.
2 I of the Lord my God will say,
　　　He is my refuge still,
　　He is my fortress, and my God,
　　　and in him trust I will.

3   Assuredly he shall thee save,
      and give deliverance
    From subtile fowler's snare, and from
      the noisome pestilence.
4   His feathers shall thee hide; thy trust
      under his wings shall be:
    His faithfulness shall be a shield
      and buckler unto thee.

5   Thou shalt not need to be afraid
      for terrors of the night;
    Nor for the arrow that doth fly
      by day, while it is light;
6   Nor for the pestilence, that walks
      in darkness secretly;
    Nor for destruction, that doth waste
      at noon-day openly.

7   A thousand at thy side shall fall,
      on thy right hand shall lie
    Ten thousand dead; yet unto thee
      it shall not once come nigh.
8   Only thou with thine eyes shalt look,
      and a beholder be;
    And thou therein the just reward
      of wicked men shalt see.

9   Because the Lord, who constantly
      my refuge is alone,
    Ev'n the most High, is made by thee
      thy habitation;
10 No plague shall near thy dwelling come;
      no ill shall thee befall:

11 For thee to keep in all thy ways
  his angels charge he shall.

12 They in their hands shall bear thee up,
  still waiting thee upon;
Lest thou at any time should'st dash
  thy foot against a stone.
13 Upon the adder thou shalt tread,
  and on the lion strong;
Thy feet on dragons trample shall,
  and on the lions young.

14 Because on me he set his love,
  I'll save and set him free;
Because my great name he hath known,
  I will him set on high.
15 He'll call on me, I'll answer him;
  I will be with him still
In trouble, to deliver him,
  and honour him I will.

16 With length of days unto his mind
  I will him satisfy;
I also my salvation
  will cause his eyes to see.

Psalm 92

A Psalm or Song for the sabbath day.

1 TO render thanks unto the Lord
  it is a comely thing,
And to thy name, O thou most High,
  due praise aloud to sing.
2 Thy loving-kindness to shew forth
  when shines the morning light;

And to declare thy faithfulness
  with pleasure ev'ry night.

3 On a ten-stringed instrument,
    upon the psaltery,
  And on the harp with solemn sound,
    and grave sweet melody.
4 For thou, Lord, by thy mighty works
    hast made my heart right glad;
  And I will triumph in the works
    which by thine hands were made.

5 How great, Lord, are thy works! each
            thought
    of thine a deep it is:
6 A brutish man it knoweth not;
    fools understand not this.
7 When those that lewd and wicked are
    spring quickly up like grass,
  And workers of iniquity
    do flourish all apace;

  It is that they for ever may
    destroyed be and slain;
8 But thou, O Lord, art the most High,
    for ever to remain.
9 For, lo, thine enemies, O Lord,
    thine en'mies perish shall;
  The workers of iniquity
    shall be dispersed all.

10 But thou shalt, like unto the horn
    of th' unicorn, exalt

My horn on high: thou with fresh oil
    anoint me also shalt.
11 Mine eyes shall also my desire
    see on mine enemies;
    Mine ears shall of the wicked hear
    that do against me rise.

12 But like the palm-tree flourishing
    shall be the righteous one;
    He shall like to the cedar grow
    that is in Lebanon.
13 Those that within the house of God
    are planted by his grace,
    They shall grow up, and flourish all
    in our God's holy place.

14 And in old age, when others fade,
    they fruit still forth shall bring;
    They shall be fat, and full of sap,
    and aye be flourishing;
15 To shew that upright is the Lord:
    he is a rock to me;
    And he from all unrighteousness
    is altogether free.

Psalm 93

1 THE Lord doth reign, and cloth'd is he
    with majesty most bright;
  His works do shew him cloth'd to be,
    and girt about with might.
  The world is also stablished,
    that it cannot depart.
2 Thy throne is fix'd of old, and thou
    from everlasting art.

3 The floods, O Lord, have lifted up,
    they lifted up their voice;
  The floods have lifted up their waves,
    and made a mighty noise.
4 But yet the Lord, that is on high,
    is more of might by far
  Than noise of many waters is,
    or great sea-billows are.

5 Thy testimonies ev'ry one
    in faithfulness excel;
  And holiness for ever, Lord,
    thine house becometh well.

Psalm 94

1 O LORD God, unto whom alone
    all vengeance doth belong;
  O mighty God, who vengeance own'st,
    shine forth, avenging wrong.
2 Lift up thyself, thou of the earth
    the sov'reign Judge that art;
  And unto those that are so proud
    a due reward impart.

3 How long, O mighty God, shall they
    who lewd and wicked be,
  How long shall they who wicked are
    thus triumph haughtily?
4 How long shall things most hard by them
    be uttered and told?
  And all that work iniquity
    to boast themselves be bold?

5 Thy folk they break in pieces, Lord,
    thine heritage oppress:

6 The widow they and stranger slay,
    and kill the fatherless.
7 Yet say they, God it shall not see,
    nor God of Jacob know.
8 Ye brutish people! understand;
    fools! when wise will ye grow?

9 The Lord did plant the ear of man,
    and hear then shall not he?
  He only form'd the eye, and then
    shall he not clearly see?
10 He that the nations doth correct,
    shall he not chastise you?
  He knowledge unto man doth teach,
    and shall himself not know?

11 Man's thoughts to be but vanity
    the Lord doth well discern.
12 Bless'd is the man thou chast'nest, Lord,
    and mak'st thy law to learn:
13 That thou may'st give him rest from days
    of sad adversity,
  Until the pit be digg'd for those
    that work iniquity.

14 For sure the Lord will not cast off
    those that his people be,
  Neither his own inheritance
    quit and forsake will he:
15 But judgment unto righteousness
    shall yet return again;
  And all shall follow after it
    that are right-hearted men.

16 Who will rise up for me against
    those that do wickedly?
  Who will stand up for me 'gainst those
    that work iniquity?
17 Unless the Lord had been my help
    when I was sore opprest,
  Almost my soul had in the house
    of silence been at rest.

18 When I had uttered this word,
    my foot doth slip away,
  Thy mercy held me up, O Lord,
    thy goodness did me stay.
19 Amidst the multitude of thoughts
    which in my heart do fight,
  My soul, lest it be overcharg'd,
    thy comforts do delight.

20 Shall of iniquity the throne
    have fellowship with thee,
  Which mischief, cunningly contriv'd,
    doth by a law decree?
21 Against the righteous souls they join,
    they guiltless blood condemn.
22 But of my refuge God's the rock,
    and my defence from them.

23 On them their own iniquity
    the Lord shall bring and lay,
  And cut them off in their own sin;
    our Lord God shall them slay.

Psalm 95

1 O COME, let us sing to the Lord:
    come, let us ev'ry one
A joyful noise make to the Rock
    of our salvation.

2 Let us before his presence come
    with praise and thankful voice;
Let us sing psalms to him with grace,
    and make a joyful noise.

3 For God, a great God, and great King,
    above all gods he is.

4 Depths of the earth are in his hand,
    the strength of hills is his.

5 To him the spacious sea belongs,
    for he the same did make;
The dry land also from his hands
    its form at first did take.

6 O come, and let us worship him,
    let us bow down withal,
And on our knees before the Lord
    our Maker let us fall.

7 For he's our God, the people we
    of his own pasture are,
And of his hand the sheep; to-day,
    if ye his voice will hear,

8 Then harden not your hearts, as in
    the provocation,
As in the desert, on the day
    of the tentation:

9 When me your fathers tempt'd and prov'd,
    and did my working see;

10 Ev'n for the space of forty years
    this race hath grieved me.

   I said, This people errs in heart,
    my ways they do not know:
11 To whom I sware in wrath, that to
    my rest they should not go.

Psalm 96

1 O SING a new song to the Lord:
    sing all the earth to God.
2 To God sing, bless his name, shew still
    his saving health abroad.
3 Among the heathen nations
    his glory do declare;
   And unto all the people shew
    his works that wondrous are.

4 For great's the Lord, and greatly he
    is to be magnify'd;
   Yea, worthy to be fear'd is he
    above all gods beside.
5 For all the gods are idols dumb,
    which blinded nations fear;
   But our God is the Lord, by whom
    the heav'ns created were.

6 Great honour is before his face,
    and majesty divine;
   Strength is within his holy place,
    and there doth beauty shine.
7 Do ye ascribe unto the Lord,
    of people ev'ry tribe,

Glory do ye unto the Lord,
   and mighty pow'r ascribe.

8 Give ye the glory to the Lord
   that to his name is due;
Come ye into his courts, and bring
   an offering with you.
9 In beauty of his holiness,
   O do the Lord adore;
Likewise let all the earth throughout
   tremble his face before.

10 Among the heathen say, God reigns;
   the world shall stedfastly
Be fix'd from moving; he shall judge
   the people righteously.
11 Let heav'ns be glad before the Lord,
   and let the earth rejoice;
Let seas, and all that is therein,
   cry out, and make a noise.

12 Let fields rejoice, and ev'ry thing
   that springeth of the earth:
Then woods and ev'ry tree shall sing
   with gladness and with mirth
13 Before the Lord; because he comes,
   to judge the earth comes he:
He'll judge the world with righteousness,
   the people faithfully.

Psalm 97

1 GOD reigneth, let the earth be glad,
   and isles rejoice each one.

2 Dark clouds him compass; and in right
    with judgment dwells his throne.
3 Fire goes before him, and his foes
    it burns up round about:
4 His lightnings lighten did the world;
    earth saw, and shook throughout.

5 Hills at the presence of the Lord,
    like wax, did melt away;
    Ev'n at the presence of the Lord
    of all the earth, I say.
6 The heav'ns declare his righteousness,
    all men his glory see.
7 All who serve graven images,
    confounded let them be.

Who do of idols boast themselves,
    let shame upon them fall:
Ye that are called gods, see that
    ye do him worship all.
8 Sion did hear, and joyful was,
    glad Judah's daughters were;
They much rejoic'd, O Lord, because
    thy judgments did appear.

9 For thou, O Lord, art high above
    all things on earth that are;
Above all other gods thou art
    exalted very far.
10 Hate ill, all ye that love the Lord:
    his saints' souls keepeth he;
And from the hands of wicked men
    he sets them safe and free.

11 For all those that be righteous
sown is a joyful light,
And gladness sown is for all those
that are in heart upright.
12 Ye righteous, in the Lord rejoice;
express your thankfulness,
When ye into your memory
do call his holiness.

Psalm 98

A Psalm.

1 O SING a new song to the Lord,
for wonders he hath done:
His right hand and his holy arm
him victory hath won.
2 The Lord God his salvation
hath caused to be known;
His justice in the heathen's sight
he openly hath shown.

3 He mindful of his grace and truth
to Isr'el's house hath been;
And the salvation of our God
all ends of th' earth have seen.
4 Let all the earth unto the Lord
send forth a joyful noise;
Lift up your voice aloud to him,
sing praises, and rejoice.

5 With harp, with harp, and voice of psalms,
unto JEHOVAH sing:
6 With trumpets, cornets, gladly sound
before the Lord the King.

7 Let seas and all their fulness roar;
   the world, and dwellers there;
8 Let floods clap hands, and let the hills
   together joy declare

9 Before the Lord; because he comes,
   to judge the earth comes he:
He'll judge the world with righteousness,
   his folk with equity.

Psalm 99

1 TH' eternal Lord doth reign as king,
   let all the people quake;
He sits between the cherubims,
   let th' earth be mov'd and shake.
2 The Lord in Sion great and high
   above all people is;
3 Thy great and dreadful name (for it
   is holy) let them bless.

4 The king's strength also judgment loves;
   thou settlest equity:
Just judgment thou dost execute
   in Jacob righteously.
5 The Lord our God exalt on high,
   and rev'rently do ye
Before his footstool worship him:
   the Holy One is he.

6 Moses and Aaron 'mong his priests,
   Samuel, with them that call
Upon his name: these call'd on God,
   and he them answer'd all.

7   Within the pillar of the cloud
      he unto them did speak:
  The testimonies he them taught,
      and laws, they did not break.

8   Thou answer'dst them, O Lord our God;
      thou wast a God that gave
  Pardon to them, though on their deeds
      thou wouldest vengeance have.

9   Do ye exalt the Lord our God,
      and at his holy hill
  Do ye him worship: for the Lord
      our God is holy still.

Psalm 100

A Psalm of praise.

1   ALL people that on earth do dwell,
      Sing to the Lord with cheerful voice.

2   Him serve with mirth, his praise forth tell,
      Come ye before him and rejoice.

3   Know that the Lord is God indeed;
      Without our aid he did us make:
  We are his flock, he doth us feed,
      And for his sheep he doth us take.

4   O enter then his gates with praise,
      Approach with joy his courts unto:
  Praise, laud, and bless his name always,
      For it is seemly so to do.

5   For why? the Lord our God is good,
      His mercy is for ever sure;
  His truth at all times firmly stood,
      And shall from age to age endure.

Another of the same

1 O ALL ye lands, unto the Lord
   make ye a joyful noise.
2 Serve God with gladness, him before
   come with a singing voice.
3 Know ye the Lord that he is God;
   not we, but he us made:
   We are his people, and the sheep
   within his pasture fed.

4 Enter his gates and courts with praise,
   to thank him go ye thither:
   To him express your thankfulness,
   and bless his name together.
5 Because the Lord our God is good,
   his mercy faileth never;
   And to all generations
   his truth endureth ever.

Psalm 101

A Psalm of David.

1 I MERCY will and judgment sing,
   Lord, I will sing to thee.
2 With wisdom in a perfect way
   shall my behaviour be.
   O when, in kindness unto me,
   wilt thou be pleas'd to come?
   I with a perfect heart will walk
   within my house at home.

3 I will endure no wicked thing
   before mine eyes to be:

I hate their work that turn aside,
  it shall not cleave to me.
4 A stubborn and a froward heart
  depart quite from me shall;
A person giv'n to wickedness
  I will not know at all.

5 I'll cut him off that slandereth
  his neighbour privily:
The haughty heart I will not bear,
  nor him that looketh high.
6 Upon the faithful of the land
  mine eyes shall be, that they
May dwell with me: he shall me serve
  that walks in perfect way.

7 Who of deceit a worker is
  in my house shall not dwell;
And in my presence shall he not
  remain that lies doth tell.
8 Yea, all the wicked of the land
  early destroy will I;
All from God's city to cut off
  that work iniquity.

Psalm 102

*A Prayer of the afflicted, when he is overwhelmed,
and poureth out his complaint before the Lord.*

1 O LORD, unto my pray'r give ear,
  my cry let come to thee;
2 And in the day of my distress
  hide not thy face from me.

Give ear to me; what time I call,
   to answer me make haste:
3 For, as an hearth, my bones are burnt,
   my days, like smoke, do waste.

4 My heart within me smitten is,
   and it is withered
Like very grass; so that I do
   forget to eat my bread.
5 By reason of my groaning voice
   my bones cleave to my skin.
6 Like pelican in wilderness
   forsaken I have been:

I like an owl in desert am,
   that nightly there doth moan;
7 I watch, and like a sparrow am
   on the house-top alone.
8 My bitter en'mies all the day
   reproaches cast on me;
And, being mad at me, with rage
   against me sworn they be.

9 For why? I ashes eaten have
   like bread, in sorrows deep;
My drink I also mingled have
   with tears that I did weep.
10 Thy wrath and indignation
   did cause this grief and pain;
For thou hast lift me up on high,
   and cast me down again.

11 My days are like unto a shade,
   which doth declining pass;

And I am dry'd and withered,
  ev'n like unto the grass.
12 But thou, Lord, everlasting art,
  and thy remembrance shall
Continually endure, and be
  to generations all.

13 Thou shalt arise, and mercy have
  upon thy Sion yet;
The time to favour her is come,
  the time that thou hast set.
14 For in her rubbish and her stones
  thy servants pleasure take;
Yea, they the very dust thereof
  do favour for her sake.

15 So shall the heathen people fear
  the Lord's most holy name;
And all the kings on earth shall dread
  thy glory and thy fame.
16 When Sion by the mighty Lord
  built up again shall be,
In glory then and majesty
  to men appear shall he.

17 The prayer of the destitute
  he surely will regard;
Their prayer will he not despise,
  by him it shall be heard.
18 For generations yet to come
  this shall be on record:
So shall the people that shall be
  created praise the Lord.

19 He from his sanctuary's height
　　hath downward cast his eye;
　And from his glorious throne in heav'n
　　the Lord the earth did spy;
20 That of the mournful prisoner
　　the groanings he might hear,
　To set them free that unto death
　　by men appointed are:

21 That they in Sion may declare
　　the Lord's most holy name,
　And publish in Jerusalem
　　the praises of the same;
22 When as the people gather shall
　　in troops with one accord,
　When kingdoms shall assembled be
　　to serve the highest Lord.

23 My wonted strength and force he hath
　　abated in the way,
　And he my days hath shortened:
24 　Thus therefore did I say,
　My God, in mid-time of my days
　　take thou me not away:
　From age to age eternally
　　thy years endure and stay.

25 The firm foundation of the earth
　　of old time thou hast laid;
　The heavens also are the work
　　which thine own hands have made.
26 Thou shalt for evermore endure,
　　but they shall perish all;

Yea, ev'ry one of them wax old,
  like to a garment, shall:

Thou, as a vesture, shalt them change,
  and they shall changed be:
27 But thou the same art, and thy years
  are to eternity.
28 The children of thy servants shall
  continually endure;
And in thy sight, O Lord, their seed
  shall be establish'd sure.

Another of the same

1 LORD, hear my pray'r, and let my cry
  Have speedy access unto thee;
2 In day of my calamity
  O hide not thou thy face from me.
Hear when I call to thee; that day
  An answer speedily return:
3 My days, like smoke, consume away,
  And, as an hearth, my bones do burn.

4 My heart is wounded very sore,
  And withered, like grass doth fade:
I am forgetful grown therefore
  To take and eat my daily bread.
5 By reason of my smart within,
  And voice of my most grievous groans,
My flesh consumed is, my skin,
  All parch'd, doth cleave unto my bones.

6 The pelican of wilderness,
  The owl in desert, I do match;
7 And, sparrow-like, companionless,
  Upon the house's top, I watch.

8 I all day long am made a scorn,
     Reproach'd by my malicious foes:
  The madmen are against me sworn,
     The men against me that arose.

9 For I have ashes eaten up,
     To me as if they had been bread;
  And with my drink I in my cup
     Of bitter tears a mixture made.

10 Because thy wrath was not appeas'd,
     And dreadful indignation:
  Therefore it was that thou me rais'd,
     And thou again didst cast me down.

11 My days are like a shade alway,
     Which doth declining swiftly pass;
  And I am withered away,
     Much like unto the fading grass.

12 But thou, O Lord, shalt still endure,
     From change and all mutation free,
  And to all generations sure
     Shall thy remembrance ever be.

13 Thou shalt arise, and mercy yet
     Thou to mount Sion shalt extend:
  Her time for favour which was set,
     Behold, is now come to an end.

14 Thy saints take pleasure in her stones,
     Her very dust to them is dear.

15 All heathen lands and kingly thrones
     On earth thy glorious name shall fear.

16 God in his glory shall appear,
     When Sion he builds and repairs.

17 He shall regard and lend his ear
   Unto the needy's humble pray'rs:
   Th' afflicted's pray'r he will not scorn.
18   All times this shall be on record:
   And generations yet unborn
      Shall praise and magnify the Lord.

19 He from his holy place look'd down,
      The earth he view'd from heav'n on high,
20 To hear the pris'ner's mourning groan,
      And free them that are doom'd to die;
21 That Sion, and Jerus'lem too,
      His name and praise may well record,
22 When people and the kingdoms do
      Assemble all to praise the Lord.

23 My strength he weaken'd in the way,
      My days of life he shortened.
24 My God, O take me not away
      In mid-time of my days, I said:
   Thy years throughout all ages last.
25   Of old thou hast established
   The earth's foundation firm and fast:
      Thy mighty hands the heav'ns have made.

26 They perish shall, as garments do,
      But thou shalt evermore endure;
   As vestures, thou shalt change them so;
      And they shall all be changed sure:
27 But from all changes thou art free;
      Thy endless years do last for aye.
28 Thy servants, and their seed who be,
      Establish'd shall before thee stay.

Psalm 103

A Psalm of David.

1 O THOU my soul, bless God the Lord;
  and all that in me is
Be stirred up his holy name
  to magnify and bless.
2 Bless, O my soul, the Lord thy God,
  and not forgetful be
Of all his gracious benefits
  he hath bestow'd on thee.

3 All thine iniquities who doth
  most graciously forgive:
Who thy diseases all and pains
  doth heal, and thee relieve.
4 Who doth redeem thy life, that thou
  to death may'st not go down;
Who thee with loving-kindness doth
  and tender mercies crown:

5 Who with abundance of good things
  doth satisfy thy mouth;
So that, ev'n as the eagle's age,
  renewed is thy youth.
6 God righteous judgment executes
  for all oppressed ones.
7 His ways to Moses, he his acts
  made known to Isr'el's sons.

8 The Lord our God is merciful,
  and he is gracious,
Long-suffering, and slow to wrath,
  in mercy plenteous.

9   He will not chide continually,
    nor keep his anger still.
10 With us he dealt not as we sinn'd,
    nor did requite our ill.

11 For as the heaven in its height
    the earth surmounteth far:
  So great to those that do him fear
    his tender mercies are:
12 As far as east is distant from
    the west, so far hath he
  From us removed, in his love,
    all our iniquity.

13 Such pity as a father hath
    unto his children dear;
  Like pity shews the Lord to such
    as worship him in fear.
14 For he remembers we are dust,
    and he our frame well knows.
15 Frail man, his days are like the grass,
    as flow'r in field he grows:

16 For over it the wind doth pass,
    and it away is gone;
  And of the place where once it was
    it shall no more be known.
17 But unto them that do him fear
    God's mercy never ends;
  And to their children's children still
    his righteousness extends:

18 To such as keep his covenant,
    and mindful are alway

Of his most just commandements,
   that they may them obey.
19 The Lord prepared hath his throne
   in heavens firm to stand;
And ev'ry thing that being hath
   his kingdom doth command.

20 O ye his angels, that excel
   in strength, bless ye the Lord;
Ye who obey what he commands,
   and hearken to his word.
21 O bless and magnify the Lord,
   ye glorious hosts of his;
Ye ministers, that do fulfil
   whate'er his pleasure is.

22 O bless the Lord, all ye his works,
   wherewith the world is stor'd
In his dominions ev'ry where.
   My soul, bless thou the Lord.

Psalm 104

1 BLESS God, my soul. O Lord my God,
   thou art exceeding great;
With honour and with majesty
   thou clothed art in state.
2 With light, as with a robe, thyself
   thou coverest about;
And, like unto a curtain, thou
   the heavens stretchest out.

3 Who of his chambers doth the beams
   within the waters lay;

Who doth the clouds his chariot make,
   on wings of wind make way.
4 Who flaming fire his ministers,
   his angels sp'rits, doth make:
5 Who earth's foundations did lay,
   that it should never shake.

6 Thou didst it cover with the deep,
   as with a garment spread:
The waters stood above the hills,
   when thou the word but said.
7 But at the voice of thy rebuke
   they fled, and would not stay;
They at thy thunder's dreadful voice
   did haste them fast away.

8 They by the mountains do ascend,
   and by the valley-ground
Descend, unto that very place
   which thou for them didst found.
9 Thou hast a bound unto them set,
   that they may not pass over,
That they do not return again
   the face of earth to cover.

10 He to the valleys sends the springs,
   which run among the hills:
11 They to all beasts of field give drink,
   wild asses drink their fills.
12 By them the fowls of heav'n shall have
   their habitation,
Which do among the branches sing
   with delectation.

13 He from his chambers watereth
    the hills, when they are dry'd:
  With fruit and increase of thy works
    the earth is satisfy'd.
14 For cattle he makes grass to grow,
    he makes the herb to spring
  For th' use of man, that food to him
    he from the earth may bring;

15 And wine, that to the heart of man
    doth cheerfulness impart,
  Oil that his face makes shine, and bread
    that strengtheneth his heart.
16 The trees of God are full of sap;
    the cedars that do stand
  In Lebanon, which planted were
    by his almighty hand.

17 Birds of the air upon their boughs
    do chuse their nests to make;
  As for the stork, the fir-tree she
    doth for her dwelling take.
18 The lofty mountains for wild goats
    a place of refuge be;
  The conies also to the rocks
    do for their safety flee.

19 He sets the moon in heav'n, thereby
    the seasons to discern:
  From him the sun his certain time
    of going down doth learn.
20 Thou darkness mak'st, 'tis night, then beasts
    of forests creep abroad.
21 The lions young roar for their prey,
    and seek their meat from God.

22 The sun doth rise, and home they flock,
    down in their dens they lie.
23 Man goes to work, his labour he
    doth to the ev'ning ply.
24 How manifold, Lord, are thy works!
    in wisdom wonderful
Thou ev'ry one of them hast made;
    earth's of thy riches full:

25 So is this great and spacious sea,
    wherein things creeping are,
Which number'd cannot be; and beasts
    both great and small are there.
26 There ships go; there thou mak'st to play
    that leviathan great.
27 These all wait on thee, that thou may'st
    in due time give them meat.

28 That which thou givest unto them
    they gather for their food;
Thine hand thou open'st lib'rally,
    they filled are with good.
29 Thou hid'st thy face; they troubled are,
    their breath thou tak'st away;
Then do they die, and to their dust
    return again do they.

30 Thy quick'ning spirit thou send'st forth,
    then they created be;
And then the earth's decayed face
    renewed is by thee.
31 The glory of the mighty Lord
    continue shall for ever:

The Lord JEHOVAH shall rejoice
  in all his works together.

32 Earth, as affrighted, trembleth all,
  if he on it but look;
And if the mountains he but touch,
  they presently do smoke.
33 I will sing to the Lord most high,
  so long as I shall live;
And while I being have I shall
  to my God praises give.

34 Of him my meditation shall
  sweet thoughts to me afford;
And as for me, I will rejoice
  in God, my only Lord.
35 From earth let sinners be consum'd,
  let ill men no more be.
O thou my soul, bless thou the Lord.
  Praise to the Lord give ye.

Psalm 105

1 GIVE thanks to God, call on his name;
  to men his deeds make known.
2 Sing ye to him, sing psalms; proclaim
  his wondrous works each one.
3 See that ye in his holy name
  to glory do accord;
And let the heart of ev'ry one
  rejoice that seeks the Lord.

4 The Lord Almighty, and his strength,
  with stedfast hearts seek ye:

His blessed and his gracious face
   seek ye continually.
5 Think on the works that he hath done,
   which admiration breed;
His wonders, and the judgments all
   which from his mouth proceed;

6 O ye that are of Abr'ham's race,
   his servant well approv'n;
And ye that Jacob's children are,
   whom he chose for his own.
7 Because he, and he only, is
   the mighty Lord our God;
And his most righteous judgments are
   in all the earth abroad.

8 His cov'nant he remember'd hath,
   that it may ever stand:
To thousand generations
   the word he did command.
9 Which covenant he firmly made
   with faithful Abraham,
And unto Isaac, by his oath,
   he did renew the same:

10 And unto Jacob, for a law,
   he made it firm and sure,
A covenant to Israel,
   which ever should endure.
11 He said, I'll give Canaan's land
   for heritage to you;
12 While they were strangers there, and few,
   in number very few:

13 While yet they went from land to land
    without a sure abode;
And while through sundry kingdoms they
    did wander far abroad;
14 Yet, notwithstanding, suffer'd he
    no man to do them wrong;
Yea, for their sakes, he did reprove
    kings, who were great and strong.

15 Thus did he say, Touch ye not those
    that mine anointed be,
Nor do the prophets any harm
    that do pertain to me.
16 He call'd for famine on the land,
    he brake the staff of bread:
17 But yet he sent a man before,
    by whom they should be fed;

Ev'n Joseph, whom unnat'rally
    sell for a slave did they;
18 Whose feet with fetters they did hurt,
    and he in irons lay;
19 Until the time that his word came
    to give him liberty;
The word and purpose of the Lord
    did him in prison try.

20 Then sent the king, and did command
    that he enlarg'd should be:
He that the people's ruler was
    did send to set him free.
21 A lord to rule his family
    he rais'd him, as most fit;

To him of all that he possess'd
   he did the charge commit:

22 That he might at his pleasure bind
   the princes of the land;
  And he might teach his senators
   wisdom to understand.
23 The people then of Israel
   down into Egypt came;
  And Jacob also sojourned
   within the land of Ham.

24 And he did greatly by his pow'r
   increase his people there;
  And stronger than their enemies
   they by his blessing were.
25 Their heart he turned to envy
   his folk maliciously,
  With those that his own servants were
   to deal in subtilty.

26 His servant Moses he did send,
   Aaron his chosen one.
27 By these his signs and wonders great
   in Ham's land were made known.
28 Darkness he sent, and made it dark;
   his word they did obey.
29 He turn'd their waters into blood,
   and he their fish did slay.

30 The land in plenty brought forth frogs
   in chambers of their kings.
31 His word all sorts of flies and lice
   in all their borders brings.

32 He hail for rain, and flaming fire
    into their land he sent:
33 And he their vines and fig-trees smote;
    trees of their coasts he rent.

34 He spake, and caterpillars came,
    locusts did much abound;
35 Which in their land all herbs consum'd,
    and all fruits of their ground.
36 He smote all first-born in their land,
    chief of their strength each one.
37 With gold and silver brought them forth,
    weak in their tribes were none.

38 Egypt was glad when forth they went,
    their fear on them did light.
39 He spread a cloud for covering,
    and fire to shine by night.
40 They ask'd, and he brought quails: with bread
    of heav'n he filled them.
41 He open'd rocks, floods gush'd, and ran
    in deserts like a stream.

42 For on his holy promise he,
    and servant Abr'ham, thought.
43 With joy his people, his elect
    with gladness, forth he brought.
44 And unto them the pleasant lands
    he of the heathen gave;
    That of the people's labour they
    inheritance might have.

45 That they his statutes might observe
    according to his word;

And that they might his laws obey.
   Give praise unto the Lord.

Psalm 106

1 GIVE praise and thanks unto the Lord,
    for bountiful is he;
His tender mercy doth endure
   unto eternity.
2 God's mighty works who can express?
   or shew forth all his praise?
3 Blessed are they that judgment keep,
   and justly do always.

4 Remember me, Lord, with that love
   which thou to thine dost bear;
With thy salvation, O my God,
   to visit me draw near:
5 That I thy chosen's good may see,
   and in their joy rejoice;
And may with thine inheritance
   triumph with cheerful voice.

6 We with our fathers sinned have,
   and of iniquity
Too long we have the workers been;
   we have done wickedly.
7 The wonders great, which thou, O Lord,
   didst work in Egypt land,
Our fathers, though they saw, yet them
   they did not understand:

And they thy mercies' multitude
   kept not in memory;

But at the sea, ev'n the Red sea,
   provok'd him grievously.
8 Nevertheless he saved them,
   ev'n for his own name's sake;
That so he might to be well known
   his mighty power make.

9 When he the Red sea did rebuke,
   then dried up it was:
Through depths, as through the wilderness,
   he safely made them pass.
10 From hands of those that hated them
   he did his people save;
And from the en'my's cruel hand
   to them redemption gave.

11 The waters overwhelm'd their foes;
   not one was left alive.
12 Then they believ'd his word, and praise
   to him in songs did give.
13 But soon did they his mighty works
   forget unthankfully,
And on his counsel and his will
   did not wait patiently;

14 But much did lust in wilderness,
   and God in desert tempt.
15 He gave them what they sought, but to
   their soul he leanness sent.
16 And against Moses in the camp
   their envy did appear;
At Aaron they, the saint of God,
   envious also were.

17 Therefore the earth did open wide,
  and Dathan did devour,
 And all Abiram's company
  did cover in that hour.
18 Likewise among their company
  a fire was kindled then;
 And so the hot consuming flame
  burnt up these wicked men.

19 Upon the hill of Horeb they
  an idol-calf did frame,
 A molten image they did make,
  and worshipped the same.
20 And thus their glory, and their God,
  most vainly changed they
 Into the likeness of an ox
  that eateth grass or hay.

21 They did forget the mighty God,
  that had their saviour been,
 By whom such great things brought to pass
  they had in Egypt seen.
22 In Ham's land he did wondrous works,
  things terrible did he,
 When he his mighty hand and arm
  stretch'd out at the Red sea.

23 Then said he, He would them destroy,
  had not, his wrath to stay,
 His chosen Moses stood in breach,
  that them he should not slay.
24 Yea, they despis'd the pleasant land,
  believed not his word:

25 But in their tents they murmured,
    not heark'ning to the Lord.

26 Therefore in desert them to slay
    he lifted up his hand:
27 'Mong nations to o'erthrow their seed,
    and scatter in each land.
28 They unto Baal-peor did
    themselves associate;
The sacrifices of the dead
    they did profanely eat.

29 Thus, by their lewd inventions,
    they did provoke his ire;
And then upon them suddenly
    the plague brake in as fire.
30 Then Phin'has rose, and justice did,
    and so the plague did cease;
31 That to all ages counted was
    to him for righteousness.

32 And at the waters, where they strove,
    they did him angry make,
In such sort, that it fared ill
    with Moses for their sake:
33 Because they there his spirit meek
    provoked bitterly,
So that he utter'd with his lips
    words unadvisedly.

34 Nor, as the Lord commanded them,
    did they the nations slay:
35 But with the heathen mingled were,
    and learn'd of them their way.

36 And they their idols serv'd, which did
    a snare unto them turn.
37 Their sons and daughters they to dev'ls
    in sacrifice did burn.

38 In their own children's guiltless blood
    their hands they did imbrue,
Whom to Canaan's idols they
    for sacrifices slew:
So was the land defil'd with blood.
39   They stain'd with their own way,
And with their own inventions
    a whoring they did stray.

40 Against his people kindled was
    the wrath of God therefore,
Insomuch that he did his own
    inheritance abhor.
41 He gave them to the heathen's hand;
    their foes did them command.
42 Their en'mies them oppress'd, they were
    made subject to their hand.

43 He many times deliver'd them;
    but with their counsel so
They him provok'd, that for their sin
    they were brought very low.
44 Yet their affliction he beheld,
    when he did hear their cry:
45 And he for them his covenant
    did call to memory;

After his mercies' multitude
46   he did repent: And made

Them to be pitied of all those
  who did them captive lead.
47 O Lord our God, us save, and gather
   the heathen from among,
That we thy holy name may praise
  in a triumphant song.

48 Bless'd be JEHOVAH, Isr'el's God,
   to all eternity:
Let all the people say, Amen.
   Praise to the Lord give ye.

Psalm 107

1 PRAISE God, for he is good: for still
  his mercies lasting be.
2 Let God's redeem'd say so, whom he
  from th' en'my's hand did free;
3 And gather'd them out of the lands,
  from north, south, east, and west.
4 They stray'd in desert's pathless way,
  no city found to rest.

5 For thirst and hunger in them faints
6   their soul. When straits them press,
They cry unto the Lord, and he
  them frees from their distress.
7 Them also in a way to walk
   that right is he did guide,
That they might to a city go,
   wherein they might abide.

8 O that men to the Lord would give
   praise for his goodness then,

And for his works of wonder done
    unto the sons of men!
9 For he the soul that longing is
    doth fully satisfy;
With goodness he the hungry soul
    doth fill abundantly.

10 Such as shut up in darkness deep,
    and in death's shade abide,
Whom strongly hath affliction bound,
    and irons fast have ty'd:
11 Because against the words of God
    they wrought rebelliously,
And they the counsel did contemn
    of him that is most High:

12 Their heart he did bring down with grief,
    they fell, no help could have.
13 In trouble then they cry'd to God,
    he them from straits did save.
14 He out of darkness did them bring,
    and from death's shade them take;
These bands, wherewith they had been
        bound,
    asunder quite he brake.

15 O that men to the Lord would give
    praise for his goodness then,
And for his works of wonder done
    unto the sons of men!
16 Because the mighty gates of brass
    in pieces he did tear,
By him in sunder also cut
    the bars of iron were.

17 Fools, for their sin, and their offence,
　　do sore affliction bear;
18 All kind of meat their soul abhors;
　　they to death's gates draw near.
19 In grief they cry to God; he saves
　　them from their miseries.
20 He sends his word, them heals, and them
　　from their destructions frees.

21 O that men to the Lord would give
　　praise for his goodness then,
　And for his works of wonder done
　　unto the sons of men!
22 And let them sacrifice to him
　　off'rings of thankfulness;
　And let them shew abroad his works
　　in songs of joyfulness.

23 Who go to sea in ships, and in
　　great waters trading be,
24 Within the deep these men God's works
　　and his great wonders see.
25 For he commands, and forth in haste
　　the stormy tempest flies,
　Which makes the sea with rolling waves
　　aloft to swell and rise.

26 They mount to heav'n, then to the depths
　　they do go down again;
　Their soul doth faint and melt away
　　with trouble and with pain.
27 They reel and stagger like one drunk,
　　at their wit's end they be:

28 Then they to God in trouble cry,
    who them from straits doth free.

29 The storm is chang'd into a calm
    at his command and will;
  So that the waves, which rag'd before,
    now quiet are and still.

30 Then are they glad, because at rest
    and quiet now they be:
  So to the haven he them brings,
    which they desir'd to see.

31 O that men to the Lord would give
    praise for his goodness then,
  And for his works of wonder done
    unto the sons of men!

32 Among the people gathered
    let them exalt his name;
  Among assembled elders spread
    his most renowned fame.

33 He to dry land turns water-springs,
    and floods to wilderness;

34 For sins of those that dwell therein,
    fat land to barrenness.

35 The burnt and parched wilderness
    to water-pools he brings;
  The ground that was dry'd up before
    he turns to water-springs:

36 And there, for dwelling, he a place
    doth to the hungry give,
  That they a city may prepare
    commodiously to live.

37 There sow they fields, and vineyards plant,
    to yield fruits of increase.
38 His blessing makes them multiply,
    lets not their beasts decrease.

39 Again they are diminished,
    and very low brought down,
Through sorrow and affliction,
    and great oppression.
40 He upon princes pours contempt
    and causeth them to stray,
And wander in a wilderness,
    wherein there is no way.

41 Yet setteth he the poor on high
    from all his miseries,
And he, much like unto a flock,
    doth make him families.
42 They that are righteous shall rejoice,
    when they the same shall see;
And, as ashamed, stop her mouth
    shall all iniquity.

43 Whoso is wise, and will these things
    observe, and them record,
Ev'n they shall understand the love
    and kindness of the Lord.

Psalm 108

A Song or Psalm of David.

1 MY heart is fix'd, Lord; I will sing,
    and with my glory praise.
2 Awake up psaltery and harp;
    myself I'll early raise.

3 I'll praise thee 'mong the people, Lord;
  'mong nations sing will I:
4 For above heav'n thy mercy's great,
  thy truth doth reach the sky.

5 Be thou above the heavens, Lord,
  exalted gloriously;
  Thy glory all the earth above
  be lifted up on high.
6 That those who thy beloved are
  delivered may be,
  O do thou save with thy right hand,
  and answer give to me.

7 God in his holiness hath said,
  Herein I will take pleasure;
  Shechem I will divide, and forth
  will Succoth's valley measure.
8 Gilead I claim as mine by right;
  Manasseh mine shall be;
  Ephraim is of my head the strength;
  Judah gives laws for me;

9 Moab's my washing-pot; my shoe
  I'll over Edom throw;
  Over the land of Palestine
  I will in triumph go.
10 O who is he will bring me to
  the city fortify'd?
  O who is he that to the land
  of Edom will me guide?

11 O God, thou who hadst cast us off,
  this thing wilt thou not do?

And wilt not thou, ev'n thou, O God,
    forth with our armies go?
12 Do thou from trouble give us help,
    for helpless is man's aid.
13 Through God we shall do valiantly;
    our foes he shall down tread.

Psalm 109

To the chief Musician, A Psalm of David.

1 O THOU the God of all my praise,
    do thou not hold thy peace;
2 For mouths of wicked men to speak
    against me do not cease:
 The mouths of vile deceitful men
    against me open'd be;
 And with a false and lying tongue
    they have accused me.

3 They did beset me round about
    with words of hateful spite:
 And though to them no cause I gave,
    against me they did fight.
4 They for my love became my foes,
    but I me set to pray.
5 Evil for good, hatred for love,
    to me they did repay.

6 Set thou the wicked over him;
    and upon his right hand
 Give thou his greatest enemy,
    ev'n Satan, leave to stand.
7 And when by thee he shall be judg'd,
    let him condemned be;

And let his pray'r be turn'd to sin,
    when he shall call on thee.

8 Few be his days, and in his room
    his charge another take.
9 His children let be fatherless,
    his wife a widow make.
10 His children let be vagabonds,
    and beg continually;
And from their places desolate
    seek bread for their supply.

11 Let covetous extortioners
    catch all he hath away:
Of all for which he labour'd hath
    let strangers make a prey.
12 Let there be none to pity him,
    let there be none at all
That on his children fatherless
    will let his mercy fall.

13 Let his posterity from earth
    cut off for ever be,
And in the foll'wing age their name
    be blotted out by thee.
14 Let God his father's wickedness
    still to remembrance call;
And never let his mother's sin
    be blotted out at all.

15 But let them all before the Lord
    appear continually,
That he may wholly from the earth
    cut off their memory.

16 Because he mercy minded not,
  but persecuted still
The poor and needy, that he might
  the broken-hearted kill.

17 As he in cursing pleasure took,
  so let it to him fall;
As he delighted not to bless,
  so bless him not at all.
18 As cursing he like clothes put on,
  into his bowels so,
Like water, and into his bones,
  like oil, down let it go.

19 Like to the garment let it be
  which doth himself array,
And for a girdle, wherewith he
  is girt about alway.
20 From God let this be their reward
  that en'mies are to me,
And their reward that speak against
  my soul maliciously.

21 But do thou, for thine own name's sake,
  O God the Lord, for me:
Sith good and sweet thy mercy is,
  from trouble set me free.
22 For I am poor and indigent,
  afflicted sore am I,
My heart within me also is
  wounded exceedingly.

23 I pass like a declining shade,
  am like the locust tost:

24 My knees through fasting weaken'd are,
    my flesh hath fatness lost.
25 I also am a vile reproach
    unto them made to be;
And they that did upon me look
    did shake their heads at me.

26 O do thou help and succour me,
    who art my God and Lord:
And, for thy tender mercy's sake,
    safety to me afford:
27 That thereby they may know that this
    is thy almighty hand;
And that thou, Lord, hast done the same,
    they may well understand.

28 Although they curse with spite, yet, Lord,
    bless thou with loving voice:
Let them asham'd be when they rise;
    thy servant let rejoice.
29 Let thou mine adversaries all
    with shame be clothed over;
And let their own confusion
    them, as a mantle, cover.

30 But as for me, I with my mouth
    will greatly praise the Lord;
And I among the multitude
    his praises will record.
31 For he shall stand at his right hand
    who is in poverty,
To save him from all those that would
    condemn his soul to die.

Psalm 110

A Psalm of David.

1 THE Lord did say unto my Lord,
    Sit thou at my right hand,
Until I make thy foes a stool,
    whereon thy feet may stand.
2 The Lord shall out of Sion send
    the rod of thy great pow'r:
In midst of all thine enemies
    be thou the governor.

3 A willing people in thy day
    of pow'r shall come to thee,
In holy beauties from morn's womb;
    thy youth like dew shall be.
4 The Lord himself hath made an oath,
    and will repent him never,
Of th' order of Melchisedec
    thou art a priest for ever.

5 The glorious and mighty Lord,
    that sits at thy right hand,
Shall, in his day of wrath, strike through
    kings that do him withstand.
6 He shall among the heathen judge,
    he shall with bodies dead
The places fill: o'er many lands
    he wound shall ev'ry head.

7 The brook that runneth in the way
    with drink shall him supply;
And, for this cause, in triumph he
    shall lift his head on high.

Psalm 111

1 PRAISE ye the Lord: with my whole
        heart
  I will God's praise declare,
Where the assemblies of the just
  and congregations are.
2 The whole works of the Lord our God
  are great above all measure,
Sought out they are of ev'ry one
  that doth therein take pleasure.

3 His work most honourable is,
  most glorious and pure,
And his untainted righteousness
  for ever doth endure.
4 His works most wonderful he hath
  made to be thought upon:
The Lord is gracious, and he is
  full of compassion.

5 He giveth meat unto all those
  that truly do him fear;
And evermore his covenant
  he in his mind will bear.
6 He did the power of his works
  unto his people show,
When he the heathen's heritage
  upon them did bestow.

7 His handy-works are truth and right;
  all his commands are sure:
8 And, done in truth and uprightness,
  they evermore endure.

9   He sent redemption to his folk;
        his covenant for aye
    He did command: holy his name
        and rev'rend is alway.

10   Wisdom's beginning is God's fear:
        good understanding they
    Have all that his commands fulfill:
        his praise endures for aye.

Psalm 112

1   PRAISE ye the Lord. The man is bless'd
        that fears the Lord aright,
    He who in his commandements
        doth greatly take delight.
2   His seed and offspring powerful
        shall be the earth upon:
    Of upright men blessed shall be
        the generation.

3   Riches and wealth shall ever be
        within his house in store;
    And his unspotted righteousness
        endures for evermore.
4   Unto the upright light doth rise,
        though he in darkness be:
    Compassionate, and merciful,
        and righteous, is he.

5   A good man doth his favour shew,
        and doth to others lend:
    He with discretion his affairs
        will guide unto the end.
6   Surely there is not any thing
        that ever shall him move:

The righteous man's memorial
   shall everlasting prove.

7 When he shall evil tidings hear,
   he shall not be afraid:
His heart is fix'd, his confidence
   upon the Lord is stay'd.
8 His heart is firmly stablished,
   afraid he shall not be,
Until upon his enemies
   he his desire shall see.

9 He hath dispers'd, giv'n to the poor;
   his righteousness shall be
To ages all; with honour shall
   his horn be raised high.
10 The wicked shall it see, and fret,
   his teeth gnash, melt away:
What wicked men do most desire
   shall utterly decay.

Psalm 113

1 PRAISE God: ye servants of the Lord,
   O praise, the Lord's name praise.
2 Yea, blessed be the name of God
   from this time forth always.
3 From rising sun to where it sets,
   God's name is to be prais'd.
4 Above all nations God is high,
   'bove heav'ns his glory rais'd.

5 Unto the Lord our God that dwells
   on high, who can compare?

6　Himself that humbleth things to see
　　in heav'n and earth that are.
7　He from the dust doth raise the poor,
　　that very low doth lie;
　　And from the dunghill lifts the man
　　oppress'd with poverty;

8　That he may highly him advance,
　　and with the princes set;
　　With those that of his people are
　　the chief, ev'n princes great.
9　The barren woman house to keep
　　he maketh, and to be
　　Of sons a mother full of joy.
　　Praise to the Lord give ye.

Psalm 114

1　WHEN Isr'el out of Egypt went,
　　and did his dwelling change,
　　When Jacob's house went out from those
　　that were of language strange,
2　He Judah did his sanctuary,
　　his kingdom Isr'el make:
3　The sea it saw, and quickly fled,
　　Jordan was driven back.

4　Like rams the mountains, and like lambs
　　the hills skipp'd to and fro.
5　O sea, why fledd'st thou? Jordan, back
　　why wast thou driven so?
6　Ye mountains great, wherefore was it
　　that ye did skip like rams?
　　And wherefore was it, little hills,
　　that ye did leap like lambs?

7   O at the presence of the Lord,
    earth, tremble thou for fear,
  While as the presence of the God
    of Jacob doth appear:
8   Who from the hard and stony rock
    did standing water bring;
  And by his pow'r did turn the flint
    into a water-spring.

Psalm 115

1   NOT unto us, Lord, not to us,
    but do thou glory take
  Unto thy name, ev'n for thy truth,
    and for thy mercy's sake.
2   O wherefore should the heathen say,
    Where is their God now gone?
3   But our God in the heavens is,
    what pleas'd him he hath done.

4   Their idols silver are and gold,
    work of men's hands they be.
5   Mouths have they, but they do not speak;
    and eyes, but do not see;
6   Ears have they, but they do not hear;
    noses, but savour not;
7   Hands, feet, but handle not, nor walk;
    nor speak they through their throat.

8   Like them their makers are, and all
    on them their trust that build.
9   O Isr'el, trust thou in the Lord,
    he is their help and shield.
10 O Aaron's house, trust in the Lord,
    their help and shield is he.

11 Ye that fear God, trust in the Lord,
　　their help and shield he'll be.

12 The Lord of us hath mindful been,
　　and he will bless us still:
　　He will the house of Isr'el bless,
　　bless Aaron's house he will.

13 Both small and great, that fear the Lord,
　　he will them surely bless.

14 The Lord will you, you and your seed,
　　aye more and more increase.

15 O blessed are ye of the Lord,
　　who made the earth and heav'n.

16 The heav'n, ev'n heav'ns, are God's, but he
　　earth to men's sons hath giv'n.

17 The dead, nor who to silence go,
　　God's praise do not record.

18 But henceforth we for ever will
　　bless God. Praise ye the Lord.

Psalm 116

1 I LOVE the Lord, because my voice
　and prayers he did hear.

2 I, while I live, will call on him,
　　who bow'd to me his ear.

3 Of death the cords and sorrows did
　　about me compass round;
　　The pains of hell took hold on me,
　　I grief and trouble found.

4 Upon the name of God the Lord
　　then did I call, and say,

Deliver thou my soul, O Lord,
   I do thee humbly pray.
5 God merciful and righteous is,
   yea, gracious is our Lord.
6 God saves the meek: I was brought low,
   he did me help afford.

7 O thou my soul, do thou return
   unto thy quiet rest;
For largely, lo, the Lord to thee
   his bounty hath exprest.
8 For my distressed soul from death
   deliver'd was by thee:
Thou didst my mourning eyes from tears,
   my feet from falling, free.

9 I in the land of those that live
   will walk the Lord before.
10 I did believe, therefore I spake:
   I was afflicted sore.
11 I said, when I was in my haste,
   that all men liars be.
12 What shall I render to the Lord
   for all his gifts to me?

13 I'll of salvation take the cup,
   on God's name will I call:
14 I'll pay my vows now to the Lord
   before his people all.
15 Dear in God's sight is his saints' death.
16   Thy servant, Lord, am I;
Thy servant sure, thine handmaid's son:
   my bands thou didst untie.

17 Thank-off'rings I to thee will give,
    and on God's name will call.
18 I'll pay my vows now to the Lord
    before his people all;
19 Within the courts of God's own house,
    within the midst of thee,
  O city of Jerusalem.
    Praise to the Lord give ye.

Psalm 117

1 O GIVE ye praise unto the Lord,
  all nations that be;
Likewise, ye people all, accord
    his name to magnify.
2 For great to us-ward ever are
    his loving-kindnesses:
His truth endures for evermore.
    The Lord O do ye bless.

Psalm 118

1 O PRAISE the Lord, for he is good;
  his mercy lasteth ever.
2 Let those of Israel now say,
    His mercy faileth never.
3 Now let the house of Aaron say,
    His mercy lasteth ever.
4 Let those that fear the Lord now say,
    His mercy faileth never.

5 I in distress call'd on the Lord;
    the Lord did answer me:
He in a large place did me set,
    from trouble made me free.

6 The mighty Lord is on my side,
    I will not be afraid;
For any thing that man can do
    I shall not be dismay'd.

7 The Lord doth take my part with them
    that help to succour me:
Therefore on those that do me hate
    I my desire shall see.
8 Better it is to trust in God
    than trust in man's defence;
9 Better to trust in God than make
    princes our confidence.

10 The nations, joining all in one,
    did compass me about:
But in the Lord's most holy name
    I shall them all root out.
11 They compass'd me about; I say,
    they compass'd me about:
But in the Lord's most holy name
    I shall them all root out.

12 Like bees they compass'd me about;
    like unto thorns that flame
They quenched are: for them shall I
    destroy in God's own name.
13 Thou sore hast thrust, that I might fall,
    but my Lord helped me.
14 God my salvation is become,
    my strength and song is he.

15 In dwellings of the righteous
    is heard the melody

Of joy and health: the Lord's right hand
   doth ever valiantly.
16 The right hand of the mighty Lord
   exalted is on high;
The right hand of the mighty Lord
   doth ever valiantly.

17 I shall not die, but live, and shall
   the works of God discover.
18 The Lord hath me chastised sore,
   but not to death giv'n over.
19 O set ye open unto me
   the gates of righteousness;
Then will I enter into them,
   and I the Lord will bless.

20 This is the gate of God, by it
   the just shall enter in.
21 Thee will I praise, for thou me heard'st
   and hast my safety been.
22 That stone is made head corner-stone,
   which builders did despise:
23 This is the doing of the Lord,
   and wondrous in our eyes.

24 This is the day God made, in it
   we'll joy triumphantly.
25 Save now, I pray thee, Lord; I pray,
   send now prosperity.
26 Blessed is he in God's great name
   that cometh us to save:
We, from the house which to the Lord
   pertains, you blessed have.

27 God is the Lord, who unto us
    hath made light to arise:
Bind ye unto the altar's horns
    with cords the sacrifice.
28 Thou art my God, I'll thee exalt;
    my God, I will thee praise.
29 Give thanks to God, for he is good:
    his mercy lasts always.

Psalm 119

Aleph: The 1st Part.

1 BLESSED are they that undefil'd,
    and straight are in the way;
Who in the Lord's most holy law
    do walk, and do not stray.
2 Blessed are they who to observe
    his statutes are inclin'd;
And who do seek the living God
    with their whole heart and mind.

3 Such in his ways do walk, and they
    do no iniquity.
4 Thou hast commanded us to keep
    thy precepts carefully.
5 O that thy statutes to observe
    thou would'st my ways direct!
6 Then shall I not be sham'd, when I
    thy precepts all respect.

7 Then with integrity of heart
    thee will I praise and bless,
When I the judgments all have learn'd
    of thy pure righteousness.

8 That I will keep thy statutes all
    firmly resolv'd have I:
  O do not then, most gracious God,
    forsake me utterly.

Beth: The 2nd Part.

9 By what means shall a young man learn
    his way to purify?
  If he according to thy word
    thereto attentive be.
10 Unfeignedly thee have I sought
    with all my soul and heart:
  O let me not from the right path
    of thy commands depart.

11 Thy word I in my heart have hid,
    that I offend not thee.
12 O Lord, thou ever blessed art,
    thy statutes teach thou me.
13 The judgments of thy mouth each one
    my lips declared have:
14 More joy thy testimonies' way
    than riches all me gave.

15 I will thy holy precepts make
    my meditation;
  And carefully I'll have respect
    unto thy ways each one.
16 Upon thy statutes my delight
    shall constantly be set:
  And, by thy grace, I never will
    thy holy word forget.

Gimel: The 3rd Part.

17 With me thy servant, in thy grace,
   deal bountifully, Lord;
That by thy favour I may live,
   and duly keep thy word.

18 Open mine eyes, that of thy law
   the wonders I may see.

19 I am a stranger on this earth,
   hide not thy laws from me.

20 My soul within me breaks, and doth
   much fainting still endure,
Through longing that it hath all times
   unto thy judgments pure.

21 Thou hast rebuk'd the cursed proud,
   who from thy precepts swerve.

22 Reproach and shame remove from me,
   for I thy laws observe.

23 Against me princes spake with spite,
   while they in council sat:
But I thy servant did upon
   thy statutes meditate.

24 My comfort, and my heart's delight,
   thy testimonies be;
And they, in all my doubts and fears,
   are counsellors to me.

Daleth: The 4th Part.

25 My soul to dust cleaves: quicken me,
   according to thy word.

26 My ways I shew'd, and me thou heard'st:
   teach me thy statutes, Lord.

27 The way of thy commandements
    make me aright to know;
So all thy works that wondrous are
    I shall to others show.

28 My soul doth melt, and drop away,
    for heaviness and grief:
To me, according to thy word,
    give strength, and send relief.
29 From me the wicked way of lies
    let far removed be;
And graciously thy holy law
    do thou grant unto me.

30 I chosen have the perfect way
    of truth and verity:
Thy judgments that most righteous are
    before me laid have I.
31 I to thy testimonies cleave;
    shame do not on me cast.
32 I'll run thy precepts' way, when thou
    my heart enlarged hast.

He: The 5th Part.

33 Teach me, O Lord, the perfect way
    of thy precepts divine,
And to observe it to the end
    I shall my heart incline.
34 Give understanding unto me,
    so keep thy law shall I;
Yea, ev'n with my whole heart I shall
    observe it carefully.

35 In thy law's path make me to go;
    for I delight therein.

36 My heart unto thy testimonies,
    and not to greed, incline.
37 Turn thou away my sight and eyes
    from viewing vanity;
And in thy good and holy way
    be pleas'd to quicken me.

38 Confirm to me thy gracious word,
    which I did gladly hear,
Ev'n to thy servant, Lord, who is
    devoted to thy fear.
39 Turn thou away my fear'd reproach;
    for good thy judgments be.
40 Lo, for thy precepts I have long'd;
    in thy truth quicken me.

Vau: The 6th Part.

41 Let thy sweet mercies also come
    and visit me, O Lord;
Ev'n thy benign salvation,
    according to thy word.
42 So shall I have wherewith I may
    give him an answer just,
Who spitefully reproacheth me;
    for in thy word I trust.

43 The word of truth out of my mouth
    take thou not utterly;
For on thy judgments righteous
    my hope doth still rely.
44 So shall I keep for evermore
    thy law continually.
45 And, sith that I thy precepts seek,
    I'll walk at liberty.

46 I'll speak thy word to kings, and I
　　with shame shall not be mov'd;
47 And will delight myself always
　　in thy laws, which I lov'd.
48 To thy commandments, which I lov'd,
　　my hands lift up I will;
　And I will also meditate
　　upon thy statutes still.

Zain: The 7th Part.

49 Remember, Lord, thy gracious word
　　thou to thy servant spake,
　Which, for a ground of my sure hope,
　　thou causedst me to take.
50 This word of thine my comfort is
　　in mine affliction:
　For in my straits I am reviv'd
　　by this thy word alone.

51 The men whose hearts with pride are
　　　　stuff'd
　　did greatly me deride;
　Yet from thy straight commandements
　　I have not turn'd aside.
52 Thy judgments righteous, O Lord,
　　which thou of old forth gave,
　I did remember, and myself
　　by them comforted have.

53 Horror took hold on me, because
　　ill men thy law forsake.
54 I in my house of pilgrimage
　　thy laws my songs do make.

55 Thy name by night, Lord, I did mind,
    and I have kept thy law.
56 And this I had, because thy word
    I kept, and stood in awe.

Cheth: The 8th Part.

57 Thou my sure portion art alone,
    which I did chuse, O Lord:
  I have resolv'd, and said, that I
    would keep thy holy word.
58 With my whole heart I did entreat
    thy face and favour free:
  According to thy gracious word
    be merciful to me.

59 I thought upon my former ways,
    and did my life well try;
  And to thy testimonies pure
    my feet then turned I.
60 I did not stay, nor linger long,
    as those that slothful are;
  But hastily thy laws to keep
    myself I did prepare.

61 Bands of ill men me robb'd; yet I
    thy precepts did not slight.
62 I'll rise at midnight thee to praise,
    ev'n for thy judgments right.
63 I am companion to all those
    who fear, and thee obey.
64 O Lord, thy mercy fills the earth:
    teach me thy laws, I pray.

Teth: The 9th Part.

65 Well hast thou with thy servant dealt,
 as thou didst promise give.
66 Good judgment me, and knowledge teach,
 for I thy word believe.
67 Ere I afflicted was I stray'd;
 but now I keep thy word.
68 Both good thou art, and good thou do'st:
 teach me thy statutes, Lord.

69 The men that are puff'd up with pride
 against me forg'd a lie;
Yet thy commandements observe
 with my whole heart will I.
70 Their hearts, through worldly ease and
   wealth,
 as fat as grease they be:
But in thy holy law I take
 delight continually.

71 It hath been very good for me
 that I afflicted was,
That I might well instructed be,
 and learn thy holy laws.
72 The word that cometh from thy mouth
 is better unto me
Than many thousands and great sums
 of gold and silver be.

Jod: The 10th Part.

73 Thou mad'st and fashion'dst me: thy laws
 to know give wisdom, Lord.
74 So who thee fear shall joy to see
 me trusting in thy word.

75 That very right thy judgments are
    I know, and do confess;
And that thou hast afflicted me
    in truth and faithfulness.

76 O let thy kindness merciful,
    I pray thee, comfort me,
As to thy servant faithfully
    was promised by thee.

77 And let thy tender mercies come
    to me, that I may live;
Because thy holy laws to me
    sweet delectation give.

78 Lord, let the proud ashamed be;
    for they, without a cause,
With me perversely dealt: but I
    will muse upon thy laws.

79 Let such as fear thee, and have known
    thy statutes, turn to me.

80 My heart let in thy laws be sound,
    that sham'd I never be.

Caph: The 11th Part.

81 My soul for thy salvation faints;
    yet I thy word believe.

82 Mine eyes fail for thy word: I say,
    When wilt thou comfort give?

83 For like a bottle I'm become,
    that in the smoke is set:
I'm black, and parch'd with grief; yet I
    thy statutes not forget.

84 How many are thy servant's days?
    when wilt thou execute

Just judgment on these wicked men
    that do me persecute?
85 The proud have digged pits for me,
    which is against thy laws.
86 Thy words all faithful are: help me,
    pursu'd without a cause.

87 They so consum'd me, that on earth
    my life they scarce did leave:
Thy precepts yet forsook I not,
    but close to them did cleave.
88 After thy loving-kindness, Lord,
    me quicken, and preserve:
The testimony of thy mouth
    so shall I still observe.

Lamed: The 12th Part.

89 Thy word for ever is, O Lord,
    in heaven settled fast;
90 Unto all generations
    thy faithfulness doth last:
The earth thou hast established,
    and it abides by thee.
91 This day they stand as thou ordain'dst;
    for all thy servants be.

92 Unless in thy most perfect law
    my soul delights had found,
I should have perished, when as
    my troubles did abound.
93 Thy precepts I will ne'er forget;
    they quick'ning to me brought.
94 Lord, I am thine; O save thou me:
    thy precepts I have sought.

95 For me the wicked have laid wait,
    me seeking to destroy:
But I thy testimonies true
    consider will with joy.
96 An end of all perfection
    here have I seen, O God:
But as for thy commandement,
    it is exceeding broad.

Mem: The 13th Part.

97 O how love I thy law! it is
    my study all the day:
98 It makes me wiser than my foes;
    for it doth with me stay.
99 Than all my teachers now I have
    more understanding far;
Because my meditation
    thy testimonies are.

100 In understanding I excel
    those that are ancients;
For I endeavoured to keep
    all thy commandements.
101 My feet from each ill way I stay'd,
    that I may keep thy word.
102 I from thy judgments have not swerv'd;
    for thou hast taught me, Lord.

103 How sweet unto my taste, O Lord,
    are all thy words of truth!
Yea, I do find them sweeter far
    than honey to my mouth.
104 I through thy precepts, that are pure,
    do understanding get;

I therefore ev'ry way that's false
with all my heart do hate.

Nun: The 14th Part.

105 Thy word is to my feet a lamp,
and to my path a light.
106 I sworn have, and I will perform,
to keep thy judgments right.
107 I am with sore affliction
ev'n overwhelm'd, O Lord:
In mercy raise and quicken me,
according to thy word.

108 The free-will-off'rings of my mouth
accept, I thee beseech:
And unto me thy servant, Lord,
thy judgments clearly teach.
109 Though still my soul be in my hand,
thy laws I'll not forget.
110 I err'd not from them, though for me
the wicked snares did set.

111 I of thy testimonies have
above all things made choice,
To be my heritage for aye;
for they my heart rejoice.
112 I carefully inclined have
my heart still to attend;
That I thy statutes may perform
alway unto the end.

Samech: The 15th Part.

113 I hate the thoughts of vanity,
but love thy law do I.

114 My shield and hiding-place thou art:
    I on thy word rely.
115 All ye that evil-doers are
    from me depart away;
  For the commandments of my God
    I purpose to obey.

116 According to thy faithful word
    uphold and stablish me,
  That I may live, and of my hope
    ashamed never be.
117 Hold thou me up, so shall I be
    in peace and safety still;
  And to thy statutes have respect
    continually I will.

118 Thou tread'st down all that love to stray;
    false their deceit doth prove.
119 Lewd men, like dross, away thou putt'st;
    therefore thy law I love.
120 For fear of thee my very flesh
    doth tremble, all dismay'd;
  And of thy righteous judgments, Lord,
    my soul is much afraid.

Ain: The 16th Part.

121 To all men I have judgment done,
    performing justice right;
  Then let me not be left unto
    my fierce oppressors' might.
122 For good unto thy servant, Lord,
    thy servant's surety be:
  From the oppression of the proud
    do thou deliver me.

123 Mine eyes do fail with looking long
    for thy salvation,
  The word of thy pure righteousness
    while I do wait upon.
124 In mercy with thy servant deal,
    thy laws me teach and show.
125 I am thy servant, wisdom give,
    that I thy laws may know.

126 'Tis time thou work, Lord; for they have
    made void thy law divine.
127 Therefore thy precepts more I love
    than gold, yea, gold most fine.
128 Concerning all things thy commands
    all right I judge therefore;
  And ev'ry false and wicked way
    I perfectly abhor.

Pe: The 17th Part.

129 Thy statutes, Lord, are wonderful,
    my soul them keeps with care.
130 The entrance of thy words gives light,
    makes wise who simple are.
131 My mouth I have wide opened,
    and panted earnestly,
  While after thy commandements
    I long'd exceedingly.

132 Look on me, Lord, and merciful
    do thou unto me prove,
  As thou art wont to do to those
    thy name who truly love.
133 O let my footsteps in thy word
    aright still order'd be:

Let no iniquity obtain
dominion over me.

134 From man's oppression save thou me;
so keep thy laws I will.
135 Thy face make on thy servant shine;
teach me thy statutes still.
136 Rivers of waters from mine eyes
did run down, when I saw
How wicked men run on in sin,
and do not keep thy law.

Tsaddi: The 18th Part.

137 O Lord, thou art most righteous;
thy judgments are upright.
138 Thy testimonies thou command'st
most faithful are and right.
139 My zeal hath ev'n consumed me,
because mine enemies
Thy holy words forgotten have,
and do thy laws despise.

140 Thy word's most pure, therefore on it
thy servant's love is set.
141 Small, and despis'd I am, yet I
thy precepts not forget.
142 Thy righteousness is righteousness
which ever doth endure:
Thy holy law, Lord, also is
the very truth most pure.

143 Trouble and anguish have me found,
and taken hold on me:

Yet in my trouble my delight
　　thy just commandments be.
144 Eternal righteousness is in
　　　thy testimonies all:
　　Lord, to me understanding give,
　　　and ever live I shall.

Qoph: The 19th Part.

145 With my whole heart I cry'd, Lord, hear;
　　　I will thy word obey.
146 I cry'd to thee; save me, and I
　　　will keep thy laws alway.
147 I of the morning did prevent
　　　the dawning, and did cry:
　　For all mine expectation
　　　did on thy word rely.

148 Mine eyes did timeously prevent
　　　the watches of the night,
　　That in thy word with careful mind
　　　then meditate I might.
149 After thy loving-kindness hear
　　　my voice, that calls on thee:
　　According to thy judgment, Lord,
　　　revive and quicken me.

150 Who follow mischief they draw nigh;
　　　they from thy law are far:
151 But thou art near, Lord; most firm truth
　　　all thy commandments are.
152 As for thy testimonies all,
　　　of old this have I try'd,
　　That thou hast surely founded them
　　　for ever to abide.

Resh: The 20th Part.

153 Consider mine affliction,
   in safety do me set:
   Deliver me, O Lord, for I
   thy law do not forget.
154 After thy word revive thou me:
   save me, and plead my cause.
155 Salvation is from sinners far;
   for they seek not thy laws.

156 O Lord, both great and manifold
   thy tender mercies be:
   According to thy judgments just,
   revive and quicken me.
157 My persecutors many are,
   and foes that do combine;
   Yet from thy testimonies pure
   my heart doth not decline.

158 I saw transgressors, and was griev'd;
   for they keep not thy word.
159 See how I love thy law! as thou
   art kind, me quicken, Lord.
160 From the beginning all thy word
   hath been most true and sure:
   Thy righteous judgments ev'ry one
   for evermore endure.

Schin: The 21st Part.

161 Princes have persecuted me,
   although no cause they saw:
   But still of thy most holy word
   my heart doth stand in awe.

162 I at thy word rejoice, as one
  of spoil that finds great store.
163 Thy law I love; but lying all
  I hate and do abhor.

164 Sev'n times a-day it is my care
  to give due praise to thee;
  Because of all thy judgments, Lord,
  which righteous ever be.
165 Great peace have they who love thy law;
  offence they shall have none.
166 I hop'd for thy salvation, Lord,
  and thy commands have done.

167 My soul thy testimonies pure
  observed carefully;
  On them my heart is set, and them
  I love exceedingly.
168 Thy testimonies and thy laws
  I kept with special care;
  For all my works and ways each one
  before thee open are.

Tau: The 22nd Part.

169 O let my earnest pray'r and cry
  come near before thee, Lord:
  Give understanding unto me,
  according to thy word.
170 Let my request before thee come:
  after thy word me free.
171 My lips shall utter praise, when thou
  hast taught thy laws to me.

172 My tongue of thy most blessed word
  shall speak, and it confess;

Because all thy commandements
    are perfect righteousness.
173 Let thy strong hand make help to me:
    thy precepts are my choice.
174 I long'd for thy salvation, Lord,
    and in thy law rejoice.

175 O let my soul live, and it shall
    give praises unto thee;
    And let thy judgments gracious
    be helpful unto me.
176 I, like a lost sheep, went astray;
    thy servant seek, and find:
    For thy commands I suffer'd not
    to slip out of my mind.

Psalm 120

A Song of degrees.

1 IN my distress to God I cry'd,
    and he gave ear to me.
2 From lying lips, and guileful tongue,
    O Lord, my soul set free.
3 What shall be giv'n thee? or what shall
    be done to thee, false tongue?
4 Ev'n burning coals of juniper,
    sharp arrows of the strong.

5 Woe's me that I in Mesech am
    a sojourner so long;
    That I in tabernacles dwell
    to Kedar that belong.
6 My soul with him that hateth peace
    hath long a dweller been.

7   I am for peace; but when I speak,
    for battle they are keen.

Psalm 121

A Song of degrees.

1   I TO the hills will lift mine eyes,
    from whence doth come mine aid.
2   My safety cometh from the Lord,
    who heav'n and earth hath made.
3   Thy foot he'll not let slide, nor will
    he slumber that thee keeps.
4   Behold, he that keeps Israel,
    he slumbers not, nor sleeps.

5   The Lord thee keeps, the Lord thy shade
    on thy right hand doth stay:
6   The moon by night thee shall not smite,
    nor yet the sun by day.
7   The Lord shall keep thy soul; he shall
    preserve thee from all ill.
8   Henceforth thy going out and in
    God keep for ever will.

Psalm 122

A Song of degrees of David.

1   I JOY'D when to the house of God,
    Go up, they said to me.
2   Jerusalem, within thy gates
    our feet shall standing be.
3   Jerus'lem, as a city, is
    compactly built together:
4   Unto that place the tribes go up,
    the tribes of God go thither:

To Isr'el's testimony, there
  to God's name thanks to pay.
5 For thrones of judgment, ev'n the thrones
  of David's house, there stay.
6 Pray that Jerusalem may have
  peace and felicity:
Let them that love thee and thy peace
  have still prosperity.

7 Therefore I wish that peace may still
  within thy walls remain,
And ever may thy palaces
  prosperity retain.
8 Now, for my friends' and brethren's sakes,
  Peace be in thee, I'll say.
9 And for the house of God our Lord,
  I'll seek thy good alway.

Psalm 123

A Song of degrees.

1 O THOU that dwellest in the heav'ns,
  I lift mine eyes to thee.
2 Behold, as servants' eyes do look
  their masters' hand to see,
As handmaid's eyes her mistress' hand;
  so do our eyes attend
Upon the Lord our God, until
  to us he mercy send.

3 O Lord, be gracious to us,
  unto us gracious be;
Because replenish'd with contempt
  exceedingly are we.

4   Our soul is fill'd with scorn of those
      that at their ease abide,
  And with the insolent contempt
      of those that swell in pride.

Psalm 124

A Song of degrees of David.

1   **H**AD not the Lord been on our side,
      may Israel now say;
2   Had not the Lord been on our side,
      when men rose us to slay;
3   They had us swallow'd quick, when as
      their wrath 'gainst us did flame:
4   Waters had cover'd us, our soul
      had sunk beneath the stream.

5   Then had the waters, swelling high,
      over our soul made way.
6   Bless'd be the Lord, who to their teeth
      us gave not for a prey.
7   Our soul's escaped, as a bird
      out of the fowler's snare;
  The snare asunder broken is,
      and we escaped are.

8   Our sure and all-sufficient help
      is in JEHOVAH's name;
  His name who did the heav'n create,
      and who the earth did frame.

Another of the same

1   **N**OW Israel
      may say, and that truly,

If that the Lord
   had not our cause maintain'd;
2 If that the Lord
   had not our right sustain'd,
When cruel men
   against us furiously
Rose up in wrath,
   to make of us their prey;

3 Then certainly
   they had devour'd us all,
And swallow'd quick,
   for ought that we could deem;
Such was their rage,
   as we might well esteem.
4 And as fierce floods
   before them all things drown,
So had they brought
   our soul to death quite down.

5 The raging streams,
   with their proud swelling waves,
Had then our soul
   o'erwhelmed in the deep.
6 But bless'd be God,
   who doth us safely keep,
And hath not giv'n
   us for a living prey
Unto their teeth,
   and bloody cruelty.

7 Ev'n as a bird
   out of the fowler's snare
Escapes away,
   so is our soul set free:

Broke are their nets,
    and thus escaped we.
8 Therefore our help
    is in the Lord's great name,
Who heav'n and earth
    by his great pow'r did frame.

Psalm 125

A Song of degrees.

1 THEY in the Lord that firmly trust
    shall be like Sion hill,
Which at no time can be remov'd,
    but standeth ever still.
2 As round about Jerusalem
    the mountains stand alway,
The Lord his folk doth compass so,
    from henceforth and for aye.

3 For ill men's rod upon the lot
    of just men shall not lie;
Lest righteous men stretch forth their hands
    unto iniquity.
4 Do thou to all those that be good
    thy goodness, Lord, impart;
And do thou good to those that are
    upright within their heart.

5 But as for such as turn aside
    after their crooked way,
God shall lead forth with wicked men:
    on Isr'el peace shall stay.

Psalm 126

A Song of degrees.

1 WHEN Sion's bondage God turn'd back,
      as men that dream'd were we.
2 Then fill'd with laughter was our mouth,
      our tongue with melody:
   They 'mong the heathen said, The Lord
      great things for them hath wrought.
3 The Lord hath done great things for us,
      whence joy to us is brought.

4 As streams of water in the south,
      our bondage, Lord, recall.
5 Who sow in tears, a reaping time
      of joy enjoy they shall.
6 That man who, bearing precious seed,
      in going forth doth mourn,
   He doubtless, bringing back his sheaves,
      rejoicing shall return.

Psalm 127

A Song of degrees for Solomon.

1 EXCEPT the Lord do build the house,
      the builders lose their pain:
   Except the Lord the city keep,
      the watchmen watch in vain.
2 'Tis vain for you to rise betimes,
      or late from rest to keep,
   To feed on sorrows' bread; so gives
      he his beloved sleep.

3 Lo, children are God's heritage,
      the womb's fruit his reward.

4 The sons of youth as arrows are,
    for strong men's hands prepar'd.
5 O happy is the man that hath
    his quiver fill'd with those;
They unashamed in the gate
    shall speak unto their foes.

Psalm 128

A Song of degrees.

1 **B**LESS'D is each one that fears the Lord,
    and walketh in his ways;
2 For of thy labour thou shalt eat,
    and happy be always.
3 Thy wife shall as a fruitful vine
    by thy house' sides be found:
Thy children like to olive-plants
    about thy table round.

4 Behold, the man that fears the Lord,
    thus blessed shall he be.
5 The Lord shall out of Sion give
    his blessing unto thee:
Thou shalt Jerus'lem's good behold
    whilst thou on earth dost dwell.
6 Thou shalt thy children's children see,
    and peace on Israel.

Psalm 129

A Song of degrees.

1 **O**FT did they vex me from my youth,
    may Isr'el now declare;
2 Oft did they vex me from my youth,
    yet not victorious were.

3 The plowers plow'd upon my back;
  they long their furrows drew.
4 The righteous Lord did cut the cords
  of the ungodly crew.

5 Let Sion's haters all be turn'd
  back with confusion.
6 As grass on houses' tops be they,
  which fades ere it be grown:
7 Whereof enough to fill his hand
  the mower cannot find;
  Nor can the man his bosom fill,
  whose work is sheaves to bind.

8 Neither say they who do go by,
  God's blessing on you rest:
  We in the name of God the Lord
  do wish you to be blest.

Psalm 130

A Song of degrees.

1 LORD, from the depths to thee I cry'd.
2 My voice, Lord, do thou hear:
  Unto my supplication's voice
  give an attentive ear.
3 Lord, who shall stand, if thou, O Lord,
  should'st mark iniquity?
4 But yet with thee forgiveness is,
  that fear'd thou mayest be.

5 I wait for God, my soul doth wait,
  my hope is in his word.
6 More than they that for morning watch,
  my soul waits for the Lord;

I say, more than they that do watch
   the morning light to see.
7 Let Israel hope in the Lord,
   for with him mercies be;

And plenteous redemption
   is ever found with him.
8 And from all his iniquities
   he Isr'el shall redeem.

Psalm 131

A Song of degrees of David.

1 MY heart not haughty is, O Lord,
   mine eyes not lofty be;
Nor do I deal in matters great,
   or things too high for me.
2 I surely have myself behav'd
   with quiet sp'rit and mild,
As child of mother wean'd: my soul
   is like a weaned child.

3 Upon the Lord let all the hope
   of Israel rely,
Ev'n from the time that present is
   unto eternity.

Psalm 132

A Song of degrees.

1 DAVID, and his afflictions all,
   Lord, do thou think upon;
2 How unto God he sware, and vow'd
   to Jacob's mighty One.
3 I will not come within my house,
   nor rest in bed at all;

4 Nor shall mine eyes take any sleep,
   nor eyelids slumber shall;

5 Till for the Lord a place I find,
   where he may make abode;
A place of habitation
   for Jacob's mighty God.
6 Lo, at the place of Ephratah
   of it we understood;
And we did find it in the fields,
   and city of the wood.

7 We'll go into his tabernacles,
   and at his footstool bow.
8 Arise, O Lord, into thy rest,
   th' ark of thy strength, and thou.
9 O let thy priests be clothed, Lord,
   with truth and righteousness;
And let all those that are thy saints
   shout loud for joyfulness.

10 For thine own servant David's sake,
   do not deny thy grace;
Nor of thine own anointed one
   turn thou away the face.
11 The Lord in truth to David sware,
   he will not turn from it,
I of thy body's fruit will make
   upon thy throne to sit.

12 My cov'nant if thy sons will keep,
   and laws to them made known,
Their children then shall also sit
   for ever on thy throne.

13 For God of Sion hath made choice;
   there he desires to dwell.
14 This is my rest, here still I'll stay;
   for I do like it well.

15 Her food I'll greatly bless; her poor
   with bread will satisfy.
16 Her priests I'll clothe with health; her saints
   shall shout forth joyfully.
17 And there will I make David's horn
   to bud forth pleasantly:
For him that mine anointed is
   a lamp ordain'd have I.

18 As with a garment I will clothe
   with shame his en'mies all:
But yet the crown that he doth wear
   upon him flourish shall.

Psalm 133

A Song of degrees of David.

1 BEHOLD, how good a thing it is,
   and how becoming well,
Together such as brethren are
   in unity to dwell!
2 Like precious ointment on the head,
   that down the beard did flow,
Ev'n Aaron's beard, and to the skirts
   did of his garments go.

3 As Hermon's dew, the dew that doth
   on Sion' hills descend:
For there the blessing God commands,
   life that shall never end.

Psalm 134

A Song of degrees.

1 BEHOLD, bless ye the Lord, all ye
   that his attendants are,
   Ev'n you that in God's temple be,
      and praise him nightly there.
2 Your hands within God's holy place
      lift up, and praise his name.
3 From Sion' hill the Lord thee bless,
      that heav'n and earth did frame.

Psalm 135

1 PRAISE ye the Lord, the Lord's name
         praise;
   his servants, praise ye God.
2 Who stand in God's house, in the courts
      of our God make abode.
3 Praise ye the Lord, for he is good;
      unto him praises sing:
   Sing praises to his name, because
      it is a pleasant thing.

4 For Jacob to himself the Lord
      did chuse of his good pleasure,
   And he hath chosen Israel
      for his peculiar treasure.
5 Because I know assuredly
      the Lord is very great,
   And that our Lord above all gods
      in glory hath his seat.

6 What things soever pleas'd the Lord,
      that in the heav'n did he,

And in the earth, the seas, and all
    the places deep that be.
7 He from the ends of earth doth make
    the vapours to ascend;
With rain he lightnings makes, and wind
    doth from his treasures send.

8 Egypt's first-born, from man to beast
9   who smote. Strange tokens he
On Phar'oh and his servants sent,
    Egypt, in midst of thee.
10 He smote great nations, slew great kings:
11   Sihon of Heshbon king,
And Og of Bashan, and to nought
    did Canaan's kingdoms bring:

12 And for a wealthy heritage
    their pleasant land he gave,
An heritage which Israel,
    his chosen folk, should have.
13 Thy name, O Lord, shall still endure,
    and thy memorial
With honour shall continu'd be
    to generations all.

14 For why? the righteous God will judge
    his people righteously;
Concerning those that do him serve,
    himself repent will he.
15 The idols of the nations
    of silver are and gold,
And by the hands of men is made
    their fashion and mould.

16 Mouths have they, but they do not speak;
    eyes, but they do not see;
17 Ears have they, but hear not; and in
    their mouths no breathing be.
18 Their makers are like them; so are
    all that on them rely.
19 O Isr'el's house, bless God; bless God,
    O Aaron's family.

20 O bless the Lord, of Levi's house
    ye who his servants are;
    And bless the holy name of God,
    all ye the Lord that fear.
21 And blessed be the Lord our God
    from Sion's holy hill,
    Who dwelleth at Jerusalem.
    The Lord O praise ye still.

Psalm 136

1 GIVE thanks to God, for good is he:
    for mercy hath he ever.
2 Thanks to the God of gods give ye:
    for his grace faileth never.
3 Thanks give the Lord of lords unto:
    for mercy hath he ever.
4 Who only wonders great can do:
    for his grace faileth never.

5 Who by his wisdom made heav'ns high:
    for mercy hath he ever.
6 Who stretch'd the earth above the sea:
    for his grace faileth never.
7 To him that made the great lights shine:
    for mercy hath he ever.

8 The sun to rule till day decline:
        for his grace faileth never.

9 The moon and stars to rule by night:
        for mercy hath he ever.
10 Who Egypt's first-born kill'd outright:
        for his grace faileth never.
11 And Isr'el brought from Egypt land:
        for mercy hath he ever.
12 With stretch'd-out arm, and with strong
                hand:
        for his grace faileth never.

13 By whom the Red sea parted was:
        for mercy hath he ever.
14 And through its midst made Isr'el pass:
        for his grace faileth never.
15 But Phar'oh and his host did drown:
        for mercy hath he ever.
16 Who through the desert led his own:
        for his grace faileth never.

17 To him great kings who overthrew:
        for he hath mercy ever.
18 Yea, famous kings in battle slew:
        for his grace faileth never.
19 Ev'n Sihon king of Amorites:
        for he hath mercy ever.
20 And Og the king of Bashanites:
        for his grace faileth never.

21 Their land in heritage to have:
        for mercy hath he ever.

22 His servant Isr'el right he gave:
    for his grace faileth never.
23 In our low state who on us thought:
    for he hath mercy ever.
24 And from our foes our freedom wrought:
    for his grace faileth never.

25 Who doth all flesh with food relieve:
    for he hath mercy ever.
26 Thanks to the God of heaven give:
    for his grace faileth never.

Another of the same

1 PRAISE God, for he is kind:
    His mercy lasts for aye.
2 Give thanks with heart and mind
  To God of gods alway:
    For certainly
    His mercies dure
    Most firm and sure
    Eternally.

3 The Lord of lords praise ye,
  Whose mercies still endure.
4 Great wonders only he
  Doth work by his great pow'r
    For certainly
    His mercies dure
    Most firm and sure
    Eternally.

5 Which God omnipotent,
  By might and wisdom high,
  The heav'n and firmament
  Did frame, as we may see:

> For certainly
> His mercies dure
> Most firm and sure
> Eternally.

6 To him who did outstretch
This earth so great and wide,
Above the waters' reach
Making it to abide:
> For certainly
> His mercies dure
> Most firm and sure
> Eternally.

7 Great lights he made to be;
For his grace lasteth aye:
8 Such as the sun we see,
To rule the lightsome day:
> For certainly
> His mercies dure
> Most firm and sure
> Eternally.

9 Also the moon so clear,
Which shineth in our sight;
The stars that do appear,
To guide the darksome night:
> For certainly
> His mercies dure
> Most firm and sure
> Eternally.

10 To him that Egypt smote,
Who did his message scorn;

And in his anger hot
Did kill all their first-born:
   For certainly
   His mercies dure
   Most firm and sure
   Eternally.

11 Thence Isr'el out he brought;
   For his grace lasteth ever.
12 With a strong hand he wrought,
   And stretch'd-out arm deliver:
     For certainly
     His mercies dure
     Most firm and sure
     Eternally.

13 The sea he cut in two;
   For his grace lasteth still.
14 And through its midst to go
   Made his own Israel:
     For certainly
     His mercies dure
     Most firm and sure
     Eternally.

15 But overwhelm'd and lost
   Was proud king Pharaoh,
   With all his mighty host,
   And chariots there also:
     For certainly
     His mercies dure
     Most firm and sure
     Eternally.

16 To him who pow'rfully
   His chosen people led,
   Ev'n through the desert dry,
   And in that place them fed:
      For certainly
      His mercies dure
      Most firm and sure
      Eternally.

17 To him great kings who smote;
   For his grace hath no bound.
18 Who slew, and spared not
   Kings famous and renown'd:
      For certainly
      His mercies dure
      Most firm and sure
      Eternally.

19 Sihon the Am'rites' king;
   For his grace lasteth ever:
20 Og also, who did reign
   The land of Bashan over:
      For certainly
      His mercies dure
      Most firm and sure
      Eternally.

21 Their land by lot he gave;
   For his grace faileth never,
22 That Isr'el might it have
   In heritage for ever:
      For certainly
      His mercies dure
      Most firm and sure
      Eternally.

23 Who hath remembered
Us in our low estate;
24 And us delivered
From foes which did us hate:
    For certainly
    His mercies dure
    Most firm and sure
    Eternally.

25 Who to all flesh gives food;
For his grace faileth never.
26 Give thanks to God most good,
The God of heav'n, for ever:
    For certainly
    His mercies dure
    Most firm and sure
    Eternally.

Psalm 137

1 **B**Y Babel's streams we sat and wept,
    when Sion we thought on.
2 In midst thereof we hang'd our harps
    the willow-trees upon.
3 For there a song required they,
    who did us captive bring:
Our spoilers call'd for mirth, and said,
    A song of Sion sing.

4 O how the Lord's song shall we sing
    within a foreign land?
5 If thee, Jerus'lem, I forget,
    skill part from my right hand.
6 My tongue to my mouth's roof let cleave,
    if I do thee forget,

Jerusalem, and thee above
  my chief joy do not set.

7   Remember Edom's children, Lord,
      who in Jerus'lem's day,
    Ev'n unto its foundation,
      Raze, raze it quite, did say.
8   O daughter thou of Babylon,
      near to destruction;
    Bless'd shall he be that thee rewards,
      as thou to us hast done.

9   Yea, happy surely shall he be
      thy tender little ones
    Who shall lay hold upon, and them
      shall dash against the stones.

Psalm 138

A Psalm of David.

1   THEE will I praise with all my heart,
      I will sing praise to thee
2   Before the gods: And worship will
      toward thy sanctuary.
    I'll praise thy name, ev'n for thy truth,
      and kindness of thy love;
    For thou thy word hast magnify'd
      all thy great name above.

3   Thou didst me answer in the day
      when I to thee did cry;
    And thou my fainting soul with strength
      didst strengthen inwardly.
4   All kings upon the earth that are
      shall give thee praise, O Lord;

When as they from thy mouth shall hear
    thy true and faithful word.

5 Yea, in the righteous ways of God
    with gladness they shall sing:
For great's the glory of the Lord,
    who doth for ever reign.
6 Though God be high, yet he respects
    all those that lowly be;
Whereas the proud and lofty ones
    afar off knoweth he.

7 Though I in midst of trouble walk,
    I life from thee shall have:
'Gainst my foes' wrath thou'lt stretch thine
          hand;
    thy right hand shall me save.
8 Surely that which concerneth me
    the Lord will perfect make:
Lord, still thy mercy lasts; do not
    thine own hands' works forsake.

Psalm 139

To the chief Musician, A Psalm of David.

1 O LORD, thou hast me search'd and
         known.
2   Thou know'st my sitting down,
And rising up; yea, all my thoughts
    afar to thee are known.
3 My footsteps, and my lying down,
    thou compassest always;
Thou also most entirely art
    acquaint with all my ways.

4 For in my tongue, before I speak,
    not any word can be,
  But altogether, lo, O Lord,
    it is well known to thee.
5 Behind, before, thou hast beset,
    and laid on me thine hand.
6 Such knowledge is too strange for me,
    too high to understand.

7 From thy Sp'rit whither shall I go?
    or from thy presence fly?
8 Ascend I heav'n, lo, thou art there;
    there, if in hell I lie.
9 Take I the morning wings, and dwell
    in utmost parts of sea;
10 Ev'n there, Lord, shall thy hand me lead,
    thy right hand hold shall me.

11 If I do say that darkness shall
    me cover from thy sight,
  Then surely shall the very night
    about me be as light.
12 Yea, darkness hideth not from thee,
    but night doth shine as day:
  To thee the darkness and the light
    are both alike alway.

13 For thou possessed hast my reins,
    and thou hast cover'd me,
  When I within my mother's womb
    inclosed was by thee.
14 Thee will I praise; for fearfully
    and strangely made I am;

Thy works are marv'llous, and right well
  my soul doth know the same.

15 My substance was not hid from thee,
    when as in secret I
  Was made; and in earth's lowest parts
    was wrought most curiously.
16 Thine eyes my substance did behold,
    yet being unperfect;
  And in the volume of thy book
    my members all were writ;

  Which after in continuance
    were fashion'd ev'ry one,
  When as they yet all shapeless were,
    and of them there was none.
17 How precious also are thy thoughts,
    O gracious God, to me!
  And in their sum how passing great
    and numberless they be!

18 If I should count them, than the sand
    they more in number be:
  What time soever I awake,
    I ever am with thee.
19 Thou, Lord, wilt sure the wicked slay:
    hence from me bloody men.
20 Thy foes against thee loudly speak,
    and take thy name in vain.

21 Do not I hate all those, O Lord,
    that hatred bear to thee?
  With those that up against thee rise
    can I but grieved be?

22 With perfect hatred them I hate,
    my foes I them do hold.
23 Search me, O God, and know my heart,
    try me, my thoughts unfold:

24 And see if any wicked way
    there be at all in me;
And in thine everlasting way
    to me a leader be.

Psalm 140

To the chief Musician, A Psalm of David.

1 LORD, from the ill and froward man
    give me deliverance,
And do thou safe preserve me from
    the man of violence:
2 Who in their heart mischievous things
    are meditating ever;
And they for war assembled are
    continually together.

3 Much like unto a serpent's tongue
    their tongues they sharp do make;
And underneath their lips there lies
    the poison of a snake.
4 Lord, keep me from the wicked's hands,
    from vi'lent men me save;
Who utterly to overthrow
    my goings purpos'd have.

5 The proud for me a snare have hid,
    and cords; yea, they a net
Have by the way-side for me spread;
    they gins for me have set.

6   I said unto the Lord, Thou art
      my God: unto the cry
  Of all my supplications,
      Lord, do thine ear apply.

7   O God the Lord, who art the strength
      of my salvation:
  A cov'ring in the day of war
      my head thou hast put on.
8   Unto the wicked man, O Lord,
      his wishes do not grant;
  Nor further thou his ill device,
      lest they themselves should vaunt.

9   As for the head and chief of those
      about that compass me,
  Ev'n by the mischief of their lips
      let thou them cover'd be.
10 Let burning coals upon them fall,
      them throw in fiery flame,
  And in deep pits, that they no more
      may rise out of the same.

11 Let not an evil speaker be
      on earth established:
  Mischief shall hunt the vi'lent man,
      till he be ruined.
12 I know God will th' afflicted's cause
      maintain, and poor men's right.
13 Surely the just shall praise thy name;
      th' upright dwell in thy sight.

Psalm 141

A Psalm of David.

1 O LORD, I unto thee do cry,
    do thou make haste to me,
And give an ear unto my voice,
    when I cry unto thee.
2 As incense let my prayer be
    directed in thine eyes;
And the uplifting of my hands
    as th' ev'ning sacrifice.

3 Set, Lord, a watch before my mouth,
    keep of my lips the door.
4 My heart incline thou not unto
    the ills I should abhor,
To practise wicked works with men
    that work iniquity;
And with their delicates my taste
    let me not satisfy.

5 Let him that righteous is me smite,
    it shall a kindness be;
Let him reprove, I shall it count
    a precious oil to me:
Such smiting shall not break my head;
    for yet the time shall fall,
When I in their calamities
    to God pray for them shall.

6 When as their judges down shall be
    in stony places cast,
Then shall they hear my words; for they
    shall sweet be to their taste.

7 About the grave's devouring mouth
      our bones are scatter'd round,
   As wood which men do cut and cleave
      lies scatter'd on the ground.

8 But unto thee, O God the Lord,
      mine eyes uplifted be:
   My soul do not leave destitute;
      my trust is set on thee.

9 Lord, keep me safely from the snares
      which they for me prepare;
   And from the subtile gins of them
      that wicked workers are.

10 Let workers of iniquity
      into their own nets fall,
   Whilst I do, by thine help, escape
      the danger of them all.

Psalm 142

Maschil of David; A Prayer when he was in the cave.

1 I WITH my voice cry'd to the Lord,
      with it made my request:
2 Pour'd out to him my plaint, to him
      my trouble I exprest.
3 When in me was o'erwhelm'd my sp'rit,
      then well thou knew'st my way;
   Where I did walk a snare for me
      they privily did lay.

4 I look'd on my right hand, and view'd,
      but none to know me were;
   All refuge failed me, no man
      did for my soul take care.

5   I cry'd to thee; I said, Thou art
      my refuge, Lord, alone;
    And in the land of those that live
      thou art my portion.

6   Because I am brought very low,
      attend unto my cry:
    Me from my persecutors save,
      who stronger are than I.
7   From prison bring my soul, that I
      thy name may glorify:
    The just shall compass me, when thou
      with me deal'st bounteously.

Psalm 143

A Psalm of David.

1   LORD, hear my pray'r, attend my suits;
      and in thy faithfulness
    Give thou an answer unto me,
      and in thy righteousness.
2   Thy servant also bring thou not
      in judgment to be try'd:
    Because no living man can be
      in thy sight justify'd.

3   For th' en'my hath pursu'd my soul,
      my life to ground down tread:
    In darkness he hath made me dwell,
      as who have long been dead.
4   My sp'rit is therefore overwhelm'd
      in me perplexedly;
    Within me is my very heart
      amazed wondrously.

5   I call to mind the days of old,
     to meditate I use
   On all thy works; upon the deeds
     I of thy hands do muse.

6   My hands to thee I stretch; my soul
     thirsts, as dry land, for thee.

7   Haste, Lord, to hear, my spirit fails:
     hide not thy face from me;

   Lest like to them I do become
     that go down to the dust.

8   At morn let me thy kindness hear;
     for in thee do I trust.
   Teach me the way that I should walk:
     I lift my soul to thee.

9   Lord, free me from my foes; I flee
     to thee to cover me.

10 Because thou art my God, to do
     thy will do me instruct:
   Thy Sp'rit is good, me to the land
     of uprightness conduct.

11 Revive and quicken me, O Lord,
     ev'n for thine own name's sake;
   And do thou, for thy righteousness,
     my soul from trouble take.

12 And of thy mercy slay my foes;
     let all destroyed be
   That do afflict my soul: for I
     a servant am to thee.

Another of the same

1   O H, hear my prayer, Lord,
     And unto my desire

To bow thine ear accord,
  I humbly thee require;
And, in thy faithfulness,
  Unto me answer make,
And, in thy righteousness,
  Upon me pity take.

2 In judgment enter not
    With me thy servant poor;
  For why, this well I wot,
    No sinner can endure
  The sight of thee, O God:
    If thou his deeds shalt try,
  He dare make none abode
    Himself to justify.

3 Behold, the cruel foe
    Me persecutes with spite,
  My soul to overthrow:
    Yea, he my life down quite
  Unto the ground hath smote,
    And made me dwell full low
  In darkness, as forgot,
    Or men dead long ago.

4 Therefore my sp'rit much vex'd,
    O'erwhelm'd is me within;
  My heart right sore perplex'd
    And desolate hath been.
5 Yet I do call to mind
    What ancient days record,
  Thy works of ev'ry kind
    I think upon, O Lord.

6 Lo, I do stretch my hands
    To thee, my help alone;
For thou well understands
    All my complaint and moan:
My thirsting soul desires,
    And longeth after thee,
As thirsty ground requires
    With rain refresh'd to be.

7 Lord, let my pray'r prevail,
    To answer it make speed;
For, lo, my sp'rit doth fail:
    Hide not thy face in need;
Lest I be like to those
    That do in darkness sit,
Or him that downward goes
    Into the dreadful pit.

8 Because I trust in thee,
    O Lord, cause me to hear
Thy loving-kindness free,
    When morning doth appear:
Cause me to know the way
    Wherein my path should be;
For why, my soul on high
    I do lift up to thee.

9 From my fierce enemy
    In safety do me guide,
Because I flee to thee,
    Lord, that thou may'st me hide.
10 My God alone art thou,
    Teach me thy righteousness:

Thy Sp'rit's good, lead me to
  The land of uprightness.

11 O Lord, for thy name's sake,
  Be pleas'd to quicken me;
And, for thy truth, forth take
  My soul from misery.
12 And of thy grace destroy
  My foes, and put to shame
All who my soul annoy;
  For I thy servant am.

Psalm 144

A Psalm of David.

1 O BLESSED ever be the Lord,
  who is my strength and might,
Who doth instruct my hands to war,
  my fingers teach to fight.
2 My goodness, fortress, my high tow'r,
  deliverer, and shield,
In whom I trust: who under me
  my people makes to yield.

3 Lord, what is man, that thou of him
  dost so much knowledge take?
Or son of man, that thou of him
  so great account dost make?
4 Man is like vanity; his days,
  as shadows, pass away.
5 Lord, bow thy heav'ns, come down, touch
      thou
  the hills, and smoke shall they.

6 Cast forth thy lightning, scatter them;
  thine arrows shoot, them rout.

7 Thine hand send from above, me save;
    from great depths draw me out;
And from the hand of children strange,
8   Whose mouth speaks vanity;
And their right hand is a right hand
    that works deceitfully.

9 A new song I to thee will sing,
    Lord, on a psaltery;
I on a ten-string'd instrument
    will praises sing to thee.
10 Ev'n he it is that unto kings
    salvation doth send;
Who his own servant David doth
    from hurtful sword defend.

11 O free me from strange children's hand,
    whose mouth speaks vanity;
And their right hand a right hand is
    that works deceitfully.
12 That, as the plants, our sons may be
    in youth grown up that are;
Our daughters like to corner-stones,
    carv'd like a palace fair.

13 That to afford all kind of store
    our garners may be fill'd;
That our sheep thousands, in our streets
    ten thousands they may yield.
14 That strong our oxen be for work,
    that no in-breaking be,
Nor going out; and that our streets
    may from complaints be free.

15 Those people blessed are who be
        in such a case as this;
     Yea, blessed all those people are,
        whose God JEHOVAH is.

Psalm 145

David's Psalm of praise.

1   I'LL thee extol, my God, O King;
        I'll bless thy name always.
2   Thee will I bless each day, and will
        thy name for ever praise.
3   Great is the Lord, much to be prais'd;
        his greatness search exceeds.
4   Race unto race shall praise thy works,
        and shew thy mighty deeds.

5   I of thy glorious majesty
        the honour will record;
     I'll speak of all thy mighty works,
        which wondrous are, O Lord.
6   Men of thine acts the might shall show,
        thine acts that dreadful are;
     And I, thy glory to advance,
        thy greatness will declare.

7   The mem'ry of thy goodness great
        they largely shall express;
     With songs of praise they shall extol
        thy perfect righteousness.
8   The Lord is very gracious,
        in him compassions flow;
     In mercy he is very great,
        and is to anger slow.

9   The Lord JEHOVAH unto all
      his goodness doth declare;
   And over all his other works
      his tender mercies are.
10 Thee all thy works shall praise, O Lord,
      and thee thy saints shall bless;
11 They shall thy kingdom's glory show,
      thy pow'r by speech express:

12 To make the sons of men to know
      his acts done mightily,
   And of his kingdom th' excellent
      and glorious majesty.
13 Thy kingdom shall for ever stand,
      thy reign through ages all.
14 God raiseth all that are bow'd down,
      upholdeth all that fall.

15 The eyes of all things wait on thee,
      the giver of all good;
   And thou, in time convenient,
      bestow'st on them their food:
16 Thine hand thou open'st lib'rally,
      and of thy bounty gives
   Enough to satisfy the need
      of ev'ry thing that lives.

17 The Lord is just in all his ways,
      holy in his works all.
18 God's near to all that call on him,
      in truth that on him call.
19 He will accomplish the desire
      of those that do him fear:

He also will deliver them,
    and he their cry will hear.

20 The Lord preserves all who him love,
    that nought can them annoy:
But he all those that wicked are
    will utterly destroy.
21 My mouth the praises of the Lord
    to publish cease shall never:
Let all flesh bless his holy name
    for ever and for ever.

Another of the same

1 **O** LORD, thou art my God and King;
    Thee will I magnify and praise:
I will thee bless, and gladly sing
    Unto thy holy name always.
2 Each day I rise I will thee bless,
    And praise thy name time without end.
3 Much to be prais'd, and great God is;
    His greatness none can comprehend.

4 Race shall thy works praise unto race,
    The mighty acts show done by thee.
5 I will speak of the glorious grace,
    And honour of thy majesty;
Thy wondrous works I will record.
6   By men the might shall be extoll'd
Of all thy dreadful acts, O Lord:
    And I thy greatness will unfold.

7 They utter shall abundantly
    The mem'ry of thy goodness great;

And shall sing praises cheerfully,
  Whilst they thy righteousness relate.
8 The Lord our God is gracious,
  Compassionate is he also;
In mercy he is plenteous,
  But unto wrath and anger slow.

9 Good unto all men is the Lord:
  O'er all his works his mercy is.
10 Thy works all praise to thee afford:
  Thy saints, O Lord, thy name shall bless.
11 The glory of thy kingdom show
  Shall they, and of thy power tell;
12 That so men's sons his deeds may know,
  His kingdom's grace that doth excel.

13 Thy kingdom hath none end at all,
  It doth through ages all remain.
14 The Lord upholdeth all that fall,
  The cast-down raiseth up again.
15 The eyes of all things, Lord, attend,
  And on thee wait that here do live,
And thou, in season due, dost send
  Sufficient food them to relieve.

16 Yea, thou thine hand dost open wide,
  And ev'ry thing dost satisfy
That lives, and doth on earth abide,
  Of thy great liberality.
17 The Lord is just in his ways all,
  And holy in his works each one.
18 He's near to all that on him call,
  Who call in truth on him alone.

19 God will the just desire fulfil
  Of such as do him fear and dread:
Their cry regard, and hear he will,
  And save them in the time of need.
20 The Lord preserves all, more and less,
  That bear to him a loving heart:
But workers all of wickedness
  Destroy will he, and clean subvert.

21 Therefore my mouth and lips I'll frame
  To speak the praises of the Lord:
To magnify his holy name
  For ever let all flesh accord.

Psalm 146

1 PRAISE God. The Lord praise, O my soul.
2   I'll praise God while I live;
While I have being to my God
  in songs I'll praises give.
3 Trust not in princes, nor man's son,
  in whom there is no stay:
4 His breath departs, to's earth he turns;
  that day his thoughts decay.

5 O happy is that man and blest,
  whom Jacob's God doth aid;
Whose hope upon the Lord doth rest,
  and on his God is stay'd:
6 Who made the earth and heavens high,
  who made the swelling deep,
And all that is within the same;
  who truth doth ever keep:

7 Who righteous judgment executes
  for those oppress'd that be,

Who to the hungry giveth food;
   God sets the pris'ners free.
8 The Lord doth give the blind their sight,
   the bowed down doth raise:
The Lord doth dearly love all those
   that walk in upright ways.

9 The stranger's shield, the widow's stay,
   the orphan's help, is he:
But yet by him the wicked's way
   turn'd upside down shall be.
10 The Lord shall reign for evermore:
   thy God, O Sion, he
Reigns to all generations.
   Praise to the Lord give ye.

Psalm 147

1 PRAISE ye the Lord; for it is good
   praise to our God to sing:
For it is pleasant, and to praise
   it is a comely thing.
2 God doth build up Jerusalem;
   and he it is alone
That the dispers'd of Israel
   doth gather into one.

3 Those that are broken in their heart,
   and grieved in their minds,
He healeth, and their painful wounds
   he tenderly up-binds.
4 He counts the number of the stars;
   he names them ev'ry one.
5 Great is our Lord, and of great pow'r;
   his wisdom search can none.

6   The Lord lifts up the meek; and casts
        the wicked to the ground.
7   Sing to the Lord, and give him thanks;
        on harp his praises sound;
8   Who covereth the heav'n with clouds,
        who for the earth below
    Prepareth rain, who maketh grass
        upon the mountains grow.

9   He gives the beast his food, he feeds
        the ravens young that cry.
10 His pleasure not in horses' strength,
        nor in man's legs, doth lie.
11 But in all those that do him fear
        the Lord doth pleasure take;
    In those that to his mercy do
        by hope themselves betake.

12 The Lord praise, O Jerusalem;
        Sion, thy God confess:
13 For thy gates' bars he maketh strong;
        thy sons in thee doth bless.
14 He in thy borders maketh peace;
        with fine wheat filleth thee.
15 He sends forth his command on earth,
        his word runs speedily.

16 Hoar-frost, like ashes, scatt'reth he;
        like wool he snow doth give:
17 Like morsels casteth forth his ice;
        who in its cold can live?
18 He sendeth forth his mighty word,
        and melteth them again;

His wind he makes to blow, and then
    the waters flow amain.

19 The doctrine of his holy word
    to Jacob he doth show;
His statutes and his judgments he
    gives Israel to know.
20 To any nation never he
    such favour did afford;
For they his judgments have not known.
    O do ye praise the Lord.

Psalm 148

1 PRAISE God. From heavens praise the
           Lord,
    in heights praise to him be.
2 All ye his angels, praise ye him;
    his hosts all, praise him ye.
3 O praise ye him, both sun and moon,
    praise him, all stars of light.
4 Ye heav'ns of heav'ns him praise, and floods
    above the heavens' height.

5 Let all the creatures praise the name
    of our almighty Lord:
For he commanded, and they were
    created by his word.
6 He also, for all times to come,
    hath them establish'd sure;
He hath appointed them a law,
    which ever shall endure.

7 Praise ye JEHOVAH from the earth,
    dragons, and ev'ry deep:

8　Fire, hail, snow, vapour, stormy wind,
　　his word that fully keep.
9　All hills and mountains, fruitful trees,
　　and all ye cedars high:
10　Beasts, and all cattle, creeping things,
　　and all ye birds that fly.

11　Kings of the earth, all nations,
　　princes, earth's judges all:
12　Both young men, yea, and maidens too,
　　old men, and children small.
13　Let them God's name praise; for his name
　　alone is excellent:
　　His glory reacheth far above
　　the earth and firmament.

14　His people's horn, the praise of all
　　his saints, exalteth he;
　　Ev'n Isr'el's seed, a people near
　　to him. The Lord praise ye.

Another of the same

1　THE Lord of heav'n confess,
　　On high his glory raise.
2　Him let all angels bless,
　　Him all his armies praise.
3　　Him glorify
　　　Sun, moon, and stars;
4　　Ye higher spheres,
　　　And cloudy sky.

5　From God your beings are,
　　Him therefore famous make;

You all created were,
When he the word but spake.
6   And from that place,
      Where fix'd you be
      By his decree,
      You cannot pass.

7   Praise God from earth below,
    Ye dragons, and ye deeps:
8   Fire, hail, clouds, wind, and snow,
    Whom in command he keeps.
9   Praise ye his name,
      Hills great and small,
      Trees low and tall;
10   Beasts wild and tame;

      All things that creep or fly.
11 Ye kings, ye vulgar throng,
    All princes mean or high;
12 Both men and virgins young,
      Ev'n young and old,
13   Exalt his name;
      For much his fame
      Should be extoll'd.

      O let God's name be prais'd
      Above both earth and sky;
14 For he his saints hath rais'd,
    And set their horn on high:
      Ev'n those that be
      Of Isr'el's race,
      Near to his grace.
      The Lord praise ye.

Psalm 149

1 PRAISE ye the Lord: unto him sing
    a new song, and his praise
In the assembly of his saints
    in sweet psalms do ye raise.
2 Let Isr'el in his Maker joy,
    and to him praises sing:
Let all that Sion's children are
    be joyful in their King.

3 O let them unto his great name
    give praises in the dance;
Let them with timbrel and with harp
    in songs his praise advance.
4 For God doth pleasure take in those
    that his own people be;
And he with his salvation
    the meek will beautify.

5 And in his glory excellent
    let all his saints rejoice:
Let them to him upon their beds
    aloud lift up their voice.
6 Let in their mouth aloft be rais'd
    the high praise of the Lord,
And let them have in their right hand
    a sharp two-edged sword;

7 To execute the vengeance due
    upon the heathen all,
And make deserved punishment
    upon the people fall.

8   And ev'n with chains, as pris'ners, bind
        their kings that them command;
    Yea, and with iron fetters strong,
        the nobles of their land.

9   On them the judgment to perform
        found written in his word:
    This honour is to all his saints.
        O do ye praise the Lord.

Psalm 150

1   PRAISE ye the Lord. God's praise within
        his sanctuary raise;
    And to him in the firmament
        of his pow'r give ye praise.
2   Because of all his mighty acts,
        with praise him magnify:
    O praise him, as he doth excel
        in glorious majesty.

3   Praise him with trumpet's sound; his praise
        with psaltery advance:
4   With timbrel, harp, string'd instruments,
        and organs, in the dance.
5   Praise him on cymbals loud; him praise
        on cymbals sounding high.
6   Let each thing breathing praise the Lord.
        Praise to the Lord give ye.